THE
Shakespeare
Code

THE
Shakespeare
Code

Virginia M. Fellows

SNOW MOUNTAIN PRESS

THE SHAKESPEARE CODE
by Virginia M. Fellows
Copyright © 2006 Summit Publications, Inc.
All rights reserved

Originally published 2000
First Snow Mountain Press edition, revised and expanded, 2006

Library of Congress Control Number: 2006921901
ISBN: 1-932890-02-5

SNOW MOUNTAIN PRESS

Snow Mountain Press is an imprint of Summit University Press®.

Cover portrait: the Chandos painting, widely believed to be of William Shakespeare (National Portrait Gallery, London)
Some images copyright © 2006 Jupiterimages Corporation

10 09 08 07 06   5 4 3 2 1

I dedicate this book to my wonderful
family and all the patient ones
whose help made it possible to bring it to a finish.
I thank each one of you
from the bottom of my heart.
I want to thank the dedicated members
of the Francis Bacon Society of London
for your many years of tireless probing
into every possible aspect
of the Shakespeare-Bacon anatomy.
I owe much to your thorough scholarship.

* * *

The editors would like to especially thank
Lawrence Gerald, Simon Miles and all who graciously
offered their feedback and comments.

CONTENTS

ILLUSTRATIONS

I am seeking not my own honour, but the honour and advancement, the dignity and enduring good of all mankind....

I keep the future ever in my plan, looking for my reward, not to my times or countrymen, but to a people very far off, and an age not like our own, but a second golden age of learning.

—Francis Bacon

NOTE FROM THE EDITORS

In November 1623, the First Folio of the plays of William Shakespeare was published. The Folio is one of the most closely studied works of English literature, yet it raises many unanswered questions. In October 1623, a month earlier, Francis Bacon, one of the leading figures of the English Renaissance, published a book containing a complete description of a new and ingenious system of concealing messages in code. Is it just a coincidence that these two books were published one month apart?

In fact, the code that Bacon described unlocks many of the mysteries of the First Folio. The key to the Shakespeare code was embedded in a book that was widely circulated in his time and to the present. Yet it was more than 250 years before anyone realized that Bacon's writings on ciphers were not just theoretical, but they were describing his method for recording a secret history of his times.

Francis Bacon used this and other codes to conceal his work in books published under his own name and under the names of Shakespeare, Spenser, Marlowe and others of the time. The hidden messages tell a startling story. They reveal state secrets and scandals—the marriage of a "Virgin Queen," murder and intrigue, corruption and lies at the highest levels of the government. And they also tell the personal life story of Francis Bacon himself.

These stories could not be safely told in Bacon's own day—more than one person was severely punished for daring to speak these truths. So Bacon concealed them in code, hoping for a future time when they could be discovered and a day when men could be free to speak and to know the truth. The codes and the secrets they contain were discovered in the late 1800s. We believe it is time for the truth to be known and the story of the cipher to reach a wider audience.

This book is an account not so much of the intricacies of ciphers and the detective work of those who discovered them, but of the hidden story itself. It does fill in details of history but, more importantly, it sets the record straight about Francis Bacon, one of the most remarkable men the world has seen.

Bacon lived in an era filled with great men and women whose names are known even today: Walter Raleigh, Francis Drake, Ben Johnson, Leicester, Essex, Queen Elizabeth I. His name may not be as well known in our time as some of the others in this list, but he has been the most influential of them all, and we are all the beneficiaries of his work.

In the idealism of his youth, he envisioned a grand plan to change the world. He sought to free the mind of man from the straitjacket of religious and secular orthodoxy. He rejected the science of his day as lacking in practical accomplishment. He foresaw a time when science and industry would lift the curse of Eden. And he outlined a new philosophy of science and nature to achieve that goal. All this is recorded in history books.

The startling story hidden in code reveals still more. It tells of Francis Bacon as the true author of the plays and poems attributed to Shakespeare. The plays are among the greatest works of English literature. They have illuminated the issues of love and life, of right and wrong, of loyalty and friendship, of mercy and justice. Even more than this, Bacon sought to create a new language and literature in England, one that could be used to express the most sublime concepts of morality and philosophy, so that great ideas and ideals could be accessible to all, not just to those who could speak and read Latin.

The codes also reveal a hidden side of Francis Bacon and the struggles he faced. They tell of a destiny denied, secrets that could not be told. They tell of tragedy and loss, a great persecution by those who saw themselves as his enemies. Yet even in the midst of all this, Bacon's spirit remained undaunted, his optimism undimmed. Against great odds, he forged a victory from the midst of seeming defeat.

The codes and their revelations are not the end of the story of Francis Bacon, but only a beginning. They are one way of entry into his fascinating life and achievements, but not the only one. This book combines their revelations with the outer story to give a picture of Francis Bacon that has not been told before.

The author, Virginia Fellows, worked for many years to bring it to fruition. We are pleased to be able to present the story in this latest edition, which has been significantly revised throughout. New for this edition are most of the illustrations, captions and notes. We have also added a section which includes an account of the codes and details of their workings.

Virginia was gratified to see the beginning of the work on the new edition in 2005. Unfortunately, she did not live to see it finished. Shortly before she died, we were able to show her the new cover and she was grateful to know that an important part of what she considered to be her own mission would finally be fulfilled.

As you read this book, we hope that you will come to know

something of the soul of Francis Bacon as Virginia knew him and as we have come to know him. There are lessons here for all of us.

Bacon was a visionary and a poet, yet someone who walked the corridors of power and held the highest offices in the land. Eventually, the rich and powerful cast him out; he was a scapegoat who might be sacrificed so that they could live another day in their own corruption. He did not become resentful or bitter. Rather, he set himself again to fulfill the aspirations of his youth, and perhaps his greatest contributions were after his retirement from public life.

Among the many works of those final years was *The New Atlantis*. It was a grand vision of a promised land. For him, the idealism of youth did not fade. With the passing of the years, he did not abandon his dreams but found ways to make them more real.

He was a prophet of the modern world—and of a future golden age. Much of what he foresaw has come to pass, but not yet everything. His Great Instauration, his plan for the remaking of society, awaits its fulfillment. The building of that new world is not yet complete. Therefore, the story is not finished. There is work to do. And each of us is called to play a part.

And perhaps the soul of Francis Bacon yet holds the key to a golden age foretold by him—a destiny yet written in the stars.

THE EDITORS

PREFACE

"It is impossible," one critic has noted, "to write an uninteresting book about Shakespeare." Certainly a broad statement considering the reams of print published about that famous genius in the past four centuries, and yet it is not entirely without logic.

Although the name William Shakespeare tops the list as one of the most influential writers of the Western world, readers have sensed an indefinable aura of mystery surrounding the great dramas. Something seems to be missing, and indeed it is. Only half the story has been told. The half that is omitted is filled with more drama, intrigue, codes, false identity, tragedy, betrayal and mystery than any popular fiction author would dare dream up. It was this distinct element of mystery that first caught my interest.

When I learned that there was doubt about the authenticity of the tale told by orthodox sources—not from any ill will on their part but from a conspiracy of silence on the part of the play-wright—I was hooked. A baffling enigma seems to have been carefully hidden behind the screen of these incredibly brilliant plays.

Next I learned that some researchers believed that Francis

Bacon was the real author. That was all the inspiration I needed. Unaware of the complexity of the story I was about to encounter, I was off with the enthusiasm of a novice on an eager search for clues to these enigmas—enigmas that appear to have surrounded the whole question of authorship from the beginning.

Could the plays really have been the work of the famous British philosopher-statesman-author known as Francis Bacon? I was soon to be, and am still these many years later, in constant amazement at what I learned.

The influence and reflection on our modern world of the life of this remarkable man is little known or understood by the mainstream historian. Much of what is taught about him is either in error or misinterpreted. Neither the exact time nor the circumstances of his birth are known, nor is the true identity of his parents. His life is a puzzle, his death a mystery. A mere fraction of his real contribution to the world has been revealed.

This twenty-first century promises to be a time of many disclosures; it is the time when the full details of the "Shakespeare controversy" may finally be resolved. "Thou stand'st as if some mystery thou didst?" wrote Bacon's friend Ben Jonson. Only a handful of serious "detectives" have cared to pierce to the heart of the enigma.

The first step of my research was a visit to the Francis Bacon Library in Claremont, California, where a fine collection of Bacon-related books endowed by philanthropist Walter Arensberg had been preserved. Arensberg, staunch and enthusiastic, was a great Bacon admirer during the early twentieth century. (The attractive little library has now been closed and the collection taken over by the prestigious Huntington Library in San Marino.) I asked the then director, Elizabeth Wrigley, to recommend one single book that would give the true history of Francis Bacon. "There is no such thing," she answered, "you will have to be the one to write it."

Since that time I have visited dozens of fine university and public libraries; I have prowled through new and used bookstores and interviewed many people through letters and personal contacts. I have acquired a collection of Baconian books and have kept in close touch with the Francis Bacon Society in London. This scholarly group was formed in the nineteenth century to explore the real facts of the Bacon-Shakespeare story. They are devoted seekers after the truth and have revealed many fascinating facts about the Elizabethan aristocrat, but even they have not reached a final conclusion about him. The one fact they *do* agree on is that Bacon was the true author of the works of Shakespeare.

Early in my research, that strange phenomenon which Carl Jung called synchronicity brought me in touch with the single most amazing Baconian artifact I could have imagined. Most readers are familiar with such surprising events. Suddenly out of nowhere, just at the right time and the right place, some essential object or information will appear, as though a genie had been at work behind the scenes. For me this surprise came in the shape of a strange wooden contraption known as a cipher wheel. On the printed pages affixed to it, in a most ingenious code is recorded the true story of Francis Bacon—an account actually and incredibly written by him in his own words. It is a story that changes the current concept of English history.

No longer was guesswork necessary. Now the task was to fit the details of Bacon's life, as the cipher gives it, into accepted records of history. *The Shakespeare Code* is my attempt to do just that and to explain what the cipher wheel is and why Bacon felt the need to create the ciphers. It is a poignant and tragic tale— but one that ends on an unexpected note of triumph.

It is a story that is crying out to be told.

Chapter One

A Tale of Two Strangers

The revealing [of secrets] is not for worldly use,
but for the ease of a man's heart.

In the last quarter of the nineteenth century, a lone horse and buggy could be seen at almost any hour of the day or night jogging along the dusty roads surrounding the city of Detroit. Dr. Orville Owen, a young physician, possessed not only an amazing memory but also a commendable sense of responsibility. People who knew him best were certain that one day he would become the most outstanding surgeon in the state.

As the doctor drove his horse and buggy on his daily rounds, he became aware that he was allowing his concerns about one patient to be carried over to the next. In order to clear his mind between calls, he took to reciting poetry aloud to the clop-clop-clop of his horse's hooves. As a great lover of Shakespeare, he eventually decided to commit to memory all the plays of this favorite poet of his, memorizing a modern, amended edition and then the original 1623 First Folio. In due time, Dr. Owen had learned them all so well that his dinner companions considered it a fine parlor trick to test his memory by reciting a line from a play and challenging Owen to identify the right act and scene.

This was no problem for Owen. He could easily quote even the following and the preceding lines. The only times he was uncertain was when he found lines in Shakespeare that were nearly identical from one play to another. In this case, he would have to ask that further lines be quoted.

These repetitions puzzled Owen, just as they have puzzled other scholars before and after this time. He pondered over them and even more over the out-of-context passages that occurred so frequently in the plays. There were also strange passages that made no sense. No one seemed to be able to explain these any more than they could explain certain oddly related sections that appeared from play to play at random and for no apparent reason.

The more familiar the doctor became with the plays, the more mystified he was. Why so much repeating? Nonsense passages from the most talented playwright in the world? Why were some words needlessly italicized while others were wrongly capitalized? Owen was well aware of the inconsistencies of Elizabethan spelling and printing, but these oddities were more than could be explained by that fact alone.

And he began to wonder, as the American scholar Delia Bacon had wondered before him,[1] why did Shakespeare make so many of his settings resemble scenes in Elizabethan England? Why had Hamlet attended a university that had not yet been founded? Why did he write about firearms before firearms had been invented, clocks when there were no clocks? What was the point of all this? A man as well acquainted with English history as the writer of the history plays would certainly have known that there had been no cannons in King John's reign.

Owen puzzled over these anomalies and finally came to believe that these and other similar errors had been deliberate "mistakes" on the part of the dramatist and not just ignorance or carelessness. But why? What could have been the point? Most of all, he puzzled over the many references to ships and the sea that began to appear seemingly at random and totally out of context in play after play. In *The Merry Wives of Windsor*, for instance, he remembered an oddly unrelated passage:

> This Puncke is one of Cupid's carriers,
> Clap on more sailes, pursue: up with your sights;
> Give fire: she is my prize, or ocean whelm them all.
>
> *act II, sc. 2*

This peculiar passage had nothing whatsoever to do with the ridiculous Falstaff's pursuit of the merry housewives. What was it doing there? Owen could find no explanation. He found other passages equally confusing.

By now the good doctor's curiosity was piqued beyond limit. Painstakingly he wrote out all the passages in which these nautical references occur. Then he read them together and found, to his utter astonishment, that he was reading a more or less recognizable account of a great sea battle, specifically that amazing victory achieved by the Elizabethans over the Spanish fleet, the Armada, sent to attack them in 1588. It seemed impossible to believe, but there it was—two different stories being told by the same words used in different sequences.[2]

Dr. Owen was not only shocked, he was hooked. Every minute he could spare was devoted to combing through the plays line by line. A passage in the prologue to *Troilus and Cressida* attracted his attention.

> Beginning in the middle, starting thence away
> To what may be digested in a play.

Beginning in the middle of what? And why? What was the playwright trying to say? On and on went his search.

After many trials and errors, Owen found "the middle"—in the middle group of plays, the history plays. In the first history play, *King John*, he found the following: "Thus, leaning on mine elbow, I begin" (act I, scene 1).

This is a phrase we are familiar with now, but it was not an idiom of the time. It was the opening Owen had been looking for. From that moment on, he was on his way to one of the most amazing literary discoveries of all time—the plays of William Shakespeare were cover text for a cipher biography, a story totally different from the plots around which the plays revolved. The doctor from Detroit was receiving glimpses of a poignant and secret life story, and it was told in great detail and in the same blank-verse style so typical of Shakespeare.

As he continued his work, Owen found that certain key words—such as reputation, fortune, honor, time, nature—marked the passages with sentences belonging to the cipher story. Entire plays and even poems had been most ingeniously buried under the cover of outer stories that have become familiar to the entire world.

The demands of his discovery forced Owen to give up much of his practice to spend time on the work, and before long he realized that he needed help. Elizabeth Wells Gallup, a respected teacher in a Michigan high school, Kate Wells, her sister, and others were hired to type out the passages as he read them aloud. After these secretaries typed the passages, they would sort them into various boxes according to the subject matter and keywords. When they had collected a pile, Owen would check them over and join the phrases according to the rules he had discovered in the cipher itself.

As he went along, he discovered that eventually he had enough new material to fill five separate small books. These were

Elizabeth Wells Gallup
While assisting Dr. Owens in decoding Bacon's Word Cipher, Mrs. Gallup discovered a second cipher, the Bi-literal Cipher, embedded in the same works of Shakespeare.

published by the Howard Publishing Company as *Sir Francis Bacon's Cipher Story*. These little books are now out of print, but many large libraries still carry copies of them (and some are available through the Web).

As the work continued, Mrs. Gallup became aware of the odd use of italics in the original publications. No more reasonable explanation could be found for this than for the misplaced subject matter. She remembered that Francis Bacon had described, in great detail, a style of cipher-writing which he called the Bi-literal Cipher in his own 1623 *De Augmentis Scientiarum*. Mrs. Gallup studied it closely and discovered that in addition to the Word Cipher being disclosed by Owen, the same plays and texts contained a Bi-literal Cipher just as described by Bacon.

In both styles the message was the same. And what it revealed was at least as startling as the existence of the ciphers themselves. They said that Francis Bacon was not the son of Sir Nicholas Bacon and his wife. He was, incredibly, the son of Elizabeth Tudor, England's "Virgin" Queen, and was a child whom she recognized privately but not publicly.

The great Elizabeth, determined to present herself as the image of the mythic Virgo, the Virgin Queen, had concealed from the general public the birth of her son, whose father was her favorite, Robert Dudley, later Lord Leicester. Yet she had told Parliament: "This shall be for me sufficient, that a marble stone shall declare that a Queen, having reigned such a time, lived and died a virgin."[3] She was not about to give up this carefully created image of herself; neither was she going to give up her personal and sensual pleasures.

Bacon dared not oppose the queen by revealing his true identity. His only recourse was to hide his true story in cipher, and hope that one day it would be discovered and revealed to the world. His greatest fear was that the cipher might never be discovered and that his work would be a true case of "love's labor lost."

Dr. Owen found that the Word Cipher used phrases lifted from various plays, giving a totally different context or story in the same blank verse. The Bi-literal Cipher, discovered by Mrs. Gallup, used two different fonts, or styles of type, on the original printed pages. These fonts were distinct but quite close in appearance, and the hidden message was discovered by decoding the pattern they formed. What Mrs. Gallup had deciphered was a text in short prose sentences that eventually corroborated all that Owen had found in the poetic lines of the Word Cipher.

The scheme of the triple content of the plays (the original and the two cipher stories) was far more brilliant than anything either Gallup or Owen could have conceived of, as they well knew. They had no choice but to accept, in amazement, the awesome story that was being unfolded as they applied the rules, play by play. As they continued their work, they found that the same methods could be applied to certain other writings of the sixteenth and seventeenth centuries—and these revealed the same ciphers that had been inserted by Bacon himself.

It was an absolute impossibility that such material could be extracted from the works if it had not been purposely placed there in the beginning. Owen thought about the adage "Nothing comes from nothing." No man could have had the genius to find a play where there was none. If he had done the impossible, he would have been a far greater genius than Bacon and "Shakespeare" combined.

Owen's editor, George Goodale, wrote his opinion on the subject:

> The existence of a cipher by use of which these stories are revealed is an indisputable fact. The stories are not Dr. Owen's inventions. He did not compose them, for the reason that neither he nor any man that lives is gifted with the surpassing genius to do it. Nobody has the right to pass judgment ... who has not first read the book.[4]

Owen had long been aware that some people believed the wondrous plays loved by all the world were not the work of an actor from Stratford but of the brilliant philosopher Francis Bacon. The doctor had not paid much attention to the idea before because he could see no valid reason for such a deception; but here, revealed line by line, was a more than adequate explanation. Here was the man who had gone to an enormous amount of effort to leave his secret biography hidden in the plays, claiming that he was the son, unacknowledged of course, of Queen

Elizabeth. Quite unintentionally, Owen had stumbled upon a state secret that would rewrite the history of Tudor England if it were known.

Doubts about who had written the works accredited to a young peasant lad from a country village in Warwickshire had been tossed about publicly for more than two hundred years by the time Owen came along. And who knows how long before that private manuscripts had been exchanged by those who were in on the secret.

In 1769, an odd little pamphlet was circulated publicly—*The Life and Adventures of Common Sense*. In this peculiar tract, a man called Common Sense is having a conversation with a stranger about "a person belonging to the playhouse":

> This man was a profligate in his youth, and, as some say, had been a deer-stealer.... [He] took the first opportunity that presented itself to rob [men] of everything he could lay his hands on.... He presently cast his eye upon a common place book, in which was contained an infinite variety of modes and forms to express all the different sentiments of the human mind, together with rules ... upon every subject or occasion that might occur in dramatic writing.... With these materials and with good parts of his own he commenced play-writer. How he succeeded is needless to say when I tell the reader that his name was Shakespear.[5]

A few years later, in 1786, another little tract appeared, *The Story of the Learned Pig*. The author claimed to be "an Officer of the Royal Navy." Witty and satirical, it is a supposed account of the reincarnation of a pig at Sadler's Wells (an old medicinal springs where a theater that frequently produced plays of Shakespeare was built).

Formerly this pig had been embodied as Romulus, founder of Rome, and later as Brutus, legendary founder of England. During Elizabeth's reign, the pig, now known as Pimping Billy, had been embodied as the son of Ben Jonson's fictional character Cob. One of Billy's friends was Will Shakspeare, whom he accuses of certain inelegant hi-jinx, including having been "falsely fathered" with plays not belonging to him. The plays mentioned were *Hamlet, Othello, As You Like It, The Tempest* and *A Midsummer Night's Dream.* It would be hard to say who "fathered" this little jibe at Shakespeare, but we can make an educated guess that it was a member of a secret society, possibly a Rosicrucian, who was aware of the true story of "Shakespeare."

Little tracts such as these barely rippled the surface of the literary seas. But at about the same time in the 1780s, another dissenter came along who raised a larger tempest. He was the Reverend James Wilmot, rector of the little village of Barton-on-the-Heath, which was a few miles to the north of Stratford-on-Avon, Shakespeare's hometown.

Wilmot was commissioned by a London firm to write a biography of William Shakespeare, a poet and playwright who was becoming more popular day by day. Wilmot accepted the offer and vigorously set about the task of collecting data, stories, personal remembrances—anything and everything he could find about the man from Stratford. Trip after trip to the neighboring village, however, failed to turn up anything of the least significance. About the most famous resident of Stratford there seemed to be nothing at all. No one seemed to know anything about him. There were no anecdotes about his youth or his retirement days in the village, no schoolboy tales—nothing!

Wilmot's enthusiasm ebbed lower and lower after each visit. He could not find the slightest reason for believing that the immortal *Lucrece*, the mystic *Tempest*, the enigmatic sonnets or even a single line of the most beautiful blank verse in the English language had been written by a man who had lived in the squalid little market town that was the Stratford of the time.

Wilmot found not even a trace of the necessary cultural and educational opportunities that would have been essential for the writing of the plays. Did a boy named Shaksper or Shastpur or Shaxper (there were many spellings of such a name—never Shake-speare with a hyphen, as it was sometimes printed) ever study at the one-room local grammar school? No records existed to show that he did. Were there books available that he might have used? Wilmot combed the countryside for fifty miles around and found not a single book that had belonged to Shakespeare.

Could the writer of the most magnificent English ever spoken have learned it from the dull and almost incomprehensible dialect of the uneducated Warwickshire villagers? Both the mother and father of Will Shaksper had been illiterate and signed their names with an X.

Stratford-on-Avon revealed itself to Wilmot as nothing but a dreary little country town whose inhabitants were, for the most part, illiterate, whose town council had difficulty in persuading the citizens to keep their trash out of the streets, whose gutters were "full of foulness" and whose one-room school did not possess even one book on grammar. A grammar book would have been a necessary item for an adequate education, the kind of education that was available in those days only to children of the higher classes.

Reluctantly Wilmot conceded that the roots of education, culture and learning that would have been an indispensable background for the writing of the sublime literature of Shakespeare did not grow in Stratford. He gave up in discouragement and went back home to Barton.

Shocked by his discovery, Wilmot kept his thoughts to himself, but he did share his findings from time to time with a few favored visitors. Only once did his beliefs see print, in a paper that one of these visitors presented at the prestigious Ipswich Philosophical Society. One man in all of England, Wilmot was convinced, had the brilliance of mind and the scholarship to have written the glorious plays. That man, he said, was none other than the great philosopher-scholar Francis Bacon.

As might be expected, this paper about Wilmot's discovery caused quite an uproar at the Ipswich Society. The information was presented there on two occasions, with the same results—disbelief and condemnation. It wasn't until 1932 that a professor came across the paper with Wilmot's great secret and published it for the world to see.[6]

Meanwhile, the ranks of those who doubted Shakespeare's authorship had been steadily growing. John Greenleaf Whittier wrote, "Whether Bacon wrote the wonderful plays or not, I am quite sure the man Shakspere neither did nor could."[7] Dr. W. H. Furness wrote: "I am one of the many who have never been able to bring the life of William Shakespeare and the plays of Shakespeare within planetary space of each other.... I think we could have found no one of that day but F. Bacon to whom to assign the crown."[8] Henry James wrote: "I am ... sort of haunted by the conviction that the divine William is the biggest and most successful fraud ever practiced on a patient world."[9] Even Mark Twain joined the fray: "That man could not have been the Stratford Shakespeare—and *wasn't.*"[10]

In the late nineteenth century, an American congressman from Minnesota by the name of Ignatius Donnelly took up the quest. Donnelly was the author of one of the earliest books on Atlantis.[11] He was also one of the first to claim to have discovered a cipher in the Shakespeare works. Using a complicated system based on certain key numbers, he extracted several intriguing passages on the lives of Will Shaksper and Francis Bacon. However, Donnelly never managed to form his ideas into a methodical system, and when his book on this subject, *The Great Cryptogram,* was finally published in 1888, it was met with such ridicule that he gave up in despair and never completed the development of his theories. (My personal opinion is that he was on to a legitimate discovery, and it is unfortunate that this particular style of cipher has never been carried further.)

There are several good books on the market, new and old, discussing the controversy about Shakespeare, fascinating and detailed explanations as to why the uneducated Will could not have written the remarkable plays that are attributed to him. Each writer has his own favorite contender for the honor. Edward de Vere, Christopher Marlowe, William Stanley, Roger Manners, Sir Walter Raleigh and numerous others have been proposed as candidates, and even Queen Elizabeth herself. All of them were friends and acquaintances of Francis Bacon.

It is not the intent of this book to go into a controversy about why Will Shaksper or any of the other claimants cannot be considered the true author. This has been adequately examined and explained by others. This book is about Francis Bacon, about the nearly incredible drama of his life, especially as he himself reveals it through the codes in his many writings.

Owen, to assist in his deciphering work, built a one-of-a-kind contraption known as the cipher wheel. A description of it and of my personal connection with it is now due.

We find that Owen, as he went on with his deciphering, discovered that the original author, Francis Bacon, had inserted into the works themselves coded instructions to aid in the tiring task of extracting the cipher.

The fact that instructions were given about cipher in cipher has caused some ridicule by those who deny the legitimacy of Owen's work. What would be the purpose of giving instructions about the code if you have to first break the code in order to find the instructions? The objection may seem valid enough, except for the fact that the instructions are there and no one could have inserted them except the original author:

> The easiest way to carry on the work is to
> Take your knife and cut all our books asunder,
> And set the leaves on a great firm wheel
> Which rolls and rolls.[12]

Dr. Owen followed these instructions carefully. After numerous experiments he had two large wooden wheels, or cylinders, built. Around the cylinders, which measured 36 inches in diameter and 48 inches in height, was wound a thousand feet of waterproof, linenlike material. The wheels were mounted in a frame in such a way that they could be turned backward and forward, much in the way that a parchment scroll or a modern tape player works. Onto the linen he glued printed pages cut from valuable books or copies of books from the period of the English Renaissance. When the big wooden wheels are rolled back and forth, the pages of the old books are exposed for easy viewing, thus allowing hundreds of pages to be rolled in and out of view with just a turn of the wheels. The cipher wheel is large and ungainly and awkward, but it serves its purpose admirably.

When I first heard of the strange contraption, it was owned by Elizabeth Hovhaness of Massachusetts and her former husband, Alan Hovhaness, both well-known musicians. The wheel, crated and untouched for years, had been stored on the fifth floor of an unheated, concrete warehouse in a rundown section of Detroit, sixty easy miles from the city of Flint, where I lived at the

Dr. Orville Owen's cipher wheel
This illustration, from Dr. Owen's original publication of the cipher story, shows the cipher wheel set up as he used it in his workshop. As he read passages from the wheel, his assistant would type them. The sheets would then be sorted according to the key-words typed at the top of each page.

time. Mrs. Hovhaness planned to move to England and did not intend to take the heavy crate with her. (It weighed almost four hundred pounds and was about as easy to ship as a grand piano.)

I had long been fascinated by the existence of this intriguing cipher wheel but never expected to be fortunate enough to actually see it, let alone possess it. I learned through Elizabeth Wrigley of the Bacon Library, now in San Marino, that Mrs. Hovhaness was looking for a permanent home for the wheel. The small Bacon Library had no room for it. Excitedly I contacted Mrs. Hovhaness at her home in the East. Within days, she said, she would be on her way to London. She was nearly as happy as I was to find a home for the wheel before she left. She made only one stipulation—the wheel must have a permanent home where it would be secure, appreciated and readily available for serious examination. I was able to promise her that eventually the wheel would go to Summit University in Montana, where it is now in storage and occasionally on display.

Mrs. Hovhaness graciously called the warehouse with immediate orders to release the huge crate to me. Within a few days, I was on my way with a friend and a truck to pick up this treasure. I could hardly have chosen a worse day for it. We had no sooner collected the huge crate from the warehouse and loaded it on the open bed of the truck when the funnel of a tornado came barreling down over the city, missing us by less than a mile. The tumult overhead slammed down ice balls large enough to leave dents in the truck. Fortunately, they bounced off the tarpaulin that covered the crate, preventing serious damage.

The sixty-mile drive home through the storm was slow and hazardous, and it was with genuine relief that we finally arrived with our cargo intact. It took three husky men to slide the big box down the planks from the truck bed to the concrete floor of a room attached to our garage. My treasure was intact and safe.

The value of this unique object is certainly not in terms of money. But it is the product of the eye-straining, exhausting labors of two dedicated men—Francis Bacon and Orville Owen. They were born three hundred years apart, yet together they created a marvelous machine on which are recorded secrets of history that the world little dreams of. It is my hope that this book will aid in vindicating the reputations of both of these remarkable men, for their stories are crying out to be told.

This is such a strange story—Francis Bacon's life as revealed in the cipher—that it has been difficult for people saturated by "orthodox" history to believe, but the writer of the cipher himself had anticipated this. The Word Cipher takes the clever form of a conversation between Bacon and the man of the future whom he expects will someday be his decipherer.[13] He speaks to him as to his dearest friend. The decipherer makes some objections:

But may they not say it is chance that doth this?

Bacon answers:

> We thought of that; and if any man conceive
> That it is done without any system...
> Let him proceed to form a history
> And neglect the guides. He cannot go through with it
> To its completion....
> No man can know the shiftings, or how to go
> Forward...
> Until he finds our four beginnings.

In another place the Decipherer complains:

> Men, no doubt, will think that I am a liar.
> I may not conceal from you that I shall appear
> For a time to be a fool.
> I shall be met with universal ridicule.

Bacon's challenge to all his objections:

> What mean you?
> Will you lose your reputation for truth?[14]

Mrs. Gallup's and Dr. Owen's tireless efforts to unravel the mystery led to many converts; they also failed to convince others. The vicar of the church in Stratford-on-Avon appears to have been convinced against his will. This gentleman had come to the United States on a lecture tour hoping to interest affluent Americans in making contributions to the Shakespeare Memorial in Stratford. Having heard of Owen's discoveries, he made a trip to Detroit to point out to the doctor the error of his ways. Planning to expose the fraud once and for all, he visited Owen at his studio and requested to see the workings of the cipher. Dr. Owen courteously demonstrated his work to the vicar and allowed him to participate in some of the extractions from the wheel. He reduced the good man to silence. According to Owen's colleague Dr. William Prescott, the vicar canceled the remainder of his lecture tour and soon returned to England, apparently unwilling to raise money for a project he no longer believed in.[15]

There are other stories of the successes of Dr. Owen. A leading Detroit newspaper printed a scathing report of one of Owen's lectures. Owen considered it libelous and got an injunction against the paper. To settle the dispute, the paper sent one of its best writers to witness a demonstration of the deciphering work. Soon, to the writer's enormous surprise, Owen had her not only convinced but actually working the cipher herself. The paper printed a front-page apology to Owen and the case was dropped.[16]

Any and all skeptics were cordially invited by both Mrs. Gallup and Dr. Owen to attend demonstrations of the methods of deciphering. Interestingly enough, and perhaps to be expected, not one so-called scholar of the academic community seems to have responded.

The idea that Francis Bacon was the true author of the works attributed to Shakespeare (the Baconian theory) has always been controversial. Some critics have claimed that Bacon could not possibly have written the plays because "he didn't have a poetic bone in his body."

This statement is so far from reality that one must question whether such commentators had ever read a word that Bacon wrote. In simplicity, rhythm and clarity, his *Essays* have been compared to the writings of Shakespeare, and this by persons who had no idea of the connection between the two. Even in Bacon's mundane, scientific writings, the soul of a poet shines through his works. His very thoughts framed themselves in poetry. Eulogies that were written after his so-called death leave no doubt that his contemporaries thought of him as a poet. The court masques that Bacon is known to have written (and there are several) are as original, imaginative, lyrical and poetic as it is possible for the stage to be. Even the poet Shelley recognized the poetry of Bacon's soul:

> Lord Bacon was a poet. His language has a sweet and majestic rhythm which satisfies the sense, no less than the almost super human wisdom of his philosophy satisfies the intellect. It ... distends and then bursts the circumference of the reader's mind, and pours itself forth ... into the universal element with which it has perpetual sympathy.[17]

Shelley claimed he would rather be "damned with Plato and Lord Bacon than go to heaven with Paley and Malthus."[18] And who could better recognize a great poet than another poet?

Some have asked an obvious question: If Bacon was the author, why isn't this widely known? The secret history revealed in the coded passages explains all we need to know about why this great poet and philosopher was denied the recognition he so richly deserved.

Now let us take up the life of Francis Bacon as it is revealed in history and in the Shakespeare Code. As we do so, we will discover secrets that have lain hidden for hundreds of years. We will also gain new insights into the man who, perhaps more than any other individual, has been responsible for the birth of the modern world.

Chapter Two

A Childhood Eden

The joys of parents are secret,
and so are their griefs and fears.

Now we go back to England in the early 1560s. If there was a question about the birthplace of Nicholas Bacon's youngest child or even about his parentage, the boy himself was happily unaware of it. Francis thrived in his life as the son of Sir Nicholas Bacon and his Lady Anne. It wasn't until Francis was fifteen that he learned of his true identity, and that in a most disturbing manner. Only after this crucial discovery was the cipher work begun, and most of the cipher story tells of events that occurred after that time. What we know about the childhood of Francis Bacon has to be stitched together mostly from a patchwork of other sources.

Whether or not the Bacons were his real parents, they were certainly good parents. Honorable, kindly, loving Sir Nicholas descended from yeoman ancestors and had been elevated to prominence early in the reign of young Queen Elizabeth, who recognized his reliability, integrity and wisdom. He was the man she chose as her first lord keeper of the Great Seal, a title especially coined for him (*lord* was added to the existing title).

The father of six children by his first marriage, Sir Nicholas had made arrangements for one of the scholarly daughters of the noted educator Sir Anthony Cooke to come into his household to help his ailing wife, Jane. The youngest Cooke daughter, Anne, got the job because of her vigor and her lively, self-assured ways, and she loved every minute of her task. Jane Bacon did not survive, and before long Anne was left to cope with the large household alone.

Sir Nicholas soon became aware of Anne's obvious devotion to him and asked her to be his wife. Young as she was, Anne willingly became the mistress of the burgeoning Bacon household, a career that would take all the strength and wisdom she could muster as the strange destinies of the various individuals under her care unfolded. Anne not only assumed the care of Nicholas's six existing children but she added two of her own—one she undoubtedly bore herself and the other, if we accept the cipher story, she secretly carried home in a round painted box shortly following his birth and raised and loved as dearly as if he had been her own.

The older of the two lads, Anthony, was named after his maternal grandfather. Never a robust child, he was frequently ill, and as he grew older he walked with a limp. Anne had lost two babies before he was born, and we can imagine that she would have hovered with the greatest anxiety and solicitude over this little one, whose round head and wispy hair so much resembled her own. Although physically handicapped, there was nothing wrong with Anthony's mind except, perhaps, for an abnormal shyness. He possessed an exceptionally original and lively intellect, a clever wit and, as time would prove, an enormous capacity for humor, loyalty, generosity and friendship, traits for which his younger brother would have cause to be grateful many times over as the years went by.

Sir Nicholas and Lady Anne Bacon

The younger boy, Francis, was a much different child. He joined the family about three years after Anthony, in the early months of 1561, and was named after the French king François II, who had recently died at the age of sixteen, leaving his young widow, Mary Queen of Scots, to her strange destiny. The little English Francis was strong from birth, attractive in appearance and gracefully built.

Francis's charming looks, sunny disposition, easy grace and a certain natural courtesy endeared him to everyone who touched his young life. It was said of him that there was a hint of indefinable mystery that surrounded even his infant years. He seemed to attract more attention than would have been expected of a child of the kindly but unremarkable Bacons.

The exact date of Francis's birth was not recorded, but the date of his baptism in the church of St. Martin-in-the-Fields was January 25, 1561. Three quarters of a century later, his secretary and chaplain, William Rawley, would give January 22, 1561, for his birth[1] and there seems to be no reason to question it.

York House, Nicholas Bacon's London residence
Orthodox history records that Francis Bacon was born at York House.
Bacon's first biographer, William Rawley, enigmatically records that Francis
was born at "York House or York Place." The latter was Elizabeth's royal
palace, next door to York House. Was he leaving a clue to Francis's true
origins? The cipher story reveals he was born to the queen and secretly
carried to York House by Lady Anne Bacon soon after his birth.

This date is well within the influence of Aquarius,[2] the
astrological sign that, according to some theorists, would have
such importance in the future of the child. Jean Overton Fuller in
her 1981 biography, *Francis Bacon,* says that a contemporary
astrologer, William Lily, gave Bacon's birth hour as 7 a.m. on the
date given by Rawley.[3] This would give him an astrological chart
with the sun and the ascendant both in Aquarius and the moon in
Aries, a meaningful chart to those interested in astrology.

One might see Aquarius as the sign of the truth seeker and
the scientist, and the double Aquarius configuration could be
interpreted as lending a double measure of Aquarian qualities—
a highly individual and unique personality; a farseeing and

outgoing nature; a friendly, dignified and humanitarian spirit; and a more than usual interest in mysticism and philosophy. It would show a nature willing to learn from everyone and everything and a desire to pass on what he had learned for the benefit of others. Other personalities sharing this sign would be the scientific experimenter Galileo, the poet Lord Byron, the farseeing lawyer Abraham Lincoln, the space-conquering aviator Charles Lindbergh, and the great actors John Barrymore and Clark Gable. The influence of Aries could indicate strong qualities of leadership, a love of independence and the ability to forge ahead in imaginative adventures of a positive and innovative nature. These positive qualities would be markedly expressed throughout the many years of Francis's life.

Certain circumstances noted by various biographers have lent mystery to the birth of Francis. The baptismal registry of St. Martin-in-the-Fields lists the name of the tiny newborn as "Mr. Franciscus Bacon,"[4] thus including a title not generally used for baptism (and not used for the other Bacon sons). Why was it added to Francis's name? Could it have been an unexpected note of respect for this particular child? Even more puzzling, there seems to have been an attempt by later hands to erase the title from the registry, although the original writing can still be seen. Much has been made of these curious facts by modern commentators in their attempts to reconstruct the circumstances of the child's birth.

Perhaps no clue to the parentage of Francis is as reliable as the testimony of the looks of the child himself. There was no one in the Bacon family whom he resembled in the slightest degree. He alone had high coloring, curly dark hair, and hazel or brown, almost black, eyes—far more spectacular features than those of his supposed parents with their middle-class English faces and their rather colorless complexions. The Bacons' faces were round

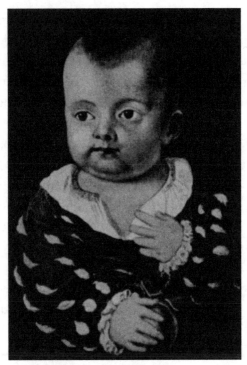

Francis Bacon as a young child
from a painting at Gorhambury

or square and pallid; Francis's was smooth and oval, tapering to a pointed chin. Their eyes were gray or blue, his dark and intense. (Later writers would say that his eyes looked as though he could read one's thoughts.) Their hair was light and straight, while his was thick, dark and curly. In researching her biography, Fuller consulted genetic specialists on the probability of parents such as the Bacons having a child such as Francis. According to Mendel's law, she learned, it was highly unlikely that the blue-eyed Bacons could have parented the brown-eyed Francis.[5]

If Francis was not a Bacon, then who was he? A careful study of portraits of Elizabeth Tudor and her lover, Robert Dudley, Lord Leicester, tells a revealing story. The face of the Bacons' "son" bore a remarkable resemblance to the very Tudor appearance

Robert Dudley, Queen Elizabeth and Francis Bacon
These miniatures by Nicholas Hilliard show the family resemblance
between Elizabeth, Robert Dudley and their unacknowledged son, Francis
Bacon.

of Elizabeth herself, except for the coloring. Her coloring was fair
with red or tawny hair, whereas his was dark. There was aristocracy imprinted in every line of his anatomy—in the lift of the
well-shaped head, in the high brow, in the expressive eyebrows
and the deep-set eyes. As for coloring and other features, the
similarity of the narrow, intellectual face and dark good looks of
Lord Leicester and young Francis is so clear that it almost seems
amusing. It can hardly be missed.

This trio of portraits—Elizabeth, Leicester and Francis—tells
a strange story. Surely, worshipers at the shrine of "Gloriana,"
her courtiers, would not have missed the resemblance. However,
there was a conspiracy of silence abroad in the land and, as we
shall see, the cipher story explains why.

We know what the young Francis looked like because of a

miniature portrait of him at the age of eighteen created by Nicholas Hilliard, Elizabeth's favorite court painter. Hilliard painted many portraits of Elizabeth and one of Leicester but, as far as we know, not one of the Bacons except for Francis. Comparing the miniatures of Francis and Leicester, one might think that they were portraits of the same man at different ages. The portrait painter was so impressed by the unusual brilliance of the boy that he made a note of it for posterity, painting around the border the Latin phrase "Si tabula daretur digna animum mallem." Loosely translated it reads: "O that I could have drawn a picture worthy of his mind."

On the Bacon side of the story, there are extant three painted terra-cotta busts, which had been commissioned as a set by their family. There is one of Sir Nicholas—stolid, square faced and heavyset. There is Lady Anne—solemn, round faced, with a small round nose and slightly protruding eyes. Then there is one of a small round-faced boy, looking for all the world like his mother. For years it has been claimed that this child was Francis, the son Anthony being left out. However, Daphne du Maurier in her *Golden Lads* gives convincing evidence that the bust is of young Anthony rather than Francis.[6] Museum authorities point out that the bust was done at a time when Francis would have been but four years old, much too young to have been the subject of the sculpture. Anthony was exactly the right age. So it was Francis, not Anthony, who was left out of the Bacon family group. Francis, on the other hand, was included with the portraits done by the court painter who worked under commission of the queen.

Whatever the truth of his birth, little dark-eyed Francis was unaware of a problem in those happy, early childhood days. He was closely guarded and deeply loved by both Lady Anne and the lord keeper. It is said that he was always the favorite in this household, and perhaps it is true. Both Bacons must have been painfully aware of the responsibilities as well as the honor of having a royal child in their care; they could hardly have avoided treating him with an extra touch of respect. As the boys grew into young men, it was always Anthony who received letters of admonition from their mother, scolding them for what she considered to be the error of their ways. Francis was usually included in the scoldings, but the letters were addressed to Anthony. Perhaps Anne was a mother who did not hesitate to admonish a child of her own, but she preferred not to scold an adopted son of such noble birth.

Lady Anne's life as the wife of the older Sir Nicholas was a busy one. Besides running two huge households and their staffs—over a hundred servants, it is said, between their country estate at Gorhambury and their official city residence, York House—she also managed to keep at her translations of religious tracts, turning Latin into English, for the famous Bishop Jewel. This and other intellectual activities would have influenced little Francis as he himself grew more interested in the literary world.

If it was indeed Queen Elizabeth who had chosen Anne Cooke Bacon to be the foster mother of her child, she could not have chosen more wisely. Anne was capable, wise, warm and conscientious. However, keeping harmony with the high-handed, impetuous queen could not have been easy for her. They had been friends from childhood, when Anne's father, Sir Anthony, was tutor to little Prince Edward, Elizabeth's brother, who died so tragically young. Both Princess Elizabeth and Anne Cooke had often been included in the schoolroom lessons along with little Edward. The princess Elizabeth was a lonely and insecure little redheaded figure in those days, her father fluctuating almost daily as to whether to consider her, the child of Anne Boleyn, a legitimate heir or not. The psychological effect on the small child can hardly be measured. Anne Bacon's practical common sense and the stability of her home life must have appealed greatly to the lonely princess, whose temperament was so radically different.

Sir Nicholas and Lady Anne's position was not always an easy one to be in. Elizabeth expected much of her favorites, and although her favor brought special privileges and wealth, it was also an expensive matter to keep up with her demands. Aware of what the queen expected of her ministers, the Bacons felt obliged to provide themselves with a large country estate that the queen would deem suitable for her lord keeper (and, perhaps, her child).

The Bacons started work on a beautiful country estate, Gorhambury, close to the ruins of the Abbey at Saint Albans. It was surely disheartening for Sir Nicholas when the queen, on her first visit to their new estate, remarked sourly: "My Lord, what a little house you have gotten!" The lord keeper managed to cover his consternation with a witty reply: "Madam, my house is well, but it is you who have made me too big for my house!" This was the kind of sharp wit that Elizabeth adored. Nevertheless, construction would have to go on a few years longer, for the queen's demands must be satisfied. Sir Nicholas could not be blamed if he breathed a sigh of frustration.

Another of the Cooke sisters, Mildred, was married to William Cecil, later Lord Burghley, the great secretary of state, who would be so essential to the queen throughout her reign. The Cecils were in the same position as the Bacons—Her Majesty must be pleased. The Cecils must build a house to suit the queen. They built their gorgeous estate, Theobalds, a few miles from Gorhambury, and the two families were constantly visiting back and forth.

The Cecils, too, had problems with the queen's demands. She complained that they had not provided a bedchamber large enough for her royal self when she came to visit. Also, certainly much to the Cecils' disapproval, she insisted that an apartment be

An old engraving of Gorhambury
Sir Nicholas Bacon built this house in the 1560s, and Francis spent much of
his childhood here, returning again in his final years after retirement from
public life in 1621.

Lord Burghley's Theobalds
from Morris's *Country Seats* (1880).
William Cecil, Lord Burghley, built his great country house as a place
suitable to receive the queen. The main front of the building ran for more
than a quarter of a mile. Francis probably visited here often as a child, and
it was here, many years later, that James I invested him as Viscount St.
Alban.

built for her beloved Robert Dudley, earl of Leicester, next to her own on the third floor. It was a matter of discretion not to comment too loudly on this arrangement.

The Bacons' estate—a sturdy rectangular house with square turrets on either end, surrounded by a forest of huge oak and beech trees, lovely gardens and wide lawns—was within easy riding distance of the Cecils' Theobalds. It would have made a wonderful childhood home for any little prince, and apparently the queen was finally satisfied, for she visited there often. William Cecil, always a careful note taker, recorded all of the queen's progresses and royal visits and conscientiously noted the dates of arrival and departure. When the queen visited Gorhambury, however, Cecil inexplicably followed a different policy. He duly recorded the date of arrival but not the date of departure. Curious about these omissions, historian John Nichols, author of *The Progresses and Public Processions of Queen Elizabeth* (1823), checked the records and found documents signed by Elizabeth at Gorhambury at times when her presence there was not publicly acknowledged.[7] One could perhaps find all sorts of explanations to account for these omissions, but the most logical may be that she had some special interest at Gorhambury that she was not eager to acknowledge.

In the *Progresses,* we note that Nichols was not wholly unaware of suspicious actions in the queen's private world. In 1572, he says, a certain Mr. Fisher (in just what capacity we don't know) attended Her Majesty while she traveled from Warwick to Kenilworth, one of the beautiful estates Elizabeth had given to her favorite, Robert Dudley, Lord Leicester. The things that Mr. Fisher learned during that trip, according to Nichols, were "such things … had been better untold. What these things mean is not for everyone to know."[8]

S. A. E. Hickson has suggested that Francis may have been

William Cecil, Lord Burghley
Lord Burghley was Elizabeth's trusted chief minister and also Francis's nominal uncle, having married Mildred Cooke, Anne Bacon's sister. Francis probably spent much time in his youth at Burghley's estate Theobalds.

present on the occasion of the magnificent entertainment that Leicester staged in 1575 at Kenilworth Castle in honor of the queen. The lord keeper would have seen to it that his family did not miss the fun. And it appears that Francis may have found delight in leaving a record of all he saw of the remarkable doings at Kenilworth.

Shortly after the festivities had come to an end, a beautifully descriptive little treatise in the form of a letter was published, signed by "the black Prince." It was an exuberant account of the gorgeous three-week-long affair at Kenilworth. The writer had obviously gloried in the whole spectacle and he treats his reader to detailed descriptions—the lovely gardens "respirant from the redolent plant and fragrant herbs and flowers"; the lavish refreshments; the jewels; the "melodious music and tunes of birds"; the sparkling palace, "at daytime so glittering by glass, at night by continual brightness of candle fire"; the tent receiving the queen, which was so extensive that it took "seven cart loads of pegs to anchor the ropes." Then there were the masques and pageants, one of which had a mermaid riding on the back of a dolphin, surely the inspiration for the passage in *A Midsummer Night's Dream* in which Oberon refers to "a mermaid, on a dolphin's back."[9]

The young author of this letter (we know he was young by the exuberance and boyishness of his writing) seems to have been impressed by the pageant of King Arthur's Lady of the Lake, with its inference that all had been prepared for Elizabeth, one of "Arthur's heirs by right" in direct line of succession. Neither did he pass up the opportunity to describe the debonair host, Lord Leicester himself, with his "amplitude of mind." Nor were the many charms of the lovely lady guests neglected.

Most amusing of all is the youthful writer's description of his own preparations for the festivities. His hair was made "to shine like a mallard's wing by means of a sponge dipped in a little capon's grease." His ruff (the elaborate starched collar of the times) was "marshaled [into place] by a setting stick." He was "fair starched sleeked and glistening like a pair of new shoes."[10]

The buoyant letter was published by an unknown Robert Laneham (or Langham, as this name was sometimes spelled). Whoever Laneham may have been, records of the master of requests show that the letter was banned by royal order three weeks after its appearance. The records show that six copies went to a Mr. Wilson, two copies were ordered to be sent to William Cecil (Lord Burghley) and two to Sir Nicholas Bacon. All others were to be suppressed, most likely destroyed. Somehow the duchess of Portland had managed to save a copy, according to

Hickson. She gives the age of the writer, "the Minstrel of Islington," as "XIV" (fourteen), the exact age of Francis at the time. All of this leads Hickson to suggest in *The Prince of Poets* that Laneham was none other than the lord keeper's literarily adept foster son, Francis himself.[11]

It is widely believed that this event at Kenilworth provided the inspiration for *A Midsummer Night's Dream*. It seems that the play also reflects the circumstances of Francis's own childhood. Hickson sees Queen Titania as Elizabeth and Lord Leicester as Oberon. The changeling child* over whom they had a falling out would be, of course, Francis. Perhaps Hickson is right, because the cipher tells us that at this early stage Elizabeth was not hesitant to show motherly affection for her child. And perhaps these lines from the play reflect Leicester's difficult situation, forbidden by the queen from acknowledging his own son:

> For Oberon is passing fell and wrath,
> Because that she as her attendant hath
> A lovely boy, stolen from an Indian king;
> She never had so sweet a changeling.
> And jealous Oberon would have the child
> Knight of his train, to trace the forests wild.
> But she perforce withholds the lovèd boy,
> Crowns him with flowers, and makes him all her joy.
> *act II, sc.1*

During his youth and childhood, Francis, of course, was unaware of any of this. He knew only that the queen's attentions to him were flatteringly intense. His chaplain, Rawley, tells us that the queen loved to call the child to her side and ask him solemn questions. She would then guffaw in delight at his

---

* A changeling is an infant who has been secretly exchanged for another.

intelligent answers.[12]

Anyone could see that she doted on the child, and perhaps Lord Robert, Elizabeth's "sweet Robin," was torn between jealousy and pride as he watched the interplay between mother and son. This child might be the link that could keep him forever basking in the sunshine of the queen's favor. On the other hand, it was his ambition to be named the queen's prince consort—or maybe even king in his own name—and it was possible that a son could prevent that from taking place. Leicester was surely as confused as everyone else by these strange circumstances and by the queen's constant indecision concerning their relationship.

Another little vignette is intriguingly suggestive of a more than ordinary relationship between Elizabeth, Leicester and a child. The Duke of Norfolk tells it in his *Confessions for High Treason*. Here is a winsome view of Her Majesty at her domestic best:

> When the Court was at Guilford, I went unaware into the Queen's Privy Chamber; and found her sitting on the threshold of the door listening with one ear to a little child who was singing and playing on the lute to her; and with other to Leicester who was kneeling by her side.[13]

Surely Norfolk, who was Elizabeth's only duke, knew who the child was, but he didn't name him. He was in enough trouble already for his involvement with Mary Queen of Scots. Alfred Dodd, biographer, thinks that there is no longer any mystery about what inspired "Shakespeare" to write in sonnet 8:

> Music to hear, why hear'st thou music sadly?...
> Mark how one string, sweet husband to another,
> Strikes each in each by mutual ordering;
> Resembling sire, and child, and happy mother,
> Who all in one, one pleasing note do sing.

As Francis grew into his teenage years, the people who cared for him day by day were aware that there was something exceptional about their charge. Indeed, this child was to have an extraordinary life—and there are those who believe that this destiny was written in the stars.

It was in 1572 that nature took up the challenge of Aristotle, who had claimed more than a thousand years earlier that the heavens where immutable, that the stars were fixed, that nothing could ever change in the skies. In the fourteenth year of Elizabeth's happy reign, the heavens proved him wrong. A marvelous new star (a supernova) flashed out of the constellation Cassiopeia. The star was as short-lived as it was brilliant. Within a year and a half, it was gone, leaving behind a world startled by this awesome portent. Tycho Brahe, a Danish astronomer, was the first to record its appearance. He reported it as being brighter than Venus, so bright that it could be clearly seen even in the fullest light of day.

Some said it was a comet; others, a star. Some said it had the same luminous appearance as the star that guided the Magi, the Bethlehem Star, which had appeared so mysteriously fifteen hundred years before. Whatever it was called, it was a strange sight in the heavens during the months that it could be clearly seen.

After sixteen months the Guest Star disappeared, never to shine again, leaving even the astronomers musing over its appearance in the "unchangeable" heavens. The portent of the star of 1572 was not easily understood. But one man had claimed to know all about it—the famous Swiss mystic Theophrastus Bombastus von Hohenheim, better known as Paracelsus. He died twenty years before Francis was born, but he had been confidently prophesying the coming of the comet for many years. When it comes, he predicted, it will be "a harbinger" of a great renovation of society—"the coming revolution," he called it. The comet would announce the presence of "a marvelous being ... who as yet lives not, and who shall reveal many things." This being would be a master of all arts, bearing three divine gifts to change the face of the world.[14]

Prophecies of comets, stars and rarely gifted beings did not ring as strangely in the ears of Elizabethans as they do in our ears today. (And we, in our time, do not treat them as scornfully as did our brothers of fifty years ago.) Just who this great master of all arts would be only the gods in heaven could know for certain, but the one man of that time who came closest to fulfilling Paracelsus's prophecy was our man of mystery, Francis Bacon.

Francis was about twelve years old at the time of the appearance of the star, but already he was showing the marks of genius. He was a young prodigy coming into his adulthood, ready to leave the security and warmth of the Bacon home for a broader life as a student at Trinity College, on the River Cam at Cambridge. Was his coming of age the event prophesied by Paracelsus? Some Baconians believe that it was and that the three gifts are Bacon's outer philosophical and scientific writings, the plays of Shakespeare, and his involvement with the Rosie-Crosse and Freemasonry movements.

Whether or not Francis was the particular genius to whom Paracelsus referred, we are told, even by the orthodox, that by the age of fifteen Francis had already formed in his mind a plan by which he hoped to reform "the whole wide world." It was an admittedly comprehensive ambition for such a young man, but future events would show that he came amazingly close to accomplishing it. It is important to an understanding of his life to consider for a moment the extent of the training he received up until the time he left for Cambridge. It was an education literally fit for a king.

Elizabeth Bowen, a modern biographer of Bacon, has called

the environment of his childhood an Elizabethan Eden.[15] Indeed, there is small doubt that any environment in sixteenth century England could have been more conducive to a "felicitous childhood" than the one provided by the foster parents of Francis. The surroundings at Gorhambury were already rich with history by the time their family moved into their lavish new country estate. The ruins of the old Roman town of Verulamium, twenty miles northwest of London, still contained the only Roman theater known to have been built in England—an appropriate landmark for one who would grow to be the greatest playwright of England!

The present town of St. Albans grew on the foundation of these ruins, taking its name from the third-century man who exchanged robes with a fugitive Christian priest and was executed in his place. Alban, the first Christian martyred on English soil, was later sainted. A church was built on the site of his martyrdom, and tens of thousands of pilgrims visit there each year. It is said that miracles of healing have occurred and still occur there, even today. In *Henry V, Part 1,* Shakespeare describes a scene in which a miracle takes place:

> A miracle! a miracle!...
> Forsooth, a blind man at Saint Alban's shrine,
> Within this half hour hath received his sight—
> A man that ne'er saw in his life before.
>
> *act II, sc. 1*

It was from the ancient Roman Verulamium and the town of St. Albans that Bacon would choose his titles when James I granted what Elizabeth had steadfastly refused him for so many years—a promotion to the peerage. Francis eventually became Baron Verulam, Viscount St. Alban—man-made titles for a prince who had been born to be a king. Interestingly, he left the *s* off of *St. Albans* (although today you'll often find the *s* included), thus indicating the name of the saint (Alban), not the town. Bacon's choice may not surprise students of mysticism who believe that Alban was a former incarnation of Francis Bacon.

Summers at Gorhambury were a time of freedom for the Bacon boys. It was a place of wide open vistas and fresh country air. When the family moved to the Bacons' official residence in London (York House) for the winter season, the atmosphere was considerably changed—to the congestion of a crowded, unsanitary city and the artificial, albeit exciting, atmosphere of the British court. "I was brought up at court," Francis would later say.

Whether in town or in the country, a whole retinue of tutors followed close on their heels, and even at Gorhambury the boys did not escape their daily lessons. Wherever they were, there were books to be read. Sir Nicholas had an impressive library of hand-copied volumes of the recently discovered Greek classics. There were also newer ones, products of the recently invented printing press, which was spreading across Europe. Only a few were printed in English, and Francis quickly learned to read French, Latin, Greek, Spanish, Italian, Hebrew and even a little Dutch. He also had access to the Cecils' great library at Theobalds and to the considerable collection of Lady Anne's father, Sir Anthony Cooke, at nearby Gidea Hall. Before he entered Cambridge at the age of twelve, Francis could read easily in many languages. Later he claimed acquaintance with every language of the Western world.

That Anthony and Francis Bacon were both educated in a manner reserved for the most privileged youths of the land is a fact that cannot be doubted. It is one point upon which all historians agree. No one in England had received a finer education than did the youngest sons of Nicholas Bacon. All the best available tutors were hired. Conscientious Sir Nicholas even called for a special tutor to help with his "youthful retinue, among whom all manner of vices do increase apace, and zeal, virtue, and the true fear of God decrease through lack of due admonishment and instruction."[16]

What a constant worry it all must have been for Lady Anne too, not only her own precious son to supervise but also the children of her husband's first marriage and, most worrisome of all, a royal prince of the house of Tudor. Small wonder that the time was to come when Francis and Anthony would fear for their mother's sanity. We can imagine what a great comfort it would have been for Lady Anne to be able to call on her own father, Sir Anthony Cooke (who had been the tutor of Edward VI) for guidance in the education of these lively lads.

Although there has been what has been called a conspiracy of silence over the early years of Francis Bacon's life, we do not have to rely entirely on speculation concerning his education. We have his own statement in cipher about how he had puzzled over the queen's unusual interest in his learning:

> It doth as often recur [in memory] that the Queen, our royal mother, sometimes said in Sir Nicholas' ear on going to her coach; "Have him well instructed in knowledge that future station shall make necessary." Naturally quick of hearing, it reached our ears ... and [was a matter] long turned and pondered upon.[17]

It would be several years yet before Francis would be able to untangle the meaning of the words.

Historically, there is an odd account left by Elizabeth's tutor, the famous Roger Ascham, that casts a considerable shadow of doubt on the chastity of the queen and adds credence to the cipher story. Ascham, a pillar of integrity and respectability, gave a puzzling glance of an interview he had with Elizabeth when Francis was but two years old.

It was in December of 1563 that Ascham received a summons to be a special guest at a dinner with certain Privy Councillors at Windsor Castle. During the meal one of the councillors asked Ascham an unusual question: Would he consider writing a book on the proper training and education of a young aristocrat? Ascham was widely respected for his remarkable modern views on education, in complete opposition to the "learn by rote and the hickory rod" philosophy of the day. He stood for tolerance and kindness in instructing students and believed that children were better "allured by love than driven by beating to attain good learning" and that goodness and readiness of will to learn were the essentials of effectual scholarship. Bacon would later write extensively on these same principles—respect for a child's own individuality was the essential ingredient of proper education.

The queen, apparently appreciating the value of Ascham's theory, had sent her councillors to urge him to record his views for some purpose of her own. As enlightened as were Ascham's views, he was not inclined to write such a book and declined the invitation, making various excuses for his refusal. The next thing he knew, he was called into the presence of the queen herself. It must have been a strange interview. What Elizabeth had to say to her old tutor in the privacy of her chamber we can only guess. Apparently, some secret was discussed that thoroughly alarmed Ascham, for it cost him at least one night's sleep. He wrote: "The night following, I slept little, my head was so full of this our former talk, and I so mindful, somewhat to satisfy the honest request of so dear a friend."[18] (The orthodox understanding of Ascham's sleepless night, of course, makes no mention of the queen's secret.)

Ascham would not have been startled out of a night's sleep merely by being called into the royal presence. He and Elizabeth were truly old friends; they had read Latin or Greek together every morning when she was younger and had frequently played cards together in the evenings. He would not have been shy with his favorite student. Whatever the queen had to say to him was likely something that shocked or excited him deeply. The result was that he did change his mind and he agreed to write the book, which is titled *The Scholemaster, or plain and perfect way of teaching children to understand, write and speak the Latin tongue, but especially purposed for the private bringing up of Youth in Gentlemen's and Noblemen's Houses....* This little book with the long title is a classic guide to the education not only of aristocratic youth but, more specifically, of young princes who would be destined one day to rule. Ascham did not live to see it published, in 1570, under the title *The Scholemaster (Schoolmaster).*

Nearly two hundred years later, in 1761, when all the principal characters involved in the mysterious affair had long been gone, a preface or dedication written in the form of a letter by Ascham was discovered and published by one James Bennet. Some believe it was intended as a dedication of *The Scholemaster* to the queen, but it was an incredibly accusatory bit of writing. One would be curious to know if it had ever been read by the queen to whom it was addressed. Had it been published during her lifetime, serious repercussions would surely have followed for poor Ascham, no matter how much he was favored by Her Majesty. (A Norfolk gentleman by the name of Marsham had lost his ears for daring to say that Elizabeth had not one but two sons by Lord Leicester.)

The curious dedication was addressed to "Divae Elizabethae" and was dated October 30, 1566. It was a strange topic for anyone to have written to a young virgin queen and a dangerous one to boot, considering Elizabeth's excessive touchiness at the least hint of criticism, particularly of her much-touted chastity.

For some inscrutable reason, Ascham chose to draw Elizabeth's attention to the biblical story of King David—he who had committed the crimes of both adultery and murder in taking to himself the glamorous Bathsheba.[19] (Later we will see how Elizabeth and Leicester were accused of murdering Leicester's wife to make way for their own marriage.) Ascham seems to be reassuring his former student that although she may be as guilty as David himself, surely she would be forgiven, even though

> God suffered him [David] to fall into the deepest pit of wickedness, to commit the cruellest murder, the shamefullest adultery.... As in a fair glass [mirror], your Majesty shall see and acknowledge, by God's dealing with David, even very many like dealings of God with your Majesty ... and in the end have as David had ... prosperity and surest felicity for you, yours, and your posterity.[20]

This was an odd comparison for Ascham to make concerning a supposedly virgin queen with no prospect of children! What could he have been thinking? Did she ever see it? We may never know.

There is also further evidence of the marriage between Elizabeth and Leicester. Andrew Lyell tells the story that he heard from the earl of Pembroke:

> When Queen Victoria was staying at Wilton House, the Earl of Pembroke told her that in the muniment room was a document which formed written evidence that in 1560 Elizabeth I married the Earl of Leicester. The marriage was performed in secret oath of absolute secrecy. At the time of that marriage the Queen was pregnant by Lord Leicester. The French and Spanish ambassadors reported this and the death of Amy Robsart to their Courts. They also told the Queen that if this was confirmed by her marriage to Leicester, France and Spain would jointly invade England, to

remove the Protestant Queen and replace her by a Catholic monarch. Queen Victoria demanded that this document should be produced, and, after she had examined it, she put it on the fire, saying, "one must not interfere with history." This information was given to me by the 15th Earl of Pembroke, the grandfather of the present Earl.[21]

A surprising reference to the queen's marriage and children is found in an older edition of the *Dictionary of National Biography,* that fount of English history:

> Whatever were the Queen's relations with Dudley before his wife's death, they became closer after it. It was reported that she was formally betrothed to him, that she had secretly married him in Lord Pembroke's house, and that she was "a mother already" (January, 1560–1).... Next year (in 1562) the reports that Elizabeth had children by Dudley revived. One Robert Brooke of Devizes was sent to prison for publishing the slander.[22]

Francis's young world was filled with exciting characters of all classes and all backgrounds. At one time or another, the great and the near great of the entire kingdom passed through the halls of York House or across the lawns of Gorhambury. They would all have known Francis by name, and he would have responded courteously in his gracious way to their jolly greetings.

There were also many family relationships. The talented Cooke sisters enjoyed no one's company more than that of each other. They had married men who were leading figures in the Elizabethan establishment, and they spent their days in a continuous trek between each other's homes, visiting other Bacons as well as cousins—the Killigrews, Russells, Hobys and Cecils.

Also there were those interesting additions to the Cecil and

Bacon households, the young aristocrats taken in as wards of the Crown. Under the English law, any young nobleman whose father died before his son came of age at twenty-one became a ward of the Crown. Sudden and early death was not uncommon in the sixteenth century, and there were always a few heirs of wealthy, deceased noblemen to be cared for by the master of the court of wards, who was handsomely rewarded for his ministrations on behalf of the fatherless boys and had complete authority over the boys' affairs. Cecil held the post under Elizabeth and he ran what amounted to a boarding school for many well-known, interesting aristocratic boys.

Among the Cecil wards was Edward de Vere, seventeenth earl of Oxford. He joined the household at the age of twelve and later entered unwillingly into a disastrous marriage with Cecil's daughter Anne. There were also the earl of Rutland, who came at the age of fourteen, and the famous earl of Southampton, Henry Wriothesley, whose father had died when his son was only eight. All of these young men—Oxford, Rutland and Southampton— were to take prominent places in the later affairs of Francis Bacon and in the strange anatomy of the Shakespeare-Bacon literary circle.

Most famous of the Cecil wards was the young earl of Essex, stunning Robert Devereux, who had joined the household at the age of nine after the death of his father (some said from poison), in Dublin Castle in the year 1576. This new little earl, along with Francis Bacon, older by six years, would be an actor in one of the most tragic and poignant dramas ever performed on the broad stage of English history.

Francis and Robert were true blood brothers, both royal princes of the house of Tudor, *enfants perdus.** Both were lost children born of the secret marriage between Elizabeth and her

---

* *enfants perdus*: French, lit. "lost children."

lover, Lord Leicester. Francis's affection for his unacknowledged brother, Essex, was constant throughout his life.

> The love we bear him [Essex] is as fresh at this day as it was in his boyhood when the relationship was for some time so carefully kept unknown—as the fact was, for years, guarded of our high birth and station. Not a thought then entered the brain, that it was not a pleasure for us both to share.[23]

The bond between them from the beginning seems to have been of a more than ordinary friendship. Perhaps a subconscious recognition of their true relationship drew them together even before the truth was revealed. Francis was fifteen before he knew the true story of his birth. Bonnie little Robert Devereux was, so the cipher says, a second son born to the queen and her secret husband in November of 1566.[24]

We do not have to depend wholly on the cipher for our information. There are several hints in history giving clues that this second son was given by the queen to her beautiful cousin, Lettice Knollys, to be raised. Lettice, a granddaughter of Mary Boleyn (Ann Boleyn's sister) and therefore a cousin to Elizabeth, had been married for some time to Walter Devereux, viscount of Hereford. Marriage did not seem to curb Lettice's flirtatious style—she was a born coquette—and for a long time when Leicester felt Elizabeth's interest in him waning, he would flirt with this glamorous cousin to make her jealous. When the boy baby was born, supposedly the first son of Walter and Lettice Devereux, he was not named, as was the custom, after his supposed father, but he was given the name Robert (after Lord Leicester?). It was the next son of the family who was given the name Walter.

Another oddity about Robert's birth was that one finds no record of such a birth in the parish register. The births of the other three Devereux children—Penelope, Dorothy and Walter—

are duly recorded, as one would expect, at their estate of Chartley. Only the birth of Robert was left unrecorded (as the birth of Francis had been). History detectives, trying to discover where Elizabeth had been at the time of Robert's birth, quote historian Froude, who records that on November 11 of that year, the queen had received an important state letter to which she did not reply until a month later. During the month of Robert's birth, she was sequestered in her private apartments transacting no public business. Equally telling is the fact that Sir Henry Wotton observed that Walter Devereux had "a very cold conceit" of the child Robert[25] and showed a marked preference for his second son, a natural enough feeling if the older one was only adopted. A suspicion that Devereux was bribed to adopt the child is strengthened by the fact that shortly after the birth, Elizabeth gave Lord Walter a manor in Essex and a few years later created him the new earl of Essex. One might guess that it was compensation for taking an unwanted child off her hands.

Chapter Three

A Life-Changing Revelation

Certainly custom is most perfect when it beginneth in young years: this we call education, which is in effect but an early custom.

The gossipy and scandalous affairs of Elizabeth's court formed the environment in which Francis Bacon was to grow and mature before his plan for "the reformation of the whole wide world" could begin. But the whispered tales never reached the ears of the boys in the Bacon household. Sir Nicholas and Lady Anne would have seen to that. Francis knew of no problems during the first twelve years of his life more serious than how to relate to the fascinating world around him and how to absorb as much of the teaching of his tutors as possible without losing the creative urges of his soul. There were so many things to be carefully observed—the echoes of his voice bouncing back from the surrounding hills, the fascinating entertainers at country fairs, the vibrations of instruments when alternating strings were plucked.

Most difficult of all may have been trying to get along with his young cousin from the nearby estate at Theobalds, Robert Cecil. From the beginning, Francis had trouble with this cousin. The boy was the only surviving son of Mildred Cooke Cecil who, like her sister Anne, was a second wife to an older man with an already established family. This only child of Lady Mildred was adored and spoiled by both parents, though he was far from being an attractive boy. Perhaps their concern for him was more intense because of his shortcomings. He had a crooked back and one shoulder that hunched lower than the other. He was thin, pale and colorless and not very affectionate. But he did have an exceptionally bright mind, and he was to use that mind with great success to keep events molded to his liking as the years passed by. It is probable that little Robert was deformed from birth, although his mother claimed that the problem was caused by a nanny who dropped him on his head in his infancy.

Years later Francis would write one of his famous essays, "Of Envy," which everyone recognized as being based on his experiences with his little cousin Robert Cecil. It was a realistic but not flattering commentary:

> A man that hath no virtue in himself ever envieth virtue in others;... and whoso is out of hope to attain to another's virtue will seek to come at even hand by depressing another's fortune.[1]

As a philosopher and psychologist, Bacon considered the mind and the body to be so closely interconnected that one affects the other. In his essay "Of Deformity," he proposed that those suffering physical deformities are often "void of natural affection; and thus they have their revenge of nature." Perhaps this essay also drew on his experience with Robert Cecil, whose mental aberrations reflected the creation of his misshapen body. Bacon did admit, however, that sometimes the opposite is true and that on occasion physical weaknesses have been known to spur one on to excellence. Regarding those with physical deformities, he wrote, "sometimes they prove excellent persons; as was Agesilaus,*... Aesop,... and Socrates."[2]

It would not have been like the sunny-natured Francis to scorn his cousin without reason. Before their lives were over, he would claim more than adequate cause for his cautious wariness of Robert, and he states without apology that Robert Cecil was the cause of some of his greatest sorrows throughout the many years of his life. In cipher, he expressed his regret that he had not paid more attention to the extent of Robert's jealousy, for by the time he realized how subtle the danger was, it was too late to stem the tide of disaster.[3]

In his youth, however, Francis was unaware of disaster of any kind. He felt secure and cherished under the caring eye of Lady Anne and safe in the well-ordered household of a genuinely loving family. Surely Lady Anne's worries were many, but she loved all her boys and spared nothing of herself to see to their welfare. Her husband's health was a primary concern, with his immense corpulence to contend with. Queen Elizabeth had once remarked that "My Lord Keeper's soul is lodged well," teasing him about his size. Lady Anne did what she could to keep him comfortable and well-fed; undoubtedly she overdid it.

The time came only too soon for the boys to be cut loose from her apron strings and exposed to a broader way of life. When Francis was twelve, he was judged to be ready for college studies, not an unusually young age to matriculate at that time.

One day early in March 1573, Queen Elizabeth made an unexpected visit to the Bacons at Gorhambury. A few weeks later, Francis was packed off to the University of Cambridge, not to

---

* Agesilaus was a valiant king of Sparta, born with one leg shorter than the other.

Corpus Christi, the college Sir Nicholas had attended, but to Trinity, the newer college endowed by Henry VIII, the boy's unrecognized grandfather. Cambridge was also the university of Elizabeth's respected tutor, Roger Ascham. Anthony went with him. It seems highly probable that the queen played a major part in these decisions.

A warm welcome from Trinity's headmaster himself awaited the boys as soon as they arrived. John Whitgift, an ardent Protestant (whose policy, it was said, was to whip boys who came to chapel without their surplice and punish tutors caught with Catholic symbols in their rooms) was a special favorite of the queen. He was given direct charge of the two Bacon boys and he quartered them in rooms next to his own. The special treatment did not go unnoticed by the other students, and they often grumbled at the unfairness of it all. "Teacher's pets," they complained, and probably they were right. Several years later, Whitgift was promoted by the queen to the highest ecclesiastical office in the land, archbishop of Canterbury. He must have cared for his special charges well.

In spite of the obviously special treatment, Francis did not particularly enjoy life at Cambridge. He had anticipated great things, but his experience fell far short of expectations. Students were inclined to "riotous living," drinking and other excesses; they were less concerned with acquiring wisdom.

Even the physical surroundings of the university would have been a great disappointment after the order and beauty of Gorhambury. It wasn't that the countryside and the pink brick buildings were not lovely; they were, as they still are today. But the grounds were unkempt. Pigsties and muddy ditches were little improvement over the filthy sewers of London. A campaign to clean up the dung and mire of the streets, to remove the offensive odors, and to corral the pigs that roamed freely was unsuccessful, and it was not much better when Francis arrived.

It was not the physical surroundings that Francis and Anthony would have complained about, however; they were adaptable young men and they could, and did, adjust to whatever circumstances they faced. Nor would they have had a problem getting along with their fellow students, in spite of their preferred status. Both Bacons were said to be popular and full of fun, ready with interesting projects and conversation or an amusing joke or prank when the occasion called for it. They were not at that time, or at any other time, prudes. But they were also, or at least Francis was, serious about their studies and eager for the new learning that seemed to be almost palpably present in the atmosphere of the last quarter of the century. New and old ideas were waiting to be discovered and put to practical use. There was a great wind blowing from the West, a new breath of life from the new continent.

The possibilities were infinite, but who was there to put them to practical use? Francis felt that he was meant to be that person. By this time he had already made up his mind to "take all of learning for his province" and to use it for the groundwork of "a reformation of the whole wide world." Loren Eiseley, in *The Man Who Saw through Time*, believes that at this very young age Bacon had already visualized a promising future. He saw

> in all its splendor the invention of inventions, the experimental method which would unlock the riches of the modern world.... Bacon alone walked to the doorway of the future, flung it wide, and said to his trembling and laggard audience, "Look. There is tomorrow. Take it with charity lest it destroy you."[4]

Whether all these ambitions were clearly formed at so young an age we don't really know, but young Bacon was on the verge of formulating impressive goals and the thinking at Cambridge was not conducive to his state of mind. Later he would write that "the last thing anyone would be like to entertain [at the university] is an unfamiliar thought."[5] He also quickly learned that anyone who allowed himself freedom of inquiry or independence of judgment found himself isolated. There was little room for thinkers in the English universities.

The age of experimental science was beginning to press in on the world. Both Bacon and Galileo, across the sea in Italy, were its prophets. Copernicus had already made his discoveries about the motion of the planets, and Isaac Newton would soon observe the effects of gravity on his famous apple and prove Aristotle's theories to be just that, theories. No longer could churchmen argue without ridicule whether or not an angel could stand on the head (or the point) of a pin. Nor would they believe, simply because Aristotle said it was so, that ice was heavier than water or that lion cubs were born dead (or asleep) and came alive days later[6] or that a large object would fall faster than a small one. Observation and experimentation was what Francis was after. If it did not bear fruit, it could not pass his value test. Argumentation based only on logic was for the ancients. Only the "look and see" would do for the future, and he must be the pivot to make the wheel turn.

He was right, of course; that is what modern science is all about. Men of sharp wits were "shut up in their cells of a few authors (chiefly Aristotle their dictator), as their persons were shut up in the cells of monasteries and colleges,"[7] wrote Francis. Cambridge was too stultified for him; he and Anthony applied for permission to go home to Gorhambury before their third year was out. Permission was quickly given. For several months during their terms, Cambridge had been shut down due to plague. Thousands had perished in London alone, and Lady Anne was only too happy to have her charges safely under her own roof again. Just before Christmas 1575, the records for the Bacon boys at Trinity were closed and their formal schooling came to an end.

The abrupt departure from Cambridge may have occurred because of frustration at the poor quality of academic life there, or there may have been another more urgent reason. We cannot be sure (the exact timing of events is not quite clear). But we do know that from this time on, one no longer has to rely on what few historical reports we find of Francis's childhood. At this point Bacon's secret diary, as decoded by Gallup and Owen, takes up the story, as we'll see shortly.

Life must have seemed good to the "golden lads" as they returned home from school and anticipated with pleasure Christmas with the family at Gorhambury. Surely Lady Anne would have insisted on burning the largest Yule log to be found and on helping to prepare the holiday feast with her own hands to celebrate the gathering of the family once more. Francis and Anthony would have enjoyed it all and they undoubtedly felt themselves to be comfortably full of wisdom and maturity.

Biographers almost always comment on the delightful sense of humor Francis had, a "jesting wit" that he could never resist. (Ben Jonson later wrote that Bacon could never "pass by a jest."[8]) With a bon mot always on his tongue and a sense of the ridiculous ready at hand, he viewed lightly the divine comedy of life as it was lived in sixteenth century England. Anthony was also blessed with a fine and easy sense of humor, no doubt inherited and stimulated by his father's keen wit. Fortunately for all of them (though perhaps Lady Anne was the exception), considering what lay before them in the years ahead, they had the ability not to take themselves too seriously. It was Francis's rich humor and his deeply spiritual nature that were the anchors he credits for saving his sanity in the difficult times to come. Trouble was already peeking its unwelcome head around the corner.

That last Christmas at Gorhambury was to mark nearly the end of Francis's carefree days. In January he celebrated his fifteenth birthday. Later that year came the amazing encounter that would change the entire pattern of his life. It would catapult him into a premature adulthood that only a strong nature could bear. The faithful Anthony, always standing at his side, was swept along with him in great and unpredictable tides, which were not only to shape the course of their own lives but also to influence the course of Western history.

The stirring event that shook the foundations of the boy's world is recorded in the cipher account discovered by Dr. Owen. Whether events happened in the exact sequence as it is given in the cipher or whether they extended over longer or shorter periods of time is not clear. In the history plays written under the name of Shakespeare, Bacon was often deliberately inaccurate concerning the exact timing of events. He was first and foremost a playwright and only secondarily a historian. He often used poetic or dramatic license to condense the action of several weeks into a short space of a few days or even hours. This may have also been done in the cipher story. Far from detracting from the dramatic effect, it tends to enhance it.

In the excerpts from Owen's book, he condenses the action into the unlikely period of two days, giving a sense of the urgency of the moment. Here, as usual, he uses the royal "we" in speaking of himself:

> We were in [her] presence—as had many and often times occurred, Queen Elizabeth having a liking for our manners —with a number of the ladies and several of the gentlemen of her court.[9]

Francis gives us an intriguing look at court life in another part of his cipher:

> About her danced girls who upon her threw
> Sweet flowers and fragrant odours
> That afar did smell.[10]

These were, of course, the little ladies-in-waiting whom Elizabeth loved to have around her to keep her spirits light. Like her French counterpart, Catherine de Medici, she would have none but the prettiest to serve her. The girls often got bored and, in their idleness, they searched for gossip or scandal to divert them. Living here "solitary, alone, sequestered from all company but heart-eating melancholy, they must crucify someone."[11]

On this particular day, it is Francis's awkward little cousin, Robert Cecil, that they choose to "crucify." It is the daughter of Lord Scales, the most frivolous of the lot, who teases and dances with him, at the queen's prompting, and then laughs at his awkwardness. Furious and embarrassed, Robert quickly plots revenge. He complains to the queen, but she only laughs and taunts him further.

> This good gentleman
> Is not ashamed to confess that he takes infinite delight
> In singing, dancing, music, woman's company
> And such like pleasures, therefore,
> He wouldst have thee dance.
> And fair goddess [she jested to Lady Scales], fall not deep
> in love with him.[12]

This is too much for Robert, and he retaliates with a scheme of his own. One is inclined to sympathize a bit with him. Francis is too much of a psychologist not to do so also, although he has little respect for his sly, cunning ways. Still, he understands the underlying jealousy that motivates his every act. Francis stands by innocently watching the little drama unfolding before him, but suddenly he is drawn into the center of the fray:

It is an old saying: a blow with a word
Strikes deeper than a blow with a sword.
And he [Robert] was more galled with his royal
             mistresses' wit
Than he was with his merry companion. He went
             with the
Poor maid,... buried in silence....
And as I before have said in my essay,
Deformed persons are commonly even with nature;
For as nature hath done ill by them,
So do they by nature....
Therefore [they] are
Extreme bold, first in their own defense,...
To watch and observe the weakness of others,
That they may have somewhat to repay....
Cecil ... stood like a hapless,... sullen knave,
Plunged in melancholy, while his companions
Were busy discoursing about him
Behind his back....
He devises a way to be revenged upon
The soft, silly maid, and ... at the same time
To be honoured, admired and highly magnified.
To do this [he] cheats his fair companion
Into covert rubs of the honour
Of the queen.
   The complexion of the maid changed from pale to red
And from scarlet to pale when he
With big, thundering voice cried twice;
"All this condemns you to the death
To so much dishonour the fair queen."
As falcon to the lure, flies the queen to him
And ask'd what he had heard.
   "Madam, this innocent and pure model,
Moved by love for thee, told me
That you are an arrant whore and that thou

Bore a son to the noble Leicester.
I pray that thou give her chastisement."
   Holy St. Michael, what a change was here!
As a painted tyrant the queen stood
And like a neutral to her will and matter did nothing.
But as you often see against some storm
A silence in the heavens, the wrack stand still,
The bold winds speechless and the orb below
As hushed as death, anon the dreadful thunder
Doth rend the region. So, after a pause,
Upon mine honor you should have heard
The great queen roar against
The fair daughter of Lord Scales.[13]

There are few biographers that write about Elizabeth who don't have something to say concerning her vicious and uncontrolled temper. Agnes Strickland quotes Bohan, the queen's panegyrist, or writer:

She was subject to be vehemently transported with anger; and when she was so, she would show it by her voice, her countenance and her hand. She would chide her familiar servants so loud that they who stood afar off might sometimes hear her voice; and it was reported that for small offenses she would strike her maids-of-honor with her hand.[14]

Biographer Carolly Erickson says:

Her loud, vehement swearing and soldierly boasting made a strange counterpoint to her elegant dress and coquettish adornments. Flowers in her hair, round oaths on her lips, she stormed through her apartments, slapping and stabbing at her women when they displeased her and demanding to be told how beautiful she was.... With every whoop of her loud laughter, every stab of her mordant wit, every jerk of her restless, wiry body she undermined her womanly beauty and coarsened herself in others' eyes.[15]

From another modern biographer, Elizabeth Jenkins:

Elizabeth's nervous irritability [was] pronounced: it was known that it sometimes drove her to abandon argument in favor of a clip on the ear.... The queen broke Mary Scudamore's finger and then gave out that the injury was caused by a falling candlestick.[16]

Hearing of these temper tantrums, we are even more fascinated to read in the Owen cipher the firsthand account of an eyewitness to the raging scene with Lady Scales that was purposely precipitated by Robert Cecil:

"By Holy God!" in uncontrollable rage, said she,
"Thou liest, dishonorable vicious wench!
We were married to him by a friar—
A tried holy man—and if our dear love
Were but the child of state, it should be told.
The world should know our love,
Our master and our king of men....
And shalt thou do him shame?
By God, we will cut and mince
The throat that doth call us a common whore!"...
  With shrilling shrieks
The wretched lady turned
And in a twinkling, like the current, flies
In violent swift flight from her fair foe.
After her, in rage and malice,
The great queen chases.
As she doth bound away her sunny locks
Hang o'er her temples like a golden fleece,...
Her gown slipped from her,
And in her shift she springs along....
Whether fear, wicked fortune

Or cruel fate the girl mislead,
By some unfortunate hap or accident
Down did she tumble....
And the queen,
Who in her hand the foul knife grasps,
Did jump upon her....
"O, thou wilt kill me; forgive me;
Kill me not," and conjured her
To spare her life. But the cruelty
Of womankind is such the queen her heeded not....
I in painful silence stood,
Tears in mine eyes,
Being grieved that I, a youth,
Must mine eyes abase and be content
To see such wrong.

Francis goes to the queen, falls on his knees and begs permission to remove the lady from the room.

"Fair queen, I kiss your highness' hand.
See, see, O see what thou hast done!
Pause in God's name!
Be not as barbarous as a Roman or a Greek
Good madam, patience.
May not I remove the maiden [from your sight]?"
    The wrath of the enraged queen
Like an earthquake
Fell upon my head....
The queen like thunder spoke:
    "How now, thou cold-blooded slave,
Wilt thou forsake thy mother
And chase her honor up and down?
Curst be the time of thy nativity!...
I am thy mother. Wilt thou stoop now
And this good girl take away from me?"

I stand aghast and most astonished.
Then she said again:
   "Slave! I am thy mother.
Thou might be an emperor but that I will not
[Betray] whose son thou art;
Nor though with honourable parts
Thou art adorned, will I make thee great
For fear thyself should prove
My competitor and govern England and me."
As she spoke my legs like
Loaden branches bow to the earth,
As willing to leave their burden;
My strength fails and over
On my side I fall.
   "Fool! Unnatural, ingrateful boy!
Does it curd thy blood to hear me say
I am thy mother?"[17]

The queen's anger at this moment is expressed even more forcefully in the Bi-literal account. She makes a fateful vow:

In her look much malicious hatred burned toward me for ill-advised interference, and in hasty indignation said, "You are my own born son, but you, though truly royal, of a fresh, a masterly spirit, shall rule nor England, or your mother, nor reign o'er subjects yet to be. I bar from succession forever-more my best beloved first-born."[18]

Francis now gets up and stands in shocked amazement, scarcely believing the words he has heard. Robert also stands there, drinking in every word and calculating how he may turn this bizarre event to his own gain. No boyish fit of retaliation is this, but a deep-seated determination that someday, somehow he will destroy this hated rival. Francis continues the story:

The queen, being moved with rage,

> Thus herself bespoke and revealed
> Her secret to that devil who,
> Wrapped in the silence of his angry soul,
> Stood list'ning.
> Every word he heard,
> And as the queen
> Stooped her anointed head
> As low as mine and said,
> "Thou art my son," the fury of his heart
> He in his deforméd face portrayed.
> He shut his choler up in secret thoughts
> And did begin those deep engendered plans
> That kindled into flame first at
> My honorable brother's death,
> And my banishment from the English throne.[19]

Robert, deftly feigning innocence, then goes to the queen and says he will, to spare Her Majesty's honor, take the blame for the injury done to Lady Scales. Elizabeth scolds him,[20] but he has managed to insert himself into her good graces while Francis is left in confusion.

Chapter Four

More Revelations

If he be compassionate towards the afflictions of others,
it shows that his heart is like the noble tree that is
wounded itself when it gives the balm.

As the cipher autobiography continues, we
are witness to the turmoil of Francis's emotions. He leaves the
queen and blindly runs for home, a hurt child turning to the
mother he trusts. It is not clear from the cipher just where this
encounter occurred, perhaps at Whitehall (or York Place), for
Bacon's home is not far away, the "fair Gothic mansion" next
door at York House. He bursts into the entrance hall and finds
Lady Anne just ready to go out for a ride in her fashionable new
carriage. Lady Anne tells Francis to wait for her, that she will
return shortly; but one look at his distraught face warns her that
here is something too important to be put off. She dismisses the
carriage and enters into the withdrawing room with her adopted
son stumbling, blind with tears, behind her:

> I drop down upon my knee before her
> And, hanging my head, say:
> "Pardon me, madam. Today the queen told me

She is my mother and not you."...
"I am come to know the secret of my childhood.
Were you both my mothers?
You do not speak:
Is't so? Is my honoured name of no note?
Am I a bastard of the queen?...
You see me here so full of grief,
Why will you not answer?"[1]

A more poignant scene can scarcely be imagined—the distressed foster mother, angry because the queen has broken her promise never to speak of Francis's royal birth, and the sobbing adopted son on his knees pleading to be told the truth. "You will not relish the truth," Lady Anne warns him. But at least, she says, he need not fear that he is a bastard, that most awful of all accusations at the time. He is the legitimate offspring of a marriage between Elizabeth and "a noble gentleman" (her lover Leicester).[2]

The strange story that Anne Bacon told this lad, whom she loved as much as her own son if not more, is one that is not accepted today by orthodox historians. Nor do history books tell the dramatic story of this sudden elevation of the supposed son of Sir Nicholas Bacon from his humble but secure position as a commoner into the precarious place of the firstborn son of Elizabeth Tudor, a prince of the royal blood. This made him the highest noble in a land which revered its monarchs as near gods. And yet he was to be the victim of a cat-and-mouse game in which his mother would accept him now and the next moment deny him vehemently until he was nearly driven to despair.

If historians accepted this story—and the evidence is all there—they might find keys to some of the puzzles of the Elizabethan age. There were many oddities of the time, and few have been satisfactorily solved. Milton Waldman, in *Elizabeth and Leicester,* paraphrases a famous remark of Bacon's that "there is no excellent beauty that hath not some strangeness in the proportion"[3] when he says, "In all fascination there is an element of mystery." Waldman writes:

> Perhaps the abiding fascination of the Elizabethan Age lies in the fact that something so well known can be so little understood. By comparison with most periods of the remoter past its documentation is remarkably complete.... We can pretty well construct the whole range of properties, physical and mental, with which it carried on the business of living. And yet it somehow remains bathed in that atmosphere of strangeness, of human unrecognizability almost....
>
> Something eludes us, some vital element is needed to ... give meaning to this mass of information. We can recover the properties but not the psychology, uncover the achievements but not their source in human motive and character. We seem to possess every facility for knowing the Elizabethan Age except the power to understand its people.[4]

The late scholar Dame Frances Yates of the University of London admits to a similar puzzlement over the age:

> I have been moving for a very long time among these thoughts and these people. Almost a lifetime has been spent in trying to understand a period which has always seemed, not a dead past, but vitally important for present imaginative and spiritual life.[5]

It should be unnecessary to point out that one of the most important keys to the age is the revelation of the almost incredible relationship between the enormously talented but flawed queen and her young genius of a son, who was forced to carry out his hopes for the nation while he was tethered by his mother's selfish desire to keep him out of sight and tongue-tied by authority.

Returning to the study at York House, we find Lady Anne looking at the distressed lad at her feet and deciding that she could no longer withhold the truth. It was not she who had broken the pact of silence. The queen herself had done it.

The things she talked about during that long night's vigil,* with the shaken Francis listening miserably to her every word in a state of shock, were things that never should have been, things secret and shameful. She had desperately hoped that time would help her to forget. Such secrets were not for her telling, nor were they of her doing, and she had kept her vow scrupulously until now. But looking at the troubled face of the child she loved so well, she knew that nothing but the truth would do. He had a right to know where he had come from. How else could he plot the course ahead?

There was nowhere to start but at the beginning, and that was with the near miracle of Elizabeth's succession to the throne. So many factors had gone into the making of that miracle.

We know from history that England did not abide by the old Frankish Salic law that barred female progeny from the throne. However, in order to marry Anne Boleyn, Henry VIII had his first marriage to Catherine of Aragon, daughter of Isabella of Spain, declared void. This made Princess Mary, Catherine's daughter, illegitimate. Then, partly because she had not been able to produce the male heir he so longed for, he had his marriage to Anne Boleyn declared null on trumped-up charges. This made little Princess Elizabeth also illegitimate. Henry's third wife, Jane

---

* We find that Francis has used a little poetic license in his blank-verse account, telling the story as though the action had taken place over a period of two days. His less poetic account in the Bi-literal Cipher (Gallup) describes Lady Anne's vigil with Francis as occurring in just one long night. We present the blank-verse version but condense the action so that it takes place in one night rather than two.

Henry VIII, by Hans Holbein
Henry's single-minded quest for a male heir led to a very uncertain childhood for Elizabeth. When the princess was three, Henry had his marriage to her mother, Anne Boleyn, declared null. He accused her of incest and practicing witchcraft and had her executed. Elizabeth, now illegitimate, lived apart from her father until Henry's last wife, Catherine Parr, helped bring about a reconciliation.

Seymour, finally produced a male heir to the throne, Prince Edward, and Henry eventually called his daughters back into the fold again, treating them as offspring of royalty should be treated, as his dearest children. He had his son at last and would now recognize his daughters. In 1544 an act of parliament established their right to take the throne.

There were few who thought Elizabeth would ever become queen. Her brother and his possible progeny would come first and then her older sister and any of her offspring. But then old Harry, grown obese and dissolute with indulgences, died.

Following him came the minor King Edward VI, the only legitimate Tudor male, with his tragically short six-year reign. His untimely death of a nameless wasting disease was the sorrow of the nation. He had been their hope of glory for the future. Did the symptoms of his slow and agonizing death bear the marks of poisoning? Many thought so, and many still do.

Next in line came Henry's oldest daughter, Mary, a Catholic queen generally unpopular in a nation so recently established in the new Protestant faith. Devoutly religious, her most important aim in life was to restore England to the papal see and to the religion of her adored mother, Catherine of Aragon. Mary was not an unkind woman, but she was dedicated to the mission of restoring Catholicism in Britain, and the ruthlessness of her efforts to get rid of Protestantism and Protestants gained her the name Bloody Mary.

It was the young Elizabeth's misfortune that certain Protestant plotters saw in her noncommitment to either the Anglican Church or the Catholic Church an opportunity to use her as a spearhead for change. The existence of such a plot, of course, made Elizabeth an immediate danger to Mary. There is no one who poses more threat to a monarch than the one next in line to the throne. Mary felt she had no choice—she had to listen to her advisers and send her little sister to the Tower of London.

Two months in the dreaded Tower was a frightening experience for the twenty-year-old princess, and Lady Anne spoke to Francis that night of Elizabeth's terror during her imprisonment. Elizabeth knew that Mary's mother had been displaced by Henry's passion for her own mother, Anne Boleyn, and she also knew that Mary could have little love for Anne's only child. Their mothers had been the bitterest of enemies.

Elizabeth grew up with the knowledge that if she had been the boy her mother longed for, the situation would have been far different. Perhaps her father would not have had her mother beheaded on a trumped-up charge of infidelity. Perhaps the course of English history would have been far different. But there she was, only a little redheaded girl who looked much like her father and who lived wholly at the mercy of the daughter of her mother's worst enemy. It was a precarious position to be in; if she learned early the necessity for self-preservation and dissimulation, we should not be surprised.

Mary's day in the sun was all too brief. Broken in spirit by her failure to produce an heir, by her unpopularity with her people and, most of all, by her cruel disappointment when her adored husband, King Philip II of Spain, deserted her and returned to his own country, she died a little-admired and lonely woman after only five years on the throne.

Francis would have known much of this recent history of his country. He would have been told many times about how, in 1558, the remote chance that Elizabeth would ever become queen had, in fact, come to pass. Anne Boleyn's daughter had been wildly welcomed to the throne, not because of her mother but because of her great resemblance to old King Harry, her high-handed but queenly ways, her great sense of showmanship, her youth and her considerable charms. She was just what England wanted after the drab, bloody rule of Mary. Though her right to the succession was, by some, still questioned, she appealed to the hearts of the general public. There she was, Elizabeth, soon to be the Great, the fifth monarch of the powerful Tudor dynasty, finally established on the British throne, albeit precariously.

Since no one had expected this neglected princess to ascend as far as the throne, no one had thought to prepare her for such a contingency. All she had to offer was her own fiery spirit, an arrogant yet not ungracious personality, an excellent education, and an uncanny ability to dissemble when she knew no other course of action. These qualifications would have to do. They were enough.

The people adored Harry's slender young red-haired daughter, and though they wished she had been a boy, they welcomed her enthusiastically enough. "The Lord has caused a new star to arise. God sent us our Elizabeth that the blood of so many martyrs, so largely shed, be not in vain," they chanted. Elizabeth wholeheartedly agreed. "This is the Lord's doing and it is marvelous in our eyes." These were the words, perhaps carefully rehearsed, that she spoke at that exciting moment when William Cecil found her under the old oak tree in the park at Hatfield quietly awaiting the news of her sister's last breath. Lack of self-confidence not being one of Elizabeth's shortcomings, she was sure that she had been called to be an instrument of God and that she had been as miraculously and mercifully saved from the lion's den as had the prophet Daniel.

Francis could easily feel deep sympathy for the frightened, friendless girl who amazingly turned out to be his mother. As Lady Anne continued with her story, he became less certain of his feelings. His foster mother, having once started her revelations, knew there was nothing to do but tell it all. She recounted an incident in Elizabeth's girlhood that historians have long puzzled over. It concerns Elizabeth's real relationship with Thomas Seymour, the husband of her stepmother, Catherine Parr. The cipher story explains it clearly.

While her brother, Edward, was king, Elizabeth went to live with her father's widow, now the dowager queen, Catherine Parr. This last wife of Henry was a kind and gentle lady who had eased the dying Henry greatly during his last years and had tried to give his children what they had so long been lacking, a warm family home. For the first time in her fourteen years, Princess Elizabeth was accepted into a stable environment that could reasonably be called a home. She was grateful to Catherine for the opportunity and often expressed her gratitude warmly. She did, of course, have her own attendants with her, the only other friends she possessed—Kate Ashley, her old governess and relative of Sir Walter Raleigh; and Thomas Parry, her cofferer, whose job it was to handle her financial affairs. Elizabeth was quite fond of these two, as she was of her stepmother, and life seemed sunny enough for a time. The possibility of her ascending to the throne was so remote that it probably scarcely entered her mind. It did enter the mind of certain others, however, particularly of one Thomas Seymour.

Edward and Thomas Seymour were brothers of Henry's third wife, Jane Seymour, and therefore uncles to little Edward. When he succeeded his father, there was the usual jockeying for place and power in the new regime. The Seymour uncles lost no time in getting themselves into the most exalted positions of the state. Edward was created duke of Somerset and managed to get himself appointed protector of the realm, with limitless opportunities of influence over the boy-king. Not to be outdone, Thomas cast around for an equally lucrative opportunity for himself. He was just the kind of man Elizabeth would always adore—handsome, masculine, bold and charismatic. "Fierce in courage, courtly in fashion, in person stately, in voice magnificent, but somewhat empty in matter" was the way biographer Elizabeth Jenkins described him.[6] The "emptiness" seemed to matter little with the women he pursued, for he had a way with them that they seemed unable to resist.

Lord Thomas immediately set out to charm the young Princess Elizabeth but was promptly warned off by the Privy Council, for it was their duty to protect the royal family's interest. Having failed there, Thomas figured that the next best prospect would be to marry Henry's widow, the queen dowager, Catherine

Parr. Catherine was easy prey for the charms of Seymour, for he had courted her before she married Henry. Catherine and Thomas were married after what was considered to be an indecently short time following the death of King Henry. Seymour immediately moved in with Catherine at her house at Chelsea, and he was immensely pleased that Catherine's stepdaughter, Elizabeth, was living with them. Now he set about to charm the fourteen-year-old princess, and it wasn't long before scandalous gossip was whispered about the household.

In the early mornings before Elizabeth was dressed, the servants said, the lord admiral would visit her in her bedchamber for what he called a playful romp. A romp it may have been, but playful it wasn't. One day naive, trusting Catherine, always so eager to please her charming husband, found him holding Elizabeth in his arms. Catherine was by now pregnant, and there were those who were suspicious that Elizabeth might also be bearing Seymour's child.

Since it was the Privy Council's duty to protect the reputation of the princess, they sent a Master Tyrwhitt to investigate the unsavory affair. Poor Tyrwhitt was no match for Elizabeth—she steadfastly denied the truth of any of the rumors and kept him baffled. "In no way," he wrote "will she confess any practice by Mrs. Ashley, or the cofferer [Thomas Parry] concerning my lord admiral; and yet I do see by her face that she is guilty."[7] In time Parry, the weakest of the three, did make a partial confession of Elizabeth's guilt, but an actual pregnancy was never proven. Elizabeth made a great show of her maidenly virtue and virginity. She played to the hilt the role of injured innocence, dressing in simple maidenlike gowns and speaking with eyes downcast in the sweetest and gentlest manner. She "goes clad in every respect as becomes a young maiden," it was said. Elizabeth got away with the charade, but Seymour was not so fortunate. He paid the penalty for his infamous flirtation and lost his head at Tower Hill.

Neither the Privy Council nor later historians believed that Elizabeth had been pregnant, but it is here that we get a different account from the cipher story. Lady Anne, reluctant to again go over details that might better have been forgotten and yet convinced that Francis had a right to know the truth, told him that Elizabeth was indeed pregnant. She knew only too well because she had been on hand for the following tragic event.

In panic, the pregnant princess had turned to her childhood friend Anne Bacon for help. Always loyal and practical, Anne told her to take to her bed, to whiten her face with powder to make herself look ill, and when the time for delivery came, she would do her best to help her. The inevitable moment finally arrived and the two terrified young women struggled through the night with the unaccustomed details of childbirth. Due to their inexpertise, the baby did not live. It was Anne's unhappy task to hide the little body in the garden, but a guard saw her while she was trying to do so and the incident was reported to young King Edward.

The cipher story gives an absorbing account, all in blank verse, of the confrontation between King Edward and his wayward sister, the details of which we will not go into here, fascinating though they are. Anne said it was not until after Edward's death that she and Elizabeth were released from the "prison house of his scorn."

These details were certainly disagreeable, and it must have been unsettling indeed for Francis, a youth gentle by nature and nurtured by the prim and puritanical ministrations of Lady Anne. Such shocking details of the behavior of the woman who was not only the queen of his country but, it appeared, the mother of his own idealistic self could have been nothing but traumatic.

But Francis was a child of his time, of the rough and raucous Elizabethan age, when morals were more preached than practiced. The natural innocence that was Francis's inheritance at his birth was forced to give way to a deep-seated wisdom born of an understanding and tolerance of the foibles of the human comedy of the world around him. It was the duality of conduct, the sacred versus the profane, that he was to spend the rest of his life trying to help his fellowmen resolve.

Although it might seem unnecessary to air the unpalatable details of Elizabeth's private life once again, it is an important background for understanding the life of her son. He himself went to infinite pains to leave a true record of his times, and it would be unfair to his great efforts to leave out such a significant part of his biography. Today it seems irrelevant whether or not Elizabeth was compromised by Seymour. But at the time it was vitally important to Francis that the true story of the Tudors be left to posterity.

From the story of Elizabeth's guilty affair with Admiral Seymour, Anne progressed to the equally chaotic but more enduring relationship between the princess and Robert Dudley. Francis would have heard much, of course, of the Dudley family—one of historically ill omen but important at court. Robert's father had been John, the duke of Northumberland; his grandfather, the notorious Edmund Dudley, who had died on the scaffold during Henry VIII's reign. John Dudley was ceaselessly ambitious for his family of twelve children and was constantly plotting to marry off all of them well. He arranged for his son Guildford to marry the gentle Lady Grey, who was the grandchild of Henry VIII's sister, whom some preferred for the throne ahead of Mary.

On King Edward's death, perhaps of poison ordered by Dudley himself, he tried to circumvent Mary's accession to the throne by putting his own daughter-in-law in her place. His efforts failed and his family was attainted—stripped of all honors and properties. He, Guildford and poor innocent Lady Jane all lost their heads at the Tower. Robert Dudley, the youngest son, was spared because of his age and imprisoned there.

In spite of the Dudleys' supposed treason, Elizabeth, with her usual regard for the supernatural, considered it an act of fate that brought her and Robert Dudley into confinement in the Tower at the same time. Such matters could not be coincidence, she was convinced, when the handsome Robert began to court her. They had known each other during their school days at Edward's court, and Robert had told her that he had come into the world at exactly the same moment she had—that they had identical birthdays and therefore identical destinies. Whether this was true has often been questioned, but Elizabeth believed it and that was enough for Robert. Fate had brought them into the world at the same moment in time, and now here they were in this gloomy Tower to suffer together. Such a destiny must not be denied.

Robert was confined in Beauchamp Tower, Elizabeth in the Bell Tower. A walk connected the two and Elizabeth was allowed to take her exercise while all other prisoners were under strict orders "not to so much as look in that direction while her Grace remained therein."[8] One suspects that Robert would not have given much heed to such orders. Milton Waldman says it is not easy to understand how romance between the two prisoners could have ripened, incarcerated as they were in the grim old fortress under the vigilant eyes of Tower guards. And yet he admits

part of it cannot be dismissed, however, as altogether improbable. Love now and then circumvented the Tower's locksmiths like any other; and sometimes it even happened that a young couple, confined in different parts of it for the crime of having fallen in love contrary to public policy, managed to disconcert public policy still further by converting their prison into a maternity hospital.[9]

Before letting Francis tell the rest of the story, it is of interest to read biographer Mary M. Luke's account of Elizabeth's contact with the children who lived within the precincts of the Tower. On her daily walks in the restricted garden, Elizabeth had met a little boy, the son of the keeper of the queen's robes, and his little girl companion, whose name was Susanna. Elizabeth delighted in conversations with them, their childish talk proving a welcome respite from the tedium of imprisonment. The young princess's experience with children had been limited, but she found a genuine enjoyment in their innocent attention. Often they brought her a handful of flowers, bestowing the blooms with grubby hands, blushes and laughter. On one occasion, Susanna handed Elizabeth a ring containing some keys that had been carelessly dropped by a warder, saying she had "brought her the keys now, so she need not always stay there, but might unlock the gates and go abroad." Elizabeth did not enlighten the child further. Instead, she accepted the gift with grave seriousness before returning to her chamber. The conversations between the children and the princess as well as the exchange of flowers and keys were all duly reported to the Council, which saw in the children the means by which messages might be conveyed.

The boy was immediately brought before the commissioners and harshly questioned, but not even the stern faces and voices of his interrogators could budge him. He had carried nothing, he said, nothing but flowers for the lady. His father, reprimanded, was told to keep his "crafty knave" at home, away from Princess Elizabeth. For several days, the boy obeyed. But later, when he saw the princess walking in the enclosure, obviously looking for her young friends, he forgot the warnings. Quickly, as she

approached, he sped to the garden gate and waited. With the air
of a conspirator, Elizabeth leaned down to talk to her young
friend. Mindful of his father's wrath, the child was brief.
"Mistress," he said hurriedly, "Mistress, I can bring you no more
flowers now." And then, his courage failing, he darted off.
Elizabeth's face showed her disappointment; she could guess what
had happened.[10]

Lady Anne, in her tearful narrative, takes up the story where
the orthodox historian leaves off:

> Your father [Robert Dudley] found a little child
> Who served him in good stead;
> For he, in secret, beareth to her princess grace,
> Sweet lines that from his pen,
> Comes swiftly to her reading;
> And to elude her gentlemen, their fair leaves
> In flowers lie buried.
> Bravely could he write, did play the poet oft,
> And thus did lovely verses frame.[11]

Francis, the thorough psychologist, understood well the
power of forbidden love. He himself had undergone a desperately
unhappy love experience a short time before he undertook the
writing of the Word Cipher. His poems and plays are full of "the
puissance" of love (the power of love), especially romantic love,
which he lists, for good or for ill, second only to divine love itself.
"There is no passion in the mind of man so puissant strong as
unhappy love." Francis was speaking from experience, as the
cipher shortly reveals. But first comes the rest of the story of the
strange romance in the Tower of London:

> She received his love letters with delight,
> And in woman's fashion magnified his glory
> and his pride,
> Blushed at herself

And saw his visage in her mind and dreams.
There is no passion in the mind of man
So puissant strong as unhappy love;
It is of so flood-gate and o'erbearing nature
That it engluts and swallows other sorrows up,
And is still itself. It mates
And masters fear of death;
Nay, we read, a maiden never bold of spirit,
Still and quiet, if she fall in love,
Will give him cable that she feared to look on;
And to live with him she loves.[12]

The fact that Robert was already married to pretty little Amy Robsart seems to have been a matter of little concern to either of the lovers in the Tower. Perhaps this disregard for convention is understandable when one considers that execution was a more likely future for both of them than a return to normal living. Robert was wise enough to realize that if he were to have his way with Elizabeth, he would have to persuade her that the union would be legitimately consecrated. His method of doing this makes very interesting reading indeed. Again we take the words directly from the cipher:

Hither came one day unto the prisoners
A learned friar and his clerk,
To practice anti-Christian and tyrannical dominion;
And in the name of his beloved Pope,
To open wide the gate
Of wickedness and insolent base government,
With counterfeited keys of Peter.
This well-seeming saint your father saw,
And cozened him with a proper tale of love,
And did not spare to tell him
He hath wronged a woman's heart,
But that being a man of honour,

He would by marrying her
Save her from being held up
As a contaminated stale.
   "Father," said he, "come sit down by me;
You gentle Monks, for treasure, gold, nor fee
To our Saviour, the Eternal Redeemer, the Lord Christ,
Your lives and fortune forfeit;
You are the shepherds of the people;
Here in this prison is a maid that loves me,
And that doth deserve as full, as fortunate a bed
As ever honourable lady in the land,
And I swear in love of her,
I propose to marry her....
I have determined, by fair means or foul,
To have this one fair woman for mine own;
And so I sue to you, good father,
To declare thine office to her,
And in love and pity,
Quickly to perform the marriage."[13]

The priest, in monk's garb, goes to Elizabeth's cell to perform the ceremony, not realizing who the young bride is. Robert accompanies him disguised as a fellow monk. When they get there, the priest immediately recognizes her as the royal Princess Elizabeth. Frightened by the possible consequences of tampering with royalty, he tries to back out, but it is too late. Robert threatens to tell his superiors that he had agreed to perform the marriage against the rules of the church. Fearing for his own skin, he does perform a ceremony, which of course is bigamy. But Elizabeth is used to having things her own way and she chooses to ignore what can't be helped. She now considers herself to be the legal wife of Robert Dudley, imprisoned for treason, son of the man who had been executed as a traitor to the British Crown.

Francis is not comforted by this news; since Robert was

Elizabeth at her coronation
This portrait, by an unknown artist, shows Elizabeth in her coronation robes.

married at the time, this marriage would not be legal. He is despondent:

> Mine honour, my credit, and my name
> And all that made me happy in ruins.[14]

But Lady Anne has more to reveal. After Elizabeth's ascent to the throne, she continued her affair with Leicester. When she discovered she was pregnant, she pleaded and threatened Robert until he agreed to remove the obstacle to their marriage—his wife, Amy—so that Her Majesty's honor would be saved from bearing a child out of wedlock. His servants contrived to make Amy's death appear to be an accident. She was found at the bottom of the stairs, having fallen to her death. Lady Anne recounts the spare details of his parents' marriage, this time lawful. The queen then

> "Was married to him ...
> Not in church, but in secret.
> My gentle lord [Nicholas Bacon] performed the
>   marriage service."
> "Did you the Queen's wedding attend?"
> "I, and I alone of all the attendant train
> Of Eliza's fair ladies, in company of my Lord Puckering,
> Saw her nuptial."[15]

Alfred Dodd says the marriage took place four days after the death of Amy Robsart and was performed "at Brooke House, Hackney, belonging to the Earl of Pembroke."[16] Francis was born four months later.

If Francis was confused about this shining "goddess" who had just announced that it was she who had given him birth, one cannot be surprised. She seemed to have a dual nature, like two-faced Janus.* It was the Janus temperament of the mother-queen that would cause her sons such sorrow. As Francis sat at his foster mother's feet, silent in the dark of old York House, he remembered his early impressions of his queen-goddess. To him she was still "the lovely Gloriana," an image he would later try to convey to her British subjects for the glory of the kingdom.

In another part of the cipher story he tells us

> She was a fair young lioness,
> White as the native rose before the change.
> Upon her head, as fit her fortune best,
> She wore a wreath of laurel, gold and palm,
> And on her forehead ivory the golden crown.

---

* The Roman god Janus is depicted with two faces, each looking in a different direction. Janus is the god of doors and gates, beginnings and endings.

Upon her naked breast there shin'd a golden star.
Her robes of purple and of scarlet dye,
Her veil of white, as best befits a maid,
A thousand blushing apparitions started in her face,
A thousand innocent shames in angel whiteness
Bore away those blushes.[17]

This was her son's poetic early memory of her. But when Anne finished the sordid story of her queen's imperfections, his anguish was deep: "Oh, that deceit should dwell in such a gorgeous palace!"[18]

Chapter Five

Banished to Paris

The lighter sort of malignity turneth
but to a crossness or frowardness or aptness to oppose ...
but the deeper sort, to envy and mere mischief.

It was a devastating and exhausting ex-
perience that Francis went through that night as he listened in
shocked silence to all that Lady Anne revealed—tales of the far-
from-exemplary lives of his queen and her lover, who, it seemed,
was also his father. And he himself was living proof of their
indiscretions. How was he to handle such a jolt, one which
shocked him out of his senses? He felt sick in his whole being.

At dawn his foster mother sent him to bed with the un-
realistic advice to think no more about it. Not surprisingly, he
spent a fitful night. The following day found him tired and out of
sorts. He was in no mood to be confronted by anyone, much less
by that "wandering wasp" Robert Cecil. But here Robert comes,
hat in hand, smirking in mock servility. He enters the library
where Francis is meditating on the revelations of the night before.
Robert himself is still stinging from the humiliations at court, and
he feels that the best remedy is to inflict his hurt onto his cousin.

No doubt by now his own mother, Lady Mildred Cecil, has told him more explicit details of the birth of his "foster cousin" Francis. Far from feeling sympathy for the impossible dilemma he has put Francis in, he is motivated only by the desire to ease the pangs of his own jealous heart. In cipher Francis tells of their unpleasant interview in his own direct style:

> The next day as in the library I sat
> Meditating on my birth
> As told me by the queen,
> Robert, that wandering wasp, crept in;
> And I soon found he came me
> Not to pity, but to misuse and mock.
> The whoreson rascal bared his top
> And [bowing] low, did thus begin to work me spite:
>   "Ha, my lord,
> Now are you equal in rank with the best.
> All my services are at your command.
> Will it please your lordship
> To visit my poor house?
> I must confess, sir, I could not trust my ears
> When the queen called you her son.
> It would have been better for her not
> To have published your birth,
> Because the birth of a bastard is not an honour.
> Good Lord! why should she relate such a blot
> To her own honour? I must be content to believe
> You are her child, chiefly for because
> The princess would never have made
> So contemptible a relation of her conduct
> Had it not been true....
> The court will [curtsey] and say nothing,
> But you, my good Prince of Wales,
> Shall mourn your own mishap.
> I pray you tell me what is your parentage....

It is not yet known
Who your father is.
There are two opinions about it—
One that you are the bastard son
Of Sir Nicholas Bacon, lord keeper;
The other, that you are son and heir
To Leicester. I incline to the latter opinion,
Chiefly from a villainous trick of your eye
And a foolish hanging of your nether lip,
That does warrant me in thinking
You are son to the queen and Leicester.
What is your name,
Francis Bacon, or Francis Dudley?"...
As the rascal says this
My heart was ready to crack with impatience
And I turned and answer:
   "... I advise you
Not to call me bastard...
For though my birth may be mean,
I hope my fortunes will be great.
But I care not.
In any case the glory and honour
Of being son to the Queen of England is enough;
For by my mother's side, at least,
I fetch my life from men
Of royal siege....
Such nativity is a favour of the gods....
Let me tell you, then, once more
I will beat your boundless tongue
Into silence...
If you say I am a bastard,...
And though you and your father
Have by fortune and her highness' favours
Gone lightly o'er low steps...
I fear you not, and I will not

Undergo this sneap without reply....
I tell you I will break your neck
If you mock me; and for I would be
   loathe to kill you,
I pray you leave me."
 "By heaven! I mock you not.
This is but in way of truth, sir....
Come, bear your fortune humbly,
Like the bastard that you are,
And come away to your mother.
I was bid to come for you.
'Tis three o'clock and your noble mother
Bid me fetch you within a quarter of an hour.
Therefore, follow me to the queen....
But tell me first,...
When is the day of your royal coronation? Speak."
And then the villain laughed.[1]

Wrong though Francis may have been, he could not resist the all too human temptation of giving this insolent young sprout a thorough thrashing. Right or wrong, one cannot help but cheer him on as he reacts strongly to those intolerable insults. Although not fiery by nature, his Tudor blood rose to the surface and he struck out to protect his own good name. He reacted in the only way a healthy, self-respecting fifteen-year-old could be expected to act. He beat up the insolent Robert.

I sprang upon him [and] with a great blow
I strike him to the ground.
When he fell I made such havoc
Of the villain that hath slandered,
Scorned and dishonoured me, that
His wounded eyes from the princess
Could not be hid. It was bad policy to tear him so,
But ... he deserved punishment.

> He was a villainous and secret contriver
> Against me almost from the day I was born,
> And I was never safe until death returned him
>   to the earth
> From whence he came.[2]

But now Francis realizes that his rash reaction to Robert's taunts could rebound to his own injury, harming himself far more than he had harmed his cousin. Not only had he acted in such a manner as to be certain to infuriate the queen, he had also incurred the lifelong animosity of young Cecil. He could not fully realize at the moment how much he was to regret his foolish boyish escapade in the years ahead.

Francis was now sorry about his uncontrolled anger. When he grew older and wiser, he would write his observations on the futility of such emotions in his essay "Of Anger."

> No man is angry that feels not himself hurt; and therefore tender and delicate persons must needs be oft angry, they have so many things to trouble them which more robust natures have little sense of.... There is no other way [to calm anger] but to meditate and ruminate well upon the effects of anger, how it troubles man's life. And the best time to do this is to look back upon anger when the fit is [thoroughly] over.[3]

Wise words spoken with the voice of experience. The ebullient nature of Francis always bounced back quickly and cheerfully to its normal state of harmony. Not so with Robert; he buried his resentment deeply and it would influence his actions for the rest of his life.

Francis, sorry for his impetuosity, quickly gives Robert his hand, apologizing for the beating and helping him to wipe off the blood and dirt. Robert's pride prevents him from telling the truth to anyone about his injuries at the moment, and he promises to pretend they came from falling off his horse. But to Francis he gives fair warning:

> And if I live, I tell you, knave,
> I will be revenged, and England's ground
> Shall not yield you shelter from my wrath.
> I'll not trouble you with words, not I;
> But I will requite this dishonour
> And be revenged on you....
> I that have neither pity, love nor fear;
> I who have often heard my mother say
> When that I was born the midwife
> Wondered and the women cried
> O Jesu bless us! He is born with teeth!...
> I will destroy you, for you are mine enemy....
> I will buzz
> Abroad such prophesies that Elizabeth
> Will be fearful of her life, and then
> To purge her fear I'll be your death.
> And for this stroke upon my crest,
> And for this blood of mine, I will
> Not suffer you to sit in England's royal
> Throne.[4]

True to his word, this is exactly what Robert managed to do over the years. Like the crookback king in Shakespeare's play *Richard III,* he cannot be happy himself, so he tries to make sure that no one else is happy. He worms his way into Elizabeth's good graces by flattery and dissimulation. When she laughs, he laughs. When she cries, he is there, catering to her and humoring her with all the insincere craft of his false nature. Francis, cast in a higher mold, scorned to act with such insincerity.

'Tis said: "The curse that was not deserved never will come." Some may find it true, but to me a causeless curse did surely come and my entire life felt the blight.[5]

> It never crossed my mind that my mother, the queen,
> Would join with such a degenerate being
> To foil her own child, otherwise he could
> Have been circumvented.[6]

All this was the product of hindsight, of course, and later he realized that Robert's scheme had been to convince the queen that Francis's very existence was a threat to her position with her subjects. No approach could have been better designed for Robert's purposes, for already she was fearful to the point of paranoia that her people would rather have a king than a queen. She was suspicious of every possible threat to her throne, as later events would tragically prove.

Young Cecil, as the sly fox, played on these fears and delighted in telling Her Grace how as a boy Francis had loved to play being king. Every chair he sat on became to him a throne, and he loved to carry a make-believe scepter and to order his playmates around. It wasn't true, of course, for no one had a greater respect for the Crown than did Francis. He was always to defend the right to rule of whoever wore it, however unworthy that one may have been, and he upheld the policy of the divine right of kings until a better system could be devised. He was a defender of the Crown, not a usurper.

Francis makes one more mistake on that eventful day before obeying a summons from the queen. At first he refuses to go with the page she has sent to fetch him.[7] He is a Tudor and just as defiant as she is. He does not intend to be ordered around. In time, however, he quiets down a bit and goes to attend her at the palace. First she scolds him for his tardiness, then she upbraids him for the bad company he keeps. She vacillates between fondness for her bright son and disapproval of what she has heard about his overly free and easy ways.

Then we proceed unto the mighty Queen....
"So thou at length hast come ... hast thou?
Did I not send for thee in the afternoon,
Between the hours of three and four?...
What! Standest thou?
Down upon thy knees, and beg pardon for thy bad fault.
I'll teach thee what it is to brave my wrath....
Pass into my room."...
    When we were alone she said:
"I know not whether heaven will have it so
For some displeasing service I have done,
But thou dost, in thy passages of life,
Make me believe that thou art only marked
For the hot vengeance and the rod of heaven
To punish my mistreadings."

The queen scolds him for not behaving like a prince, a rather unfair criticism, it seems, since she herself has withheld from him knowledge of his royal beginnings. And yet she admits to a certain motherly pride in him that she has been forced to conceal:

"Thou hast lost thy princely privilege
With wild participation; not an eye
But is aweary of thy common sight
Save mine, which hath desire to see thee more,
Which now doth, that I would not have it do,
Make blind itself with foolish tenderness."[8]

Like Prince Hal, that lively young man with the charming ways who is Falstaff's fine friend in *Henry IV, Part 2*, Francis assures the queen that he would "add a luster" to the Crown, that he keeps company with the commoners for a purpose, as does Hal. In the play, Warwick explains Hal's behavior:

The prince but studies his companions
Like a strange tongue, wherein, to gain the language....

The prince will in the perfectness of time
Cast off his followers, and their memory
Shall as a pattern or a measure live,
By which his grace must mete the lives of others,
Turning past evils to advantages.

act IV, sc. 4

Francis keeps company with common people so that he may study them, learn how they talk, "gain the language"; he wants to understand their ways so he will know how to work with them. He compares his studies to laying the foundations for the building of a house. But over time, he assures her, he will mend his ways.[9]

It is clear that Robert has already been busy with his tales. To tell the truth, there was a certain amount of justification for his charge that Francis was too democratic in his ways. He was always one to live life fully, to find friends everywhere and anywhere, and to mix easily with companions he found interesting, whether or not they were of a high rank. He was royal but not a snob.

Elizabeth proceeds to give her son a valuable lesson on retaining the respect of the people through the deliberate creation of a mystique of royalty. This advice Francis was never to forget, although it became increasingly difficult to follow in the years to come when he was in the unenviable position of being neither accepted royalty nor a natural commoner. She explains the art of keeping the majesty of royalty always fresh in the people's mind—keep most often aloof; keep your presence fresh and new; don't appear too often to the public sight; keep people waiting; preserve the "sun-like majesty" of royalty by always dressing in a fashion to inspire envy and admiration; don't allow others to dress as richly as yourself; bear yourself in a regal manner; and never—no never—admit to personal flaw or error.[10] "'Much suspected, by me / Nothing proved can be,' quoth Elizabeth, prisoner" were the words she had scratched with a diamond ring on the glass of her prison window.[11] It was her personal motto.

Eventually the painful interview between mother and son approaches the end. His mother-queen admits that she has not decided just how to handle him or to arrange for his future now that he is in on the secret of who and what he is. Then she upbraids him for the low company he keeps:

> "Art thou not by birth a prince?
> Why then dost thou look so low,
> As if thou hadst been born of the worst of women?
> Thy tastes are not for royal deeds,
> And [it] were sin to stain England's throne
> By such a counterfeit image of a king."

It seems that Her Majesty was unnecessarily hard on her son, for from all reports from his contemporaries, he had an exceptionally noble and princely manner. Her scoldings sound typically motherly. She has more to say:

> "To shield thee from disasters of the world,
> I am resolved that thou shall spend some time
> In the French emperor's court.
> Muse not that I thus suddenly proceed,
> For what I will, I will; and there an end.
> Tomorrow be in readiness to go...."
>
> "Madam [says Francis], I cannot so soon be provided;
> Please you deliberate a day or two."
>
> "No more; look, what thou wantest
> Shall be sent after thee....
> For thy provision thou shalt receive
> Enough from me for thy maintenance.
> And so, my son, farewell."

The queen says that she would personally prefer keeping him at home and sending him to the universities, but he needs a bit of polish and the best place for that is at the elegant French court.

> Thus I was banished. And on the day following
> About the hour of eight, I put to sea
> With that gentle knight, Sir Amyas Paulet,
> Bound to the court of France.
> I will not here pursue the story of my life
> But rather will reserve it
> Until my return from France.[12]

One might expect Francis to have been overjoyed at the unexpected prospect and excitement of a trip to France with the new English ambassador. But at first he was not. He was devastated at what seemed to him to be a disgrace—banishment from his native land and his mother's court. Soon, however, his ebullient spirits took charge and he began to look forward to what would prove to be the happiest three years of his life.

It takes a little time for him to be made ready to go. Lady Anne at first pleads with the queen to change her mind and allow Francis to stay in England. In spite of her fears, her pleas were ignored and there was nothing else to do but to bustle around and prepare a wardrobe for him that would be suitable for the richness of sophisticated Paris.

It would appear from the cipher story that Francis left for France the following day, but historically we know that it was a while later. Biographer Alfred Dodd points out that the new ambassador, Paulet, was not due to replace the English ambassador at Paris for a few months but that suddenly plans were made to send him earlier.[13]

We know that one of Her Majesty's choicest ships, the *Dreadnought,* was commissioned to carry the party abroad. The country's most capable naval officer, Captain George Bristowe, was given orders to outfit the ship and to proceed "to such port on the other side as might be deemed most convenient to him." Though Elizabeth had not decided what to do about this unwanted son, he was a Tudor and fully royal, so until she formed a policy about him, she intended to see that he was treated as royalty should be.

Francis tells us frankly in cipher how his feelings alternated between exalted moods of excited anticipation and low ebbs of melancholic foreboding.[14] It might be, he knew, that the sojourn would be a permanent one—a total banishment from his beloved "fortunate isle." We have no record that demonstrates the condition of Francis's mind more clearly than those famous first seventeen sonnets* known as the "procreation sonnets," so named because they appear to be urging someone to marry, to have a child, and to carry on the family name for posterity.

Taking the sonnets not as poems urging someone to marry, as is generally done, but as urging someone who is already married —his mother—to admit to her marriage publicly and to recognize the child she has already created, the sonnet sequences take on a new and poignant meaning. Sonnet 13 reads as a heart cry from a child yearning for recognition from those who should love him best:

> O, that you were yourself, but, love, you are
> No longer yours than you yourself here live;
> Against this coming end you should prepare,
> And your sweet semblance to some other give.
> So should that beauty which you hold in lease
> Find no determination, then you were
> Yourself again after your self's decease,

---

* It was in France that Francis fell in love with "sonneteering," the craze for writing those fourteen-line poems that were the rage on the continent. It was a fashion that he would help to popularize on his return to England.

When your sweet issue your sweet form should bear.
Who lets so fair a house fall to decay,
Which husbandry in honor might uphold
Against the stormy gusts of winter's day
And barren rage of death's eternal cold?
 O none but unthrifts! Dear my love, you know,
 You had a father; let your son say so.

The poem takes on a deeper meaning when read as a plea from the heart of an unacknowledged prince of the Tudor dynasty to his mother, the queen, begging her not to let the royal house of Tudor fall into decay for lack of a successor. There is a successor, and he is it! "Please recognize me! You had a father! Let your son say as much!"

Chapter Six

Juliet and Her English Romeo

*As to the stage, love is ever matter of comedies
and now and then of tragedies; but in life it doth much
mischief, sometimes like a siren, sometimes like a fury.*

The Owen cipher devotes one of its five books
to Francis's sojourn in France. The writing is lengthy, overly
descriptive and, like so much Elizabethan literature, rather
tedious at times. Nevertheless, it is obvious that it was in France
that the young anonymous prince found the key to his future and
that his career was shaped by the experiences that impressed him
during his three-year visit to the French court.

Francis's departure from England as a teenager is marked by
the deeply confusing changes that have just taken place in his life.
He is wide open to new impressions and values. His return to
England finds him a sadder but more mature young man, with
new ideas that influenced him for the rest of his life. It was in the
French court that he first contacted the esoteric precepts that he
later wove into his Rosicrucian and Masonic activities.[1] These he
molded into an original and highly effective plan for service to

the world.

In retrospect, the reader may wonder at Bacon's enormous emphasis on reporting his French experience. But once again we must remember how important it was, not only to him but to his country. The all-encompassing importance of royalty is hard to understand today, with only watered-down monarchies for comparison. In Bacon's time, everything centered on the reigning monarch. The power of the throne was almost absolute and the privileges were endless. The court was then the center of the nation—the hub on which the world turned.

The first and perhaps the most important thing that happened to Francis on his arrival in France may not seem too surprising, given his youth, his romantic nature and his inborn sense of chivalry. He fell head over heels in love, with a passion that is reserved only for those with the deepest capacity of heart. For Francis, love was not a passing fancy nor an amusement lasting but a moment; his first love was also his last love, the only great "*amour*" of his life. In more mature years, when the object of his devotion proved to be faithless and tragically unworthy of so sustained an emotion, he

> banished her portrait to the walls of memory, only, where it doth hang in pure, undimmed beauty of those early days— while her most lovely presence doth possess this entire mansion, of heart and brain.[2]

Love was total and unchanging for this man. Both his friendships and his romance had the enduring and endearing quality of foreverness. Once given, the heart of Francis was eternally and permanently engaged. Certain historians and philosophers believe that Sir Francis Bacon was cold, humorless and totally incapable of romantic passion. One can only wonder that such a misunderstanding came to be, in view of the fact that it is exactly the opposite of the reality.

Few have realized the entire truth—that one of the most famous and enduring love stories of all time was written by Francis Bacon in celebration of his own great love. The enduring tale of Juliet and her Romeo exists as witness to this truth, and it is in this play that much of his cipher love story is portrayed.[3]

Marguerite of Valois, or Princess Margot (daughter of the dreaded Catherine de Médici and granddaughter of Lorenzo de Médici) was the one to whom Francis gave his heart. Dodd says that there is a tradition that when Francis first saw her, "he swooned away, so affected was he by her loveliness."[4] Had they met in lifetimes past? Some might say so.

Francis met his princess shortly after his arrival in France. The great ship *Dreadnought,* which had been commissioned to carry the ambassador and his accompanying British entourage across the Channel, had no sooner landed at the port of Calais on the twenty-fifth day of September, 1576, than the whole party set off for the court of Paris. Francis's spirits were high, his excitement at full flood, and his resentment at his "banishment" almost forgotten. He and his companions were eager for the long ride to Paris.

The exuberant spirits of the incognito prince were in no way diminished by his entrance into Paris. He and his party were greeted with great warmth. All was arranged and the visitors were to be "lodged and accommodated in great state," more than likely in the luxurious marble palace of the Louvre itself, which at that time was the home of the royal family of France. Francis was duly impressed. He had been used to the best that the English court had to offer, but that didn't compare with the lavishness that greeted him from all sides in this sophisticated metropolis, more elegant and far richer than his home city of London. He was to be even more wonder-struck a few days later by the extravagant banquet that had been arranged for the visiting Englishmen by the elegant King Henri himself. They were

immediately invited to a feast that was so grand in its richness
that it dazzled the English lad's eyes and remained vividly in his
memory years later. He recalled it in his cipher diary:

> Being arrived at Henry's kingly hall,
> That like Adonis' garden bloomed with flowers
> (For fleurs-de-lis, the lilies of the French,
> The rose of England, with sweet violets,
> Pale daffodils, and sweet honeysuckle
> Covered the walls and obscured the table.)
> Such proud luxurious pomp, excess, and pride
> Of royal arras and splendid gold
> Dazzled my eyes, I never such choice crystal saw,
> Nor such pomp of rich and glittering gold.[5]

It was enough to take his breath away. Into all this splendor,
as the banquet was about to begin, strutted the French king, le
Grand Roi, in full pomp, escorted by the most beautiful maidens
of France bearing garlands of tulips, peonies and wild thyme, and
tall young men carrying boughs of laurel. Following close behind
the king came his satin-clad and beribboned *mignons*, or minions,
effeminate favorites who were never far away. The aged Queen
Mother, Catherine de Médici, came next.[6] It was whispered by
some, and not too discreetly at that, that she was the real power
behind the French throne.

It was all most exciting, and Francis confessed to his diary
that he was "such a novice in the Paris courts" that he
"wondered at ... such rich banquetings" and was awed by the
splendor of the whole affair. "We feasted, full of mirth, but
nothing riotous," he reports.[7]

With his ready wit, high humor, and natural eloquence and
grace, the British prince would have been more than capable of
holding his own, in spite of the sophistication of the circle, and
the cipher assures us that it was so. The charm of his youthful

self-assurance was glimpsed when King Henri called him to his side and greeted him in the French tongue, not really expecting him to understand. He had underestimated his young guest. A shift in language was no problem for Francis, who had been carefully trained from childhood to converse easily in a number of tongues. He answered the king's welcome in a gracious and straightforward manner, never once stumbling over the difficulty of the French idioms usually so trying for foreigners. All eyes were on the boy, obviously delighted with his performance, to whom the king then said:

> Thou art not old enough in years for a man
> Nor young enough for a boy....
> Thou art well favored, noble by birth....
> I liked thee 'fore I saw thee, now I love and admire thee.
> Thou art thy father's joy, thy mother's comfort,
> Thy country's hope.[8]

These were the words with which he was greeted by the king of France, who seems to have had no doubt about whose son this was. A son of Lady Anne and Sir Nicholas would hardly have been called his country's hope, nor would he have been welcomed with such honor by the king. The king then presented him with a purse of gold, while the entire company stood around gazing at the newcomer "as if they saw some wondrous monument, some comet, or unusual prodigy."[9]

The extraordinary attention he received at the hands of the royal family at the French court leaves little doubt that whether or not he was openly acknowledged to be a Tudor prince, there was hardly a Frenchman who did not think he knew something of his royal origins. Sixteen years earlier, Sir Nicholas Throckmorton, the then English ambassador to the French court, had frantically written to William Cecil complaining about the shocking rumors that were openly being passed around France concerning the behavior of the young British queen.[10] Stories intimating scandalous behavior between her and Lord Leicester had circulated all over the continent—gossip knew no boundaries. In France it was not treasonous to gossip about the English queen and there were no dire consequences for doing so. The French could, and did, smile openly at things that were taboo to the English. Rumors of the birth of a British prince had been repeated freely from cottage to palace in Paris until the humiliated Throckmorton had been ready to resign in despair.

Now, sixteen years later, the French courtiers must have winked knowingly when there suddenly appeared at their door a handsome young aristocrat of just the right age, sent to Paris from the hand of the queen and placed expressly under the protection of the British ambassador. It was not difficult to add two and two together—this was no son of the Bacons! The courtiers were not fooled. They came to love the boy and they called him Monsieur Doux and Signor Dolce, the sweet young gentleman.[11]

It was hard for Francis to handle the identity of his birth, almost too much for a fifteen-year-old, especially after he met the king's sister, Princess Marguerite. No mere son of the Bacons would be permitted to aspire so high. Standing again with the king at the feast given in his honor, Francis sees for the first time this beautiful princess who is soon to capture his heart.

Marguerite's name would not have been a strange one to Francis's ears, for it had been her wedding to her cousin, the Huguenot (Protestant) king Henri of Navarre, on August 18, 1572, that had precipitated the night of horror known as the Saint Bartholomew's Day Massacre. Six days after the wedding, the streets of Paris ran red with Huguenot blood. Francis was only eleven years old when the dreadful news hit London, and the indignation and horror of the entire Protestant world would not have been forgotten by him. He would remember that the whole horrible affair had been engineered by the Catholic mother of Marguerite. Now here he was, falling in love with her daughter.

Marguerite was not a docile princess, and it angered her that her mother had forced her into an alliance with the young Henri of Navarre. At the time that Francis met her, there was supposedly a divorce in the offing. The reluctance of Marguerite to engage in even a political marriage with Navarre undoubtedly had much to do with her current love affair with the duke of Guise. Supposedly one of the handsomest men in France, he was a member of the powerful Guise family, of whom Mary Queen of Scots was the brightest hope.

The Guises were always formidable rivals to Marguerite's family, the Valois, a situation which may have added spice to their attraction for each other and undoubtedly was the inspiration for the feud between the Capulets and the Montagues of *Romeo and Juliet*. Francis lets his cipher readers in on the gossip going around the court about Marguerite, admitting that she was certainly no angel when he first met her.[12] Nevertheless, although she was eight years his senior, to him she was just short of divine. "She is the fairest Lady I have yet beheld in France and is walled about with diamonds, pearls, and gold."[13] A glamorous first impression. Soon his praises become more ardent. She is his "sweet, sweet love" and the "bright angel" of his heart.[14]

Contemporary portraits of Marguerite do not show her to have been as strikingly beautiful as nearly all descriptions make her out to be. Perhaps the artists' skills do not do her justice. They show her with a rather sour, pouty face and undistinguished features. It may be that her charm and personality were enough to give the impression of beauty even when it was physically lacking. Several verbal pictures border on idolatry in praise of her beauty, such as the account given by her admirer Don John of Austria, who once made a special trip to attend a ball at the Louvre. His sole purpose was to see the fabulous Princess Margot

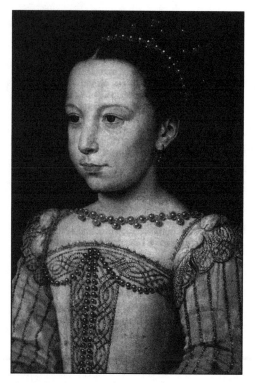

Marguerite of Valois, by Francois Clonet
The cipher story reveals that the French princess was the first love of Francis's life, the inspiration for many of his sonnets and for the tragic love story of *Romeo and Juliet*. While the portrait of Juliet in the play embodies all that was fair and noble in Marguerite, her darker nature is seen in Cressida, the unfaithful love of Troilus in *Troilus and Cressida*. Echoed in drama and poetry, we can see something of the "sweet sorrow" that afflicted Francis's heart, the pain of unrequited love.

for himself. Standing on the sidelines of the dance floor, the don watched her for a while. Then he turned to his companion and gave his opinion, "The beauty of the Princess is more divine than human, but she is made to damn and ruin men rather than to save them."[15] Francis would eventually be forced to the same conclusion.

It was not only the beauty and glamour of Princess Marguerite that captured the heart of Francis. Other qualities excited him even more. The impact on him was overwhelming. He could see that they had everything in common, even if she was a third again as old in years. They were destined for each other; he didn't doubt that for a minute. She, like Francis, had a brilliant and searching mind, a great love of music and a gift for witty repartee. She too loved poetry and could be happy for hours in reading and meditation; she too was concerned about the welfare of the common man and often gave great sums of money to the poor. These are some of the many charms that would have captivated Francis.

Most endearing of all would have been the elegant soirées she held in her quarters at the palace, evenings when the most talented and cultured of the intelligentsia were invited for discussions on poetry, music, art, literature, mysticism and, in general, all affairs of the cultural world. This was a little esoteric academy, much like those that were blossoming all over Europe at the time. An inside view of one such academy may be seen in the play *Love's Labor's Lost*.[16]

In these gatherings Francis would have met the famous Pierre de Ronsard and his Pléiade, the group of poets whose mission it was to ennoble French language and literature. The principles he encountered here would influence him for the rest of his life, even creating in him a determination to elevate his own native English language and the practically nonexistent culture of his homeland.

The cipher explains that as Francis's love for Marguerite grew, he became more enchanted with her at each encounter. The knowledge of his high birth gives him full confidence in his own worth and his right to speak his mind. He is encouraged further by the lack of love between Marguerite and Navarre. Marguerite's naturally flirtatious ways and obvious interest in the charming young visitor from England finally make him bold enough to speak to her directly. He performs a service for her, for which she thanks him.

Pierre de Ronsard (1524–1585)
Ronsard was known in his own time as the "prince of poets." He was the leader of the Pléiade, a group of French poets who made their aim the elevation of the French language and literature. By emulating forms and incorporating vocabulary from Greek and Roman classics, they sought to create a vernacular capable of the highest literary and philosophical expression. Bacon returned from France with the determination to do the same in England. The next forty years saw the full flowering of the English Renaissance and the birth of the English language as we know it today.

> I kneel to thank this lovely Queen for her sweet words,
> And beg for grace to lay my duty [kiss] on her hand:
> Frankly she gives it and her looks are gracious—
> Fain would I kiss her feet to ease my bashful heart:
> For such a passion doth embrace my bosom,
> My heart beats thicker than a feverous pulse,
> And all my powers do their bestowing lose,
> Like vassalage, at unawares encount'ring
> The eye of majesty. Lower I bend and sigh—
> F.B. "O Queen, if you deny me favor let me die!
> I kiss your hand, but not in flattery:
> Its pleasant touch hath made my heart to dance."

M. "What sayest thou, boy? Is my young Prince a
      poet?"...
  I look into the lady's face, and in her eyes
I find a wonder, or a wondrous miracle,
And I nor heard nor read so strange a thing—
A shadow of myself formed in her eye,
And in this form of beauty read I—love!
I do protest I never loved myself
Till now infixed, I behold myself
Drawn in the flattering table of her eye.
M. "Speak then, my gentle Prince; and canst thou love?"
F.B. "Nay, ask me if I can refrain from love,
For I do love thee most unfeignedly."
  With cheeks abashed I blush, and swear to serve,
Be it unto death and future misery,
This Queen of earthly queens, as goddess so divine,
Who charms with her sweet smile even the most
      saturnine....
F.B. "Fair Margaret, the beauty of thy face,
Sufficient to bewitch the heavenly powers,
Hath wrought so much in me, that now of late,
I find myself made captive unto love." [17]

Marguerite was used to the adulation of men, but she was
nevertheless impressed by the ardor of Francis's devotion. Perhaps
she was also a bit alarmed:

"Prince, stand thou up, thou art too highly moved,
Too violently carried; hear me speak:
Thy zeal must be controlled; rise, sweet boy, rise;
'Tis for thy good that I thee thus advise;
A greater power than we denies all this.
Wouldst have it said thou temp'st me to forsake
Navarre, my King, when most he needs my help?"

Marguerite's reference to ethics does not bother Francis one whit. He is convinced that his love for her is made in heaven.

> F.B. "The law of Heaven will not lead us amiss:
> And here I promise and protest withal...
> To stand in this until your final judgment."
> M. "It resteth then that thou be well content."
> F.B. "But lest my liking might too sudden seem,
> I would have salved it with a longer treatise."
> M. "What need ye bridge much broader than the
>   stream?...
> But oh! My Prince,
> I do beseech thee, hear me....
> Love is too weighty for thy youth to wear."
> F.B. "I wear it lightly; were it heavier!"...
> M. "Great lords have come and pleaded for my love,
> But thou, sweet youth, art England's only flower,
> The royal tree hath left us royal fruit."...
> Her words did tell me nothing of her heart,
> But when she bent on me the light of her sweet eyes,
> They gave to me good leave to speak again. [18]

This beautiful writing, worthy of the immortal pen of Francis Bacon, should not be lost to the world.

Inexperienced in love but faithful and trusting, and completely convinced of the sacredness of their love, Francis gives Marguerite his ring. When she accepts it, he believes she is pledging her love and loyalty in return. Would such a saint as Marguerite tamper with the love he offers so freely? It never enters his mind.

With all the fervor of his youth, Francis sets out to arrange for the completion of the divorce proceedings between Marguerite and Navarre and to sue for his mother's permission for a wedding to take place between the Tudor prince of Britain and the Valois princess of France. All things are possible in love. He takes Sir Amyas into his confidence and urges him to intercede with Elizabeth on his behalf. Paulet seems to be in favor of the alliance, perhaps realizing the sincerity of Francis's ardor. He agrees to do what he can to help bring it about.

The ambassador's efforts are not well received. Elizabeth is in no mood to take on such a difficult alliance for this son, whom she has never even admitted to having. Besides, she herself is currently involved in a political romance with her "little frog," Marguerite's singularly unattractive brother, the duke of Alençon, also known as the duke of Anjou. Relations between France and England are far too delicate to risk such an alliance, besides risking popularity with her subjects. She is furious at Paulet for his part in encouraging the affair, and it is only by adroit diplomacy on the ambassador's part that he manages to hold on to his job.[19] By the same token, Francis has taken another of the many steps that will antagonize his mother increasingly, each false move leading farther away from the throne.

It was not, however, Elizabeth's rejection of Francis's request for marriage with Marguerite that caused his eventual estrangement from his beloved. One day, says the cipher, Marguerite's old nurse, or nanny (surely the prototype for Juliet's famous nurse), drew Francis aside and whispered in his ear that the reason the princess could not give him the fullness of her love was that it was already given, not to her husband, Navarre, but to her lover, Henry the duke of Guise. Get rid of him, whispered the nurse, and all will be well.[20]

The clandestine relationship between the king's sister and the powerful duke was an unfortunate one from every point of view. For Francis, it was heartbreaking. "I cannot brook competitors in love," he moaned,[21] realizing at last that Marguerite's emotions were not as innocent as his own. The result of his discouragement was an ongoing conflict between hope and despair.

> Two loves I have, of comfort and despair,
> Which like two spirits do suggest me still;
> The better angel is a man right fair,
> The worser spirit a woman colored ill.

Sonnet 144

The "better angel ... a man right fair" has caused much consternation among Shakespeare commentators. But the "beautiful boy" (or young man) sonnets were written to his own muse, the "high-self" of his vision. In sonnet 144, the tug-of-war is between his higher ambitions and his all-too-human love for Marguerite.

Romeo and his young love, Juliet, are so familiar to us that even now in the twenty-first century, we almost forget that they are not historical characters. Change the names to Francis and Marguerite and we find that we were right in the first place—they are historical characters. *Romeo and Juliet* is a celebration of joy and tragedy in young love in a way that has seldom, if ever, been surpassed. Romeo cares for nothing in the world except for Juliet. Their love possesses him completely and nothing else can enter his thoughts, in spite of the tragedy that foreshadows itself from the beginning. Just so was Francis.

The other play that Francis says he uses to tell their love story is *Troilus and Cressida*. Noted in the Stationers' Register on February 7, 1603, it was first seen in print six years later. When the First Folio was published in 1623, this play was not listed in the catalogue, or table of contents, and the play was inserted between the histories and the tragedies as if the editors were not sure just where its right place was. Is its essence cynical, is it comical, or is it tragic? Perhaps it is a bit of all three. The author himself had been exposed to disillusionment, but he was mature enough to see a wry kind of humor in the situation—a typical Baconian attitude as an observer of the comedy of human error, even when he himself was the chief target.

The Trojan youth Troilus is represented as the "prince of chivalry" and he is described by the observant Ulysses in the following passage from the play:

> The youngest son of Priam, a true knight,
> Not yet mature, but matchless; firm of word,
> Speaking in deeds and deedless in his tongue.
>
> *act IV, sc. 5*

The virtues of Troilus are virtues that Bacon elsewhere extols. This ideal and idealistic young prince becomes infatuated with the worldly and somewhat jaded Cressida. To him she is perfect.

> Never did young man fancy
> With so eternal and so fixed a soul.
>
> *act V, sc. 2*

Cressida is a blithe spirit with a gift for witty conversation, an absence of moral conscience and a talent for pleasing men. Experienced as Cressida is, she is too clever to give in too readily to Troilus's wooing. "Men prize the thing ungained"[22] is her philosophy, and she keeps her lovers dangling until they become thoroughly obsessed with love. When she finally allows the old lecher Pandarus to arrange the meeting that Troilus has been pleading for, she confesses that she has been in love with him from the beginning and that if she should ever prove to be untrue, she hopes her name will be used as a synonym for faithlessness. All of this is a bit of coquetry which later developments show to have been less than accurate. Troilus, of course, believes her every word.

Soon, circumstances require that the lovers be separated, since she is traded to the Greeks for a prisoner of war. In an agony of apprehension and jealousy, Troilus gives her a sleeve in token of their love. (Elaborately decorated sleeves were a prized item and were often given as gifts between friends and lovers, as a scarf or jewelry might be given today.) Cressida swears fidelity to Troilus and asks if he will be true. His answer: "Who, I? Alas it is my vice, my fault."[23]

However, Cressida, true only to her frivolous nature, readily gives kisses to all the Greek commanders and behaves like the wanton flirt that she is. The Greek leader Ulysses immediately recognizes her nature through what, in these times, we call body language:

> There's language in her eye, her cheek, her lip;
> Nay, her foot speaks. Her wanton spirits look out
> At every joint and motive of her body.
> O, these encounters, so glib of tongue,
> That give a coasting welcome ere it comes,
> And wide unclasp the tables of their thoughts
> To every ticklish reader.
>
> *act IV, sc. 5*

Of course, it does not take Cressida long to take up a new *amour*, and when Troilus visits the camp, he finds her giving his gift sleeve to her new love, Diomedes. With a shrug of resignation, she tells Diomedes to keep the sleeve, and she sends one last sigh of regret to her Trojan suitor: "Troilus, farewell! One eye yet looks on thee."[24]

Through such little scenes we catch glimpses not of Troilus and Cressida in Trojan history but of Francis and Marguerite nearly thirty centuries later. It is this sense of an underlying current reality in "Shakespeare" that has kept readers fascinated since that famous folio of 1623 first appeared in print.

Chapter Seven

The Glory of a King

Prosperity doth best discover vice,
but adversity doth best discover virtue.

One gray morning, waking from a restless sleep in his quarters in Paris, Francis remembered a troubling dream which he later related to "diverse English gentlemen." In this dream, his beloved English home, the Bacons' manor house of Gorhambury, seemed to be "plastered all over with black mortar." Intuitively interpreting this as a forewarning of bad news, he was not wholly surprised when a messenger arrived with news of Sir Nicholas's death.

Francis's much-loved foster father, the lord keeper, had died of a chill caught when his barber left him napping in the raw February air before an open window. On waking, Sir Nicholas had predicted his own approaching death. When the barber explained that he had left him sleeping because he did not wish to disturb his nap, Sir Nicholas replied, "Then, by your civility, I lose my life."[1] Within a few days, Elizabeth's great keeper was dead.

As quickly as possible, Francis crossed the Channel and

returned to London, unfortunately arriving after the lavish state funeral for the queen's dear friend. One can feel how deeply moving it must have been for Francis to hear about the procession—how his foster mother, who had loved him far more than his own mother ever did, was mounted on a black-draped horse and rode alone, close behind the hearse bearing the body of the man who had been all of life to her. For Francis, this was the man who had been his protector, his counselor, his friend from the moment of his birth.

All day long the bells of St. Paul's had rung; all day long the bells of St. Martin's had rung. It had been a solemn occasion for everyone. For Francis it marked the end of a cycle, almost the end of his youth. There would be no more security other than what he could provide for himself. Who was there now to advise him? Whom could he trust? For Anthony, it was different. For him the death of his father marked the beginning of a period of relative freedom from paternal authority and restraint.

When the will of Nicholas Bacon was read, it was apparent that everyone in the family had been well provided for—with one important exception, the youngest son. An older son, Nicholas, became a rich man at his father's death. The other two sons of the first marriage, Nathaniel and Edward, were amply provided for, as were the three daughters—Elizabeth, Jane and Anne. Gorhambury Manor was deeded to Lady Anne for the remainder of her life, afterward to revert to Anthony. Anthony also received valuable manors in Middlesex and Hertfordshire. For Francis there was nothing, nothing except some questionable properties and leases that brought him a modest yearly sum. This youngest son, whom the Bacons obviously adored—he alone was left virtually penniless.

The will of Nicholas Bacon "is a puzzle," writes biographer Jean Overton Fuller.[2] Had it been written before the birth of

Francis, it would have been understandable. But that was not the case. It was written in 1577, when Francis was a teenager in France and, according to the cipher, after the revelation of his royal birth. It had been revised in 1578 just two months before the lord keeper's death.

There could have been only one explanation for the neglect of Francis—the queen's secret admission of her son's parentage. The elder Bacon must have fully expected that Elizabeth would care for her own. It may even have been at Elizabeth's orders that Nicholas had revised his will. She apparently had the full intention of restraining her offspring by controlling the purse strings, a policy she continued for the rest of her life. Only the understanding that Francis was not of his own flesh and blood can make sense out of Sir Nicholas's will.

Until the queen decreed otherwise, Francis must now be content to occupy himself in the way she ordered. Indeed it was a "melancholy thing," but Francis knew he had no alternative but to take up the study of law at Gray's Inn. He continually commented that he did not feel suited for the law. He was a poet and philosopher, and he felt that his time was wasted in the courts of law. "I would live to study, and not study to live," he would write many years later.

The only income of this young prince of England was a small stipend provided by the state (the queen). Anthony and Lady Anne did everything possible to help him finance his plans and further the expensive and expansive scheme for the "advancement of learning," the supreme goal of his life, but they soon ran short of adequate means to help him.

Francis's role was a difficult one. No one could imagine just how difficult without standing in his shoes. He suffered exceedingly from the pain of the rejection—a prince of the "blood royal," inherited from the most powerful reigning houses of

Statue of Sir Francis Bacon at Gray's Inn
After his return from Paris, Francis took up residence at Gray's Inn. At that
time, the Inns of Court served not only as colleges for the study of law,
but also as social clubs and finishing schools for sons of the aristocracy.
Francis wrote several masques and early Shakespeare plays during his
tenure here. The gardens of Gray's Inn were laid out by Francis in 1606
when he served as treasurer of the Inn.

Europe. In his veins flowed the royal blood of Valois-Plantagenet-
Tudor arrogance, nobility and pride. It was a perpetual struggle
for him to bring it under control. He was forced to stand aside
while his closest friends from childhood were given wealth,
privilege and titles. He watched other men rise from glory to
glory while he, the queen's own son, was denied a simple
knighthood. This inability to rise has caused some historians, not
knowing the truth, to conjecture that there was some intrinsic
flaw in young Bacon that kept him from advancement.

It was his very soul that told him he was born to a divine

destiny and that somehow he must fulfill this role. In his essay "Of Great Place," he would later write of the difficulty of succeeding: "The standing is slippery, and the regress is either a downfall or at least an eclipse, which is a melancholy thing."[3]

In June of 1579, Francis began to "keep his terms" in Gray's Inn (one of the Inns of Court still active today). He "kept chambers" in the rooms formerly used by Sir Nicholas. The Inns of Court were more than law schools; they also served as polishing schools to train young aristocrats in the arts of superior status in the realm, a background that no commoner from a little country village such as Stratford-on-Avon could ever hope to acquire. Such an aristocratic culture is easily apparent in all the works of Shakespeare.

Just what goes to make up the perfect English gentleman is hard to define, although many have tried. In 1497 the Venetian ambassador to the queen's court wrote in apparent frustration:

> The English are great lovers of themselves and of everything belonging to them. They think that there are no other men like themselves, and no other world but England.... Whenever they see a handsome foreigner, they say that he looks like an Englishman, and that it is a great pity he should not be an Englishman; and when they set any delicacy before a foreigner they ask him if such a thing is made in his country.[4]

These comments were quoted in 1926 by William Ralph Inge, dean of St. Paul's, who also gave his own observations on English ideals:

> If we should ever follow the example of [other] countries and abolish, in the name of democratic uniformity, the "gentlemen's schools," it is probable that the nation would suffer grievously by the loss of those traditions which impartial foreigners have admired so heartily.[5]

These ideals, he wrote, were developed during Queen Elizabeth's century by such works as Spenser's *Faerie Queene,* in which the poet tried to present a view of the ideal gentleman. (Again, we shock the academicians by pointing out that the cipher claims that Bacon himself wrote the works of Spenser.[6]) Dean Inge continues:

> [The Elizabethan character] was as a whole a new character in the world. It had not really existed in the days of feudalism and chivalry.... In the days of Elizabeth it was beginning to fill a large place in English life. It was formed amid the increasing cultivation of the nation, the increasing varieties of public service, the awakening responsibilities to duty and calls to self-command. Still making much of the prerogative of noble blood and family honours, it was something independent of nobility and beyond it.... Great birth, even great capacity, were not enough; there must be added ... new appreciation of what is beautiful and worthy of honour, a new measure of the strength and nobleness of self-control, of devotion and unselfish interests. This idea of manhood [is] based not only on force and courage, but on truth.[7]

We can thank Dean Inge for his insight into the changes that were taking place when we realize that these were the same ideals that Francis was not only incorporating into himself but that he would spend most of his life trying to instill into the persona of the British people.

A commentary by Cardinal Newman, quoted by Dean Inge in his *England*, reflects the influence of Francis Bacon on his times:

> It is almost a definition of a gentleman to say that he is one who never inflicts pain.... The true gentleman avoids whatever may cause a jar or a jolt in the minds of those with whom he is cast—all clashing of opinion, ... all suspicion or

gloom or resentment; his great concern being to make every one at their ease and at home.... He never speaks of himself except when compelled, never defends himself by a mere retort, he has no ears for slander or gossip,... and interprets everything for the best. He is never mean or little in his disputes, never takes an unfair advantage.... He has too much sense to be affronted at insult, he is too busy to remember injuries and does not bear malice.[8]

There is more and, as Inge observes, these qualities would not be reserved alone for Englishmen. But from various observations by Bacon's many friends during the course of his life, he more than fulfills the ideals of gentlemanly behavior expected of members of Gray's Inn. These young men were sons of aristocrats, however, and they were lively, high-spirited and most had pouches full of money. They were far from being prudes, and many lively adventures originated at one or another of these inns. A favorite entertainment was the staging of masques and plays. Some of Shakespeare's early plays had their beginnings here, including *The Comedy of Errors* (Gray's Inn) and *Twelfth Night* (Middle Temple).

In spite of the privileged atmosphere and the high living of the young aristocrats around him, Bacon was far from happy at Gray's Inn. He couldn't shake the feeling that he had been born for greater purposes. "The Law drinketh up too much of my time," he complained early in his career. "I wish for studies of greater delight."[9] Back home, in the nation that should have one day been his birthright to rule, he was considered more of an outsider than he had ever been in France. He was no longer a true member of the Bacon family, nor was he accepted as a Tudor.

It was a desperately unhappy time for Francis Tudor. If we detect a similarity between his feelings and the words of misery expressed by that fictional but famous young Prince of Denmark,

Interior of Gray's Inn Hall
from a drawing by H. Crichmore
The play *The Comedy of Errors* saw its first performance here as part of
the 1594 Christmas revels of the inn. The plot is based on two plays by
Plautus (the great comic dramatist of third century B.C. Rome) which were
not available in English at that time. *The Comedy of Errors* first appeared
in print in 1623 in the First Folio.

Hamlet, we can be sure it was intentional on the writer's part.
Like Francis, Hamlet felt lonely and rejected:

> I have of late, but wherefore I know not, lost all my mirth,
> forgone all custom of exercises; and indeed, it goes so
> heavily with my disposition that this goodly frame, the
> earth, seems to me a sterile promontory.
>
> *act II, sc. 2*

Even more poignant is Hamlet's longing for extinction:

O that this too sullied flesh would melt,
Thaw, and resolve itself into a dew,
Or that the Everlasting had not fixed
His canon 'gainst self-slaughter. O God, God,
How weary, stale, flat, and unprofitable
Seem to me all the uses of this world!

act I, sc. 2

To be, or not to be—that is the question…

act III, sc. 1

The *cri de coeur*, the cry of the heart, of young Hamlet has moved the compassion of audiences for centuries, but who was there to listen to the tears of young Francis? A cry of such pathos could have come only from the heart of one who had personally experienced the pain of the conflict between the need to live and the desire to die. There were to be other low ebbs in the course of Francis's life, but this one was perhaps the most hurtful of all. It was at this point of desperation, the darkest night of his soul, that a deep mystical experience occurred which helped him pull out of his murky state of melancholy and find a purpose in living once more.

Even midst the lightheartedness of his Parisian years, there had always been a part of Francis that was never out of touch with his deeper and "better" self. He called this part of himself his Muse. Often Francis turned to this deeper side for comfort. One night, alone in his chambers in Gray's Inn, he sought solace in his Bible, as he often did. Thumbing through the "holy scriptures of our great God," he came to his favorite passage in Proverbs. The cipher tells us that he began to read

That passage of Solomon, the king, wherein he
Affirmeth "That the glory of God is to conceal
A thing, but the glory of a king is to find it out."[10]

Suddenly there was a change in the atmosphere of the room. He didn't know what was happening, but he was aware that it was something not of this world and that it had the power to change his life.

> As we read and pondered the wise
> Words and lofty language of this precious
> Book of love, there comes a flame of fire which
> Fills all the room, and obscures our eyes with its
> Celestial glory. And from it swells a heavenly
> Voice that, lifting our mind above her
> Human bounds, ravisheth our soul with its sweet,
> Heavenly music. And thus it spake:
>   "My son, fear not, but take thy fortunes and thy
> Honours up. Be that thou knowest thou art,
> Then thou art as great as that thou fearest.
> Thou art not what thou seemest. At thy
> Birth the front of heaven was full of fiery
> Shapes; the goats ran from the mountains,
> And the herds were strangely clamorous
> To the frighted fields. These signs
> Have marked thee extraordinary, and all the
> Courses of thy life will show thou art not in
> The roll of common men....
>   "Be thou not, therefore, afraid of greatness,
> I charge thee. Some men become great by
>   advancement, vain
> And favour of their prince; some have greatness
> Thrust upon them by the world, and some achieve
> Greatness by reason of their wit; for there is
> A tide in the affairs of men, which when taken at the
> Flood, leads on to glorious fortune. Omitted, all the
> Voyage of their life is bound in shallows
> And miseries. In such a sea art thou now afloat,
> And thou must take the current when it serves....

"Remember that [which] thou hast just
Read, that the Divine Majesty takes delight to hide
His work, according to the innocent play of children,
To have them found out; surely for thee to
Follow the example of the most high God cannot
Be censured. Therefore put away popular applause,
And after the manner of Solomon the king, compose
A history of thy times, and fold it into
Enigmatical writings and cunning mixtures of the
Theatre, mingled as the colours in a painter's shell,
And it will in due course of time be found.
    "For there shall be born into the world
(Not in years, but in ages) a man whose pliant and
Obedient mind we, of the supernatural world, will take
Special heed, by all possible endeavour, to frame
And mould into a pipe for thy fingers to sound
What stop thou please; and this man, either led or
Driven, as we point the way, will yield himself a
Disciple of thine, and will search and seek out thy
Disordered and confuséd strings and roots with some
Peril and unsafety to himself. For men in scornful and
Arrogant manner will call him mad, and point at him
The finger of scorn; and yet they will,
Upon trial, practice and study of thy plan,
See that the secret, by great and voluminous labour
Hath been found out." And then the voice we heard
Ceased and passed away.[11]

Francis now knew that he was no longer alone. Comfort and hope flooded over him like a healing balm and his lively creative mind came immediately into play. Hadn't he studied the latest methods of secret writing and devised his own ciphers while he was in France?[12] His principal biographer, James Spedding, would later write: "He could at once imagine, like a poet, and execute like a clerk of the works. Upon the conviction, 'This may be done,' followed at once the question, 'How may it be done?' Upon that question answered, followed the resolution to try and do it."[13] This natural ability came fully into action after the inspiring visit of his mystical counselor. It needed only a Dr. Owen and a Mrs. Gallup to "roll away from the sepulchre this great stone."

Chapter Eight

The Golden Lads

*Preserve the right of thy place, but stir not questions of
jurisdiction, and rather assume thy right in silence.*

While Francis was studying law, writing and
applying the advice from his celestial vision, a new dimension
entered his life—a closer involvement with the glamorous life and
tragic death of young Robert Devereux, earl of Essex and, as the
cipher reveals, his own birth brother.[1] It was the beginning of
what would develop into one of the saddest tales ever told.

We will begin the story by turning to Dame Daphne du
Maurier's book *Golden Lads*, the first of her two biographies of
Sir Francis Bacon. Here she gives a carefully detailed and
thoroughly documented account of the lives of three of the most
interesting young men who ever walked the streets of London—
Francis Bacon, Anthony Bacon and young Robert Devereux.
Dame Daphne does not specifically reveal her opinions concerning the authorship of the Shakespeare plays, but it is difficult
not to read her reservations between the lines. In *The Winding
Stair*, the second of these biographies, she makes a revealing
statement:

It is not intended here to enter into a long and tedious argument as to whether William Shakespeare was indeed the author of all the thirty-six plays published under his name in the First Folio.[2]

She follows this with several paragraphs questioning the validity of the Shakespeare claim, then gives a quotation from a letter from Tobie Matthew to Francis Bacon, written from overseas:

> The most prodigious wit that I ever knew of my nation, and of this side of the sea, is of your Lordship's name, though he be known by another.[3]

Why should his lordship be known by another name? Du Maurier's choice of this particular passage seems to reveal her thoughts on the matter. However, we do not have to rely on guesswork about Dame du Maurier's attitude when we glimpse the title page of the journal of the Francis Bacon Society of London. For many years the name of Lady Browning, Daphne du Maurier, appeared as an honorary vice president. This journal, *Baconiana*, is a publication supporting the authorship of the Shakespeare plays by Francis Bacon. It began in 1886.

The dust jacket of *Golden Lads* is designed with portraits of three charming young men in the ruffs and laces of fashionable Elizabethan dress. On the left smiles the sweet face of the eighteen-year-old Francis Bacon, taken from the miniature portrait by Hilliard. In the center is a portrait of Anthony Bacon, and on the other side the dashing young Robert Devereux, second earl of Essex. These are the three "golden lads," so named from a passage in Shakespeare's *Cymbeline*.

> Fear no more the heat o' th' sun
>   Nor the furious winter's rages;
> Thou thy worldly task hast done,

Home art gone and ta'en thy wage.
Golden lads and girls all must,
As chimney-sweepers, come to dust.

act IV, sc. 2

It is doubtful that anywhere in history a more interesting trio of young men could be found. Their influence on their times would astonish historians if the whole truth were known.

Traditionally, of course, these three pictures are of Francis Bacon, his brother Anthony and his close friend Robert Devereux. According to the cipher story, the relationship is reversed, a far more interesting situation. The one who is Francis's brother is the earl of Essex, and the other one is not his brother but his dearest friend, Anthony Bacon. By a strange destiny, these three remarkable young men were dropped into a drama of circumstances that were beyond their power to control.

As we saw earlier, young Essex was supposed to have been the first son of Walter Devereux and his wife, Lettice. It turns out that the entire drama of the birth of little Francis (Tudor) had been replayed in a similar scenario—the same parents, a different year, a different child.

Lord Leicester had definitely been paying more than decent attention to Elizabeth's beautiful and glamorous cousin Lettice Knollys, wife of Sir Walter Devereux. It was after a violent and unsettling period of quarreling over Lettice and a subsequent and euphoric makeup that little Robert "Devereux" was born. The date was November 10, 1566. The circumstances surrounding the birth of this second child were just as peculiar as those surrounding the birth of Francis. Elizabeth temporarily disappeared from public life and she neglected to sign state papers. For an entire month she was not seen at close range by her subjects. Again the court maintained a strange silence concerning the whole affair.

In Elizabeth's England, moral ideals were more frequently talked about than acted upon, and it was often required of the members of the court to close their eyes, shut their mouths and ignore the appearance of a child whose illegitimate parentage was not a topic that could be safely discussed. If the father chose to acknowledge his offspring publicly, everything was all right. Many of the illegitimate offspring of the nobility were sooner or later given recognition by their fathers, and they often received titles as well as the right of inheritance. It was the father's right to decide. In this case, of course, the situation was complicated by Elizabeth's position and her determination to appear virtuous in spite of her intrigues.

In 1571 (at Leicester's request, says the cipher[4]), Elizabeth expressly demanded of Parliament the passing of a bill making it a penal offense to speak of any successors to the Crown other than the "natural issue" of her body. Her ministers urged her to use the more usual term, "lawful issue," but she was adamant. "Natural" it would be. Her obstinate refusal gave rise not only to suspicious speculation but also to numerous defamatory views about her motives. Biographer Alfred Dodd comments on this in *Francis Bacon's Personal Life-Story.*[5] Elizabeth's famous court historian, William Camden, remembered the time when the act was passed, and he heard it said openly that this was done by the contrivance of Leicester with a design to impose upon the nation some baseborn son of his own as the queen's offspring.[6]

Shortly after the birth of Robert, Elizabeth gave to his "father," Walter Devereux, Lord Hereford, a manor near Braintree in Essex, not far from London. A few years later, she created him earl of Essex and he was made a Knight of the Garter. The Devereux had suddenly advanced in the ranks of nobility and increased their material assets. It would seem that Walter was being well paid for his sponsorship of little Robert Tudor Dudley.

"Young Man among Roses," by Nicholas Hilliard
The young courtier in the portrait wears the queen's colors, black and white, and is surrounded by roses, her symbol. It has been suggested that he is Robert Devereux, earl of Essex.

It is not inconceivable—in fact it seems very likely—that he had been making things uncomfortable for the queen and was demanding more and more compensation for taking the little prince off her hands, an act that some might call blackmail.

Following Walter's death in 1576, the new earl of Essex, Robert, was made a ward of Lord Burghley. The boy was the poorest earl in the country, it was said. Young Robert's new guardian sent to Chartley, the Essex estate, for a description of the lad. The reply gave a glowing report: "He can express his mind in Latin and French, as well as English; very courteous and modest, rather disposed to hear than to answer; given greatly to learning; weak and tender, but very comely and bashful."[7]

Such a report would have pleased Elizabeth and Leicester. By nature they were both interested in learning and education. Their absent child seemed to have taken after them, just as Francis did—although they had not seemed to value it in his case. It was time to meet their youngest son.

Early in 1577 Burghley sent for the fledgling earl to live with him at Theobalds. On arrival, he was taken for the first time to court. "The nine-year-old Robert Devereux charmed everyone he met," writes his biographer Robert Lacey. "His beauty was breath-taking."[8] For the first time too he would meet the fabulous woman whom he did not yet know was his mother.

The queen was immediately enchanted with the boy. As she welcomed him, she leaned forward to give him a kiss. Already fiercely independent and not finding this aging, red-haired woman very appealing, he turned his head aside and refused her. The queen may not have been amused, but she was intrigued.

It is not clear when Francis first met this younger brother, for Francis was away on his fascinating three-year visit to France when Robert came to Theobalds. But surely Lady Anne would have told him of this brother during her long recital of the strange hush-hush family connections. It was probably not until the tempestuous young earl was called to court at the age of seventeen that their acquaintanceship grew into the intense friendship which played so marked a role in both their lives.

Soon after Robert came to the Cecils, he was sent up to Trinity at Cambridge, the same college that Francis had left eighteen months earlier. The younger boy, only ten years old, was entrusted to the special care of Dean Whitgift, just as Francis had been. Both lads were granted the same special privileges and solicitous treatment otherwise unprecedented in the annals of the college. Even Robert was surprised at the unexpected attention, for he wrote a letter to Burghley thanking him for the many kindnesses he encountered, all of which he attributed to Burghley's influence (not yet knowing, of course, that Burghley was acting on orders from the queen). Two years following Robert's terms at Trinity, Whitgift was made archbishop of Canterbury by the appointment of the queen.

The third portrait on the cover of *Golden Lads* is the likeness of Francis's beloved adoptive brother, Anthony, whom he often spoke of as "Anthony my comfort." No blood brothers could have been closer, and of course they had not known they weren't brothers until Francis was fifteen. When Francis published his first acknowledged works, the 1597 edition of *Essays,* he dedicated them to Anthony.

In *The Two Gentlemen of Verona,* the same value is placed on friendship as between the two brothers. It is easy to imagine that when Valentine describes his dear friend, "his other self," Proteus, the names could be transposed to Francis and Anthony. In the play, the duke of Milan asks, "You know him [Proteus] well?" Valentine answers, "I know him as myself; for from our infancy / We have conversed and spent our hours together."[9] Francis and Anthony!

An even clearer parallel is seen in *The Merchant of Venice* in the friendship between Antonio (Anthony) and Bassanio (Bacon). This is certainly a story inspired by and celebrating the love of the two foster brothers—Anthony willing to give his life for Francis as well as his fortune, which he had offered many times.

Loyal Anthony makes up the third member of the trio of "golden lads." Between the three of them, they had blood ties to nearly everyone of importance in Elizabeth's England. It has been said that Elizabeth and Lord Burghley ran England as though it were a family estate and that court gatherings were like a family reunion.[10] It was so, and Francis and Essex were major components of the whole.

When Francis returned from Europe, the two blood brothers, Robert and Francis, struck up a firm friendship. It was enhanced, no doubt, by the secret of their mutual parentage—an inheritance mixed with joy and grief—and the frustrations caused by this knowledge. Francis tells us of his consternation, part pride and part apprehension, on learning of his true nativity. It also would have been interesting to know just how Robert reacted to the first knowledge. As it is, we can only imagine it, but knowing the lad's temperament, he would not have taken it calmly. Did the queen tell him? Or Leicester? Or Francis himself? We do not know.

There is evidence that when Francis returned from France, he lived for a while in Leicester House on the Strand, close by York House, with his natural father.[11] York House would no longer have been available to him as a home since the lord keeper was gone and Lady Anne would not have the privilege of living there. This must have suited her well, for she quickly moved back to Gorhambury, which was her favorite anyway. She offered Francis a place under her roof whenever he wished it, but he needed to be in the city and near the court, where all the action was taking place. Until the queen decided on a policy concerning him, Leicester House was a logical place for him. His fate was still in the balance. Apparently, this arrangement was short-lived. Soon we find Francis ensconced in his rooms at Gray's Inn.

Philip Sidney, Leicester's nephew (and therefore Francis's cousin), and his friends were already active in literary pursuits. Francis now joined the group. Although he was younger by several years, his vast intellectual powers, his unusual maturity and his natural love of the literary arts would have made him more than the equal of those young gallants. Already this group had drawn around themselves a remarkable roster of philosopher-

Philip Sidney (1554–1586)
Sidney, a prominent courtier and diplomat in Elizabethan times, greatly influenced English poetry. Sidney was a nephew of Leicester (therefore a cousin of Francis) and a coworker in Francis's literary projects. He is most famous today for his sonnets and his work *A Defense of Poesy* (poetry).

poets. They called themselves the Areopagus, taking their name from an ancient judicial council of Athens. It was an illustrious group and it reached its flood tide when Francis and Philip got together. They made a brilliant team, and those around them seemed more brilliant than they actually were as they reflected their leaders.

Anthony Bacon would have been an important member of the group when he was in England, although he was absent during those early years, having gone abroad shortly after his father's death. The younger Lord Robert and his satellite, the wealthy young earl of Southampton, would have joined the ranks as soon as they were old enough to be interested. These and others formed the core of the "magic circle," which was primarily responsible for the remarkable literary renaissance known as the "flowering of England." Dodd says that it is at this time that the seeds for the secret society that later developed into Rosicrucianism were sown.[12]

Pallas Athena, the "Spear-shaker"
Alfred Dodd describes how Bacon, while he was at Gray's Inn, established a secret society known as "The Honourable Order of the Knights of the Helmet," which was dedicated to the ideals embodied by Pallas Athena. To the Greeks, Athena was the personification of wisdom, the goddess who presided over the intellectual and moral side of human life. She was known by them as the "Spear-Shaker." (Perhaps this gives a clue as to the identity of the real "Shake-speare.") The "helmet" in the society's name was the helmet of Athena, which, in mythology, was supposed to make the wearer invisible. The members of the order likewise served "invisible" to the world, much of the fruit of their labors being released anonymously or under pseudonyms (*Francis Bacon's Personal Life-Story*, p. 131).

Chapter Nine

Two Brothers

*Men must beware that they carry their anger
rather with scorn than with fear, so that they may seem...
to be above the injury than below it.*

During Bacon's busy years of literary activity
in the 1580s and 1590s, he and his brother Robert grew ever
closer. Their father, Lord Leicester, died shortly after England's
great victory over the Spanish Armada in 1588. Elizabeth,
forgetting and forgiving his transgressions with Lettice, had made
her "Robin" the lord lieutenant of England's southern portion, a
position of great responsibility and power.

These off-again, on-again lovers, exactly the same age according to their own reckoning, were beginning to grow old, and they
frequently dined together in private and discussed their mutual
ailments. Like an old married couple, they had mellowed beyond
the years of quarrels and controversy. Elizabeth worried about
Lord Robert's health and suggested he "take the waters" at
Buxton. This he obediently set out to do, but he never arrived at
his destination. On the way he collapsed suddenly, taken by "cold
rheums" or "continual fever," and in the fifty-sixth year of his

life, Robert Dudley, Elizabeth's sometime husband and only true love, died.

Elizabeth was devastated and she withdrew to the privacy of her bedchamber in Whitehall to grieve, allowing no one entrance, until Burghley, alarmed, ordered the door to be broken down.[1] Beside her bed in a little jeweled casket was a letter from Leicester labeled "His last letter."

Leicester's will named Robert Devereux, Lord Essex, along with Lettice,* as the chief beneficiary of his estate. Elizabeth, however, had no intention of allowing the despised Lettice to gain any more than a widow's due, and she ordered Leicester's goods to be put up for auction for payment of his debts. Twenty-year-old Essex inherited his father's "best armour," two horses, and little else. Francis, of course, inherited nothing.

Leicester was gone, and his passing marked the end of one era; the defeat of the Spanish Armada heralded the beginning of a new one. (Some believe that the importance of the defeat of the Armada lies in the fact that the full equipment of the Spanish Inquisition was aboard the Spanish ships ready to restore Catholicism to England.[2] They were thwarted by the loss of the battle.) England was now recognized as a formidable sea power in her own right, well on her way to becoming the mighty empire upon which "the sun never sets."

Elizabeth felt lonely, as she always had without Leicester, but she still had their two sons, Robert and Francis, to whom she could turn. Whatever she may have said to Francis at this time we do not know. His influence in the House of Commons was becoming greater day by day (he was first elected as a member of parliament in 1581 and reelected in 1584), and perhaps she was wary of his increased popularity. The Cecils would try to see to it that she was. At the same time, she counted on his advice. What

---

* Leicester had secretly married Lettice, Walter Devereux's widow, around 1578, thus becoming "stepfather" to his own unacknowledged son.

Queen Elizabeth in approximately 1588
This portrait commemorates the defeat of the Spanish Armada, one of the turning points of English history. The panel to the right of the queen shows the storms that scattered and destroyed the ships of the Armada. These were interpreted as intervention by God to thwart the Spanish aim of restoring Catholicism in England and a sign of divine approval for the Protestant cause.

we do know is that much of her love for Leicester was transferred to her younger son in that strange relationship between the queen and Essex that is still so puzzling to historians today. Was it actually an affair? Probably not, although Francis hints that it was far from normal.

After his return from Europe in 1591, Anthony, too, grew more intimate with Essex. Home after twelve years abroad, Anthony had put up at Gray's Inn with Francis for a few months. As always, the two foster brothers would have found much to talk about and, according to Lady Anne, they were far too lively for their own good. She wrote to Anthony scolding him with her usual motherly advice:

> Be wise and godly too, and discern what is good and what
> [is] not for your health.... Be wary of suppers late or full.
> Procure rest in convenient time. It helpeth much to
> digestion. I verily think your brother's weak stomach to
> digest hath been much caused and confirmed by untimely
> going to bed, and then musing *nescio quid* [I know not
> what].... But my sons haste not to hearken to their mother's
> good counsel.[3]

We do know that the activities of her sons were not all
frivolity, as she imagined. Their lives at Twickenham Park
(Francis's country estate, opposite Elizabeth's palace at Richmond) and Gray's Inn were simple enough according to
Elizabethan standards. Francis did not indulge in the outlandishly
expensive clothes that were the norm at the court and he
entertained only his few close friends, but he did always seem to
be in debt.

It was, of course, the literary work that ate up more money
than the brothers could raise. W. T. Smedley gives some idea of
the magnitude of the task that Francis was pursuing, inspired by
the work of the Pléiade in France:

> Translations of the classics, of histories and other
> works—with the assistance and the commandment of more
> wits than his own—were made.... Books came from his
> pen, poetry and prose, at a rate which, when the truth is
> revealed, will literally stagger humanity. Books were written
> by other men under his direction....
> From 1576 to 1623 ... the English language was
> made.... The histories of the principal nations of the world,
> practically everything that was worth knowing in the litera-
> ture of other countries, were for the first time made avail-
> able in the English tongue.... What is still more remarkable,

Richmond Palace, one of Elizabeth's favorite residences
from a drawing by Anto van den Wyngaerde (1562)
From the windows of this palace, the queen could look out and see
Twickenham Park, Francis's "Palace fit for a Prince" on the opposite bank
of the Thames. It would have been an easy row across the river for Francis
to visit the queen privately. Twickenham was where Francis established his
writing school, or scriptorium, the "good pens" who assisted him in his
literary work.

these translations were printed and published.... Being
printed in the English language, purchases were practically
confined to this country, and the number of readers was
very limited....

Books of this class were never produced with the object
of making profit. The proceeds of the sales would not cover
the cost of printing and publishing without any provision of
the translator or author. Why were they published and how
was the cost provided?[4]

"Riches are for spending; and spending for honour and good
actions," wrote Francis in his essay "Of Expense." And
furthermore, he wrote, if the project is worthy, one is justified in
spending large amounts of money on it. If this is the case,
however, spending must be limited in other areas. Bacon was
following his own advice (or at least attempting to)—spending
greatly on his project and economizing on the rest, although

never quite enough. Thus it was that this impecunious prince of the realm was constantly harassed by his creditors and professional usurers.

Anthony, always so close and supportive, tried with all his resources to help keep the expensive scheme rolling. Already he had sold (or mortgaged) much of his inherited property for the purpose as he had traveled throughout Europe contacting those with like ideals, those who could help bring about his plans for the remaking of not only England but the entire world.

Funds were dwindling, and yet those expensive "masks" always had to be paid. Francis dared not publish under his own name for fear of the queen's wrath. The Stratford actor was apparently receiving a huge amount of the proceeds from the plays without being responsible for a single halfpence of the expense, and he was constantly demanding more.[5]

In 1593 things were desperate—all their resources were exhausted and the only recourse was to appeal to Lady Anne. Anthony wrote to her, most reluctantly we can be sure. Once again Anthony was the go-between for communications between Francis and Lady Anne. What he was requesting was that Lady Anne sign a paper allowing Francis to sell a bit of property that he could not dispose of without her approval.

Lady Anne took the request amiss, but she reluctantly signed the agreement and sent it back with the expected frantic letter of disapproval: "I have been too ready for you both till nothing is left." The state of the affairs of her two beloved boys "doth much disquiet me."[6] At times her letters scarcely made sense; she was showing early signs of the unquiet and confused mental aberration that would lead to full insanity before her earthly role was outplayed. Perhaps the stresses and strains of rescuing Elizabeth's child were taking their toll.

The mounting debt was a heavy burden for the boys, and

before the decade was over Francis was to be arrested for a debt of £300 owed to a Mr. Sympson, a goldsmith. It was only by the intercession of his loyal Anthony that Francis, a royal prince by blood, was saved from spending time in the dismal debtor's prison, the Fleet, like any common criminal.

Again we see that one of the greatest dramas ever written, *The Merchant of Venice,* does biographical honor to Anthony's devotion. The play is not only about friendship, it is about justice—and usury:

> 'Tis not unknown to you, Antonio,
> How much I have disabled my estate,
> By something showing a more swelling port
> Than my faint means would grant continuance.
> Nor do I now make moan to be abridged
> From such a noble rate; but my chief care
> Is to come fairly off from the great debts
> Wherein my time, something too prodigal,
> Hath left me gaged. To you Antonio,
> I owe the most, in money and in love.
>
> *act I, sc. 1*

This was a fine tribute to Anthony, but it didn't solve their money problems.

Robert Devereux's life in these years followed a different course. He had inherited the title earl of Essex at the age of nine, when Walter had died so fortuitously (for Elizabeth) in Ireland, and from the age of seventeen he was spending most of his time at court.

Robert was of a different nature from his older brother, Francis. Born under the sign of Scorpio, astrologers may see him as having had a win-at-all-costs determination and a haughty spirit mixed with a stinging temper and a streak of self-destructive, rebellious rashness—all intermingled with a sunny and gallant

Bassanio, from *The Merchant of Venice*
In one of the most popular of the Shakespeare plays, Bassanio is poor but of noble birth. Antonio, his devoted friend, is a wealthy merchant. The relationship of these two echoes that between Francis Bacon (Bassanio) and his brother Anthony (Antonio), who provided much financial support for Francis's great endeavor.

disposition that was sure to make him popular with everyone. Astrology or no, these and more were qualities that Essex had in abundance. Although he seems to have been intelligent enough and to have enjoyed literature and poetry to a certain degree, he was a warrior at heart, while Francis loved harmony. Robert loved the sword; Francis loved the pen.

Essex was taken by Leicester on a military campaign in the Netherlands in 1585, when he was yet a teenager. He was appointed to Leicester's own former position of master of the horse in 1587 and made a Knight of the Garter by the queen in 1588. Such honors had never been given to Francis. It was obvious that both Leicester and Elizabeth delighted in this fiery son far more than they did in their wiser, brighter and more scholarly older son.

Lytton Strachey describes the boy Robert as moody and unpredictable—"lying for hours in his chamber, obscurely melancholy, with a Virgil in his hand."[7] Was he already brooding over the secret of his birth? We don't know of course. We do know that he was a handsome and charming youth, tall and graceful, with boyish enthusiasms, a great love of hunting and sports, and an odd way of walking with his head thrust forward. As he grew more popular at court, he became "the glass of fashion," a glamorous model that everyone wanted to follow. The young earl was overflowing with that elusive quality that today would be called charisma, and whether or not it was deserved, he attracted devotees from all walks of life. A further appeal inherited by young Robert was an auburn tint to his hair and a thin beard that was distinctly ginger colored, like that of his grandfather Henry VIII.

A comparison of the picture of a youthful Henry with that of Robert shows a distinct resemblance between them—another quality that would have endeared Essex to his mother, the queen. Francis says clearly in cipher that Robert's fearlessness and rashness could be traced "directly to our mother":

> His early youth was lightly passed, but after he did know that it was the Queen that gave him life, he grew imperious, and (when brought to Court by our truly ingenious father...), his will showed its true source, and revealed the origin of the young Caesar.[8]

The queen clearly adored her upstart son. The more fiery and imperious he appeared to be, the more obviously she delighted in him. By the age of nineteen, he was worshiping her at one moment and defying her the next. The cipher tells us that, like his mother, he could make quick decisions in sudden calamities and express conflicting opinions in so swift succession that one hardly knew where, in fact, he stood.[9]

> He was one of the adventurous, valiant, bold spirits not easily hidden in any place, and it was not, therefore, unseemly that the son of one so widely and favourably reputed as the first Earl of Essex made so bold [as] to woo the goddess Fortune at Court. None knew so truly as Elizabeth, our proud unbending, royal mère, the cause of many of our willful Essex' overbearing ways.... Our vain mother loved his bold manner and free spirit, his sudden quarrels, jealousy in soul of honour, strength in love. She saw in him her own spirit in masculine mold, full of youth and beauty.[10]

After the death of Leicester, Elizabeth became increasingly enamored of Essex. Biographer G. B. Harrison writes of this strange attachment with astute accuracy: "It had something of the jealous love of a widow towards her only son."[11] It was marveled that the queen was so tolerant of Robert's rude and imperious manners. She took insults from him that she would not have tolerated in another, certainly not in Francis. But then it would never have occurred to Francis to express anything except the greatest respect and honor to his queen, let alone his mother.

All accounts of the lives of Elizabeth and Essex tell of the violence of the quarrels between them, of how Robert defied Her Royal Highness and at one time even turned his back on her. How does the queen react to this ultimate insult? She boxes his ears as though he were a child and ignores the whole episode. Another time after a quarrel, she sent him to bed like a naughty boy. After a chastisement, Essex would sulk in his room for a day or a week or a fortnight, and then he would write her an impassioned letter vowing his loyalty and passionate love and complaining bitterly of her unfair treatment of him.

There is no doubt that Elizabeth put her two sons in an

intolerable position. She expected of them the devotion and loyalty owed not only to a queen but also to a mother, and yet she denied them the rights to which they were naturally entitled as princes and as her sons. At court these princes should have been given precedence over every other courtier of any rank. Yet sometimes, infuriatingly, the queen allowed someone of inferior rank—Robert Cecil or the arrogant Sir Walter Raleigh—to be placed at their head.

Francis was resilient enough to be able to bear the humiliation of the situation; Robert was not. He became increasingly nervous, touchy, volatile, paranoid. Sometimes he retreated into deep periods of depression, which alternated with periods of frantic activity and ambitious fervor—a seemingly manic-depressive condition.

More than once when Robert and Elizabeth were at odds, he tried to run away, "like a schoolboy playing truant," Robert Lacey writes.[12] Each time the queen sent her men after him to bring him back. She could not bear to let this beloved child out of her sight. When he incurred Elizabeth's wrath by secretly marrying the widow of Sir Philip Sidney (a promise he claimed to have made to the dying Sidney), it finally seemed that the breach could never be healed. But Essex "pursued and cajoled her with ardors as romantic as ever," writes Strachey,[13] and she finally gave in.

Some orthodox historians have believed that in spite of the difference in their ages, Elizabeth and Essex were lovers, although probably, they generally agree, not physically. We know that they were parent and child. Even so, the relationship was neither normal nor healthy, far from it. A letter from one Anthony Paget to his father says that Essex was seen emerging from the queen's chamber at dawn after playing cards "until the birds began to sing in the morning."[14] They were constantly together in the early stages of their relationship, taking walks in the gardens, riding together, dancing and playing at cards—laughing, flirting, paying each other extravagant compliments. When they quarreled, they were miserable; when they made up again, it was all smiles and love. Francis says in cipher:

> Great [was the] court scandal regarding love messages betwixt them, as though they had been mindful only of pleasure, so that the lords of her council winked visibly at it,... for 'twas dangerous for any onlookers if the eyesight were keen and saw behind those masques. [I was] pledged to write it as I believed it ... not ... omitting the sin of either.[15]

A strange and unhealthy relationship such as this could only end in tragedy.

Francis, with all his amiability and balance, was far from being insensitive, quite the opposite. He suffered deeply from his rejection by his parents and their obvious preference for his younger brother. In sonnet 29 his hurt and sense of injustice is clear:

> When, in disgrace with Fortune and men's eyes,
> I all alone beweep my outcast state,
> And trouble deaf heaven with my bootless cries,
> And look upon myself and curse my fate,
> Wishing me like to one more rich in hope,
> Featured like him, like him with friends possessed,
> Desiring this man's art, and that man's scope,
> With what I most enjoy contented least;
> Yet in these thoughts myself almost despising,
> Haply I think on thee, and then my state,
> Like to the lark at break of day arising
> From sullen earth, sings hymns at heaven's gate;
>   For thy sweet love rememb'red such wealth brings,
>   That then I scorn to change my state with kings.

It can also be seen in sonnet 86:

> Was it the proud full sail of his great verse,
> Bound for the prize of all too precious you,
> That did my ripe thoughts in my brain inhearse,*
> Making their tomb the womb wherein they grew?
> Was it his spirit, by spirits taught to write
> Above a mortal pitch, that struck me dead?
> No, neither he, nor his compeers by night
> Giving him aid, my verse astonishèd.
> He, nor that affable familiar ghost
> Which nightly gulls him with intelligence,
> As victors, of my silence cannot boast;
> I was not sick of any fear from thence.
>   But when your countenance filled up his line,
>   Then I lacked matter, that enfeebled mine.

Bacon's dilemma (being continually at odds with "the better part of me") and the constant battles he waged ("at mortal war" against the almost insurmountable odds to lay "great bases for eternity") are the very human tendencies that make him so endearing to those who have come to know him through his cipher. He shares fully with his fellow beings the problems and pains of this mortal life, and one cannot help but love him for it.

It must have been excruciatingly humiliating to Francis to be forced to apply himself to the study of law while his younger brother's star was shining ever more brilliantly at court, while grants and monopolies worth thousands of pounds were bestowed on this new "Robin." One of the most lucrative grants of all, the Farm of Sweet Wines (the right to levy duties on all imported wines—an enormous grant, considering the Britishers' taste for wine) was given to him. It was a huge monopoly and would allow Essex to build a fortune. There was just one hitch—the grant was for only ten years

---

* inhearse: enclose as in a coffin

and would have to be renewed at the end of that time, and the renewal would depend wholly on Elizabeth's good will.

Francis did not for a moment resent his younger brother's popularity. But when it threatened his own right of succession, it became a true burden to his heart. In secret he says:

> Daily we see cause of this constantly increasing dread, in the favor shown to our brother rather than to ourself, despite the priority of our claim to all princely honour.[16]

In 1595 Anthony moved into Essex House with Lord Robert. He had been actively involved in gathering secret intelligence during his many years in Europe and was well qualified to become what amounted to a foreign secretary to the earl. Spies and agents, poets and dramatists, courtiers and noblemen, relatives and friends passed each other constantly on the roads to and from Essex House, the old Leicester House renamed. It was becoming almost a court in miniature, a dangerous challenge in the eyes of the Cecils, which they would have made haste to point out to Her Majesty.

The chief concern of these three young patriots—Francis, Robert and Anthony, all of whom spent their time and efforts in guarding the kingdom—was to make sure that Elizabeth's ex-brother-in-law, Mary's husband, Philip of Spain, did not succeed in his efforts to return the recalcitrant England to the fold of the Roman Catholic papacy. They guarded Elizabeth's little nation like watchdogs, pledged to its total freedom in religion, politics and trade. Their duty, as they saw it, was to make sure that Elizabeth did not perform some rash act or enter into an unfortunate marriage that would jeopardize the independence of England.

Essex's influence with the queen was reaching stellar proportions in the early 1590s, as was his popularity with the public—he was the darling of London. He had only to ride through the streets on his fiery horse to be cheered and adored; heads were bared as the earl of Essex passed by. He charmed all alike by doffing his hat at these greetings and acknowledging the cheers with low, sweeping bows—a living example of the grace and chivalry that the British still adored in the nobility. Yet Francis warned him, not out of jealousy but out of concern, to beware. If his star ascended higher than that of the queen, he would be headed straight for disaster. Neither the queen nor her subjects would tolerate too much competition. No one would be allowed to replace their still beloved "Queen Bess." Francis could see the danger, but Essex was enjoying the scene too much to recognize the stumbling blocks.

As the Essex-Bacon success increased, the Cecils' antagonism grew in proportion. The gap between the Cecils and the three "golden lads" had widened with the years. Old Burghley was now grooming his own son, Robert, to fill his place, and he did not intend to encourage the advancement of Elizabeth's progeny if he could help it. He knew his aging mistress as well as any man living—they had long been together. He warned Robert not to press her, for once her mind was made up, she was almost always right. Robert Cecil heeded this warning by tactfully disguising his pressure as concern for Her Majesty's well-being. Francis gave the same advice to Essex, but with Essex it did not take.

William Cecil was also wise enough to know that if the Bacon-Essex group grasped the power of government, he and his son would be out. The elderly Burghley was safe enough as long as Elizabeth was alive, but the younger man's ambitions reached far into the future. Burghley held the Essex group back in order to clear the way for his own frail but clever offspring.

Bacon has been accused of leaving the Cecil clan and joining up with Essex to further his own ambitions, as though somehow this was a dishonorable thing to do. It was, of course, what every

Robert Cecil, Lord Burghley's ambitious son
Robert succeeded his father as Queen Elizabeth's chief minister. The cipher story reveals that he had a lifelong animosity towards Francis Bacon.

man at court tried to do. In the old court days, there was no way to follow one's choice of career other than to link up with a person of "place" with like ambitions or aims. After the final great tragedy, Bacon freely admitted that the reason he worked with Essex was that at the time he considered him to be the fittest instrument to do good to the state. And by teaming up with his brother, he might be able to more effectively carry out his program for the benefit of the country.

In the year of 1593 Essex's influence with the queen had peaked and he was seeking desperately for more clout at court. It was at this time that he decided to help Francis gain a government office of some importance, trying to right the wrong done to Francis for so long. Essex had his heart set on getting the vacant position of attorney general for him or, failing that, the lower office of solicitor general when it became vacant. In retrospect, it is easy to see that it would have been wiser to try for this lower office first. From a letter written to Essex in 1595, it is clear that in the beginning Francis was not overly enthusiastic about taking on a government position. He knew he deserved it and felt qualified to handle it; nevertheless, he often said that he was "more fitted to hold a book than to play a part" in state affairs.

Essex would have nothing but the best for his brother, more as a matter of demanding recognition from the queen than anything else, and he was determined. The timing was bad. Francis had just tweaked the nose of the queen in Parliament, as she saw it, in a debate regarding subsidies* in which he had considered the well-being of the subjects over that of the Crown. She was punishing Francis by denying him access to her presence. A courtier without access had no position at all in affairs and was temporarily shunned. So Francis was once again limited and had to depend on his volatile brother to negotiate for him.

It was not the time for Essex to push for his candidate. Also, Elizabeth would have been especially touchy just then, for in the same year a member of Parliament by the name of Peter Wentworth had suggested that the Commons draw up a bill forcing Elizabeth to name her successor. Testy and irrational on the subject, she went into one of her towering rages, sent Wentworth to the Tower for the rest of his life, and no doubt let her sons know that she would not tolerate any further discussion of the subject.

Francis's course grew daily more difficult. He knew what it would take to please the queen; he also knew the high cost of maintaining his own integrity. His struggle to achieve some sort of balance between the two is what has given historians the idea that he was too ambitious for his own good, that he was

---

* subsidy: money granted by the British parliament to the crown and raised by special taxation.

ingratiating and subservient at court.

It was one of Bacon's own observations that the higher one is in degree or birth, the more obligated he is to act with generosity, justice and nobility. *Noblesse oblige* was the keynote of his character. In a subtle way, people recognized the great worth of Francis Bacon and they expected from him the best. Later, when certain of his actions were misinterpreted because of the difficulties of his position, the disillusionment was greater than it would have been for a more ordinary man. "Lilies that fester smell far worse than weeds."[17] For Edward Coke, for Robert Cecil, for any lesser endowed individual to seek place was all right. For Francis Bacon, it was not.

While Essex was seeking office for Francis, Elizabeth kept postponing a decision on the matter until Essex's and Francis's nerves were frayed. In Birch's *Memoirs* we read of Essex riding in a coach one day with Cecil. Cecil deliberately taunted him by hinting that Bacon was so "raw a youth," unprepared for "so great a place."[18] This was particularly insulting since Francis was older than either of them and Cecil was already holding a higher place. This was the argument that the Cecils were giving the queen—Francis was too young and inexperienced for the job. (They all knew that at the age of thirty-three he was more than adequate for the position, but it was a good argument to give the queen, who, like many mothers, could not quite see that her child had grown up.) Cecil remained cool, but Essex flashed forth in uncontrollable ire:

> The attorneyship for Francis is that I must have. And in that I will spend all my power, might, authority, and amity, and with tooth and nail defend and procure the same for him against whomsoever; and whosoever getteth this office out of my hands for any other, before he have it, it shall cost him the coming by.[19]

The battle was on, the lines were drawn. Nothing but total victory would do for either side. Even Lady Anne tried to do her part for Francis; she visited her nephew "Roberto il diavolo," as he was sometimes called. She told him she believed that Francis was "but strangely used by men's dealings, God knows who and why." Anne knew "who and why" and so did Robert. "I think he is the very first young gentleman of some account and yet nothing done for him.... The world marvels in respect of his friends and his own towardness. Experience teacheth that her Majesty's nature is not to resolve but to delay."[20]

Lady Anne dared to lay the blame on the queen; nobody understood better than she how bitter was the humiliation Francis was being forced to bear. But in spite of Lady Anne's help, Essex was not to have this victory. The more he argued with the queen, the more she delayed. He insisted that Francis should be "neither stranger to her person or her service."[21] But it wasn't up to Essex or Francis to make these decisions, and the queen grew more obstinate day by day. It was stubborn Tudor against stubborn Tudor, and the best of them all caught miserably in the middle.

Essex wrote to Francis after an interview with Her Majesty that she was "very reserved." This, of course, was the whole crux of the matter. As long as Essex grew passionate on the behalf of his brother, the queen would refuse him. On his own Francis might possibly have gotten the attorneyship. With Essex raising a rumpus about it constantly, he hadn't a chance. One of Elizabeth's courtiers commented wisely that if he should ever desire a favor of the queen, the last person he would ask to plead for him would be Essex.

After more than a year of indecisiveness, Elizabeth gave the position to Edward Coke, the Cecil candidate. He was a man with few endowments of grace or charm, although admittedly well trained in the intricacies of English law. Already he was an enemy to Francis and would be more so later on. The decision in favor of Coke was a rebuff to Essex and an insult to Francis. Next they tried for the lesser job of solicitor for Francis, but by then the queen was totally irritated and she also refused him that position. The humiliation was almost more than Francis could bear. In the midst of the affair he had written in a letter to Essex:

> I cannot but conclude with myself that no man ever received a more exquisite disgrace.... My nature can take no evil ply; but I will by God's assistance, with this disgrace of my fortune, and yet with that comfort of the good opinion of so many honourable and worthy persons, retire myself with a couple of men to Cambridge, and there spend my life in my studies and contemplations, without looking back.[22]

Undoubtedly, this is exactly what Francis would have liked to do, but even that respite was not allowed. In a poem released under the name of Edmund Spenser, he had written some years earlier:

> Full little knowest thou that has not tried
> What hell it is in suing long to bide...
> To eat thy heart through comfortless despairs;
> To fawn, to crouch, to wait, to ride, to run;
> To spend, to give, to want, to be undone.
> Unhappy Wight, born to disastrous end,
> That doth his life in so long tendance spend.
>   "Mother Hubbard's Tale"

Once again we suspect that according to his vow, Francis has left an anonymous account of his sad experience without giving outward voice to complaint.

Equally poignant is the allegory of sonnet 143:

> Lo, as a careful housewife runs to catch
> One of her feathered creatures broke away,

Edmund Spenser (c. 1552–1599)
Spenser is known as one of the greatest of early English poets, most
famously for *The Faerie Queene,* a celebration of the Tudor dynasty and
the Arthurian tradition. The cipher story reveals that Francis Bacon was the
author of all the works released under the name of Spenser (Owen, *Sir
Francis Bacon's Cipher Story,* vols. I–II, p. 22).

Sets down her babe, and makes all swift dispatch
In pursuit of the thing she would have stay;
Whilst her neglected child holds her in chase,
Cries to catch her whose busy care is bent
To follow that which flies before her face,
Not prizing her poor infant's discontent;
So run'st thou after that which flies from thee,
Whilst I, thy babe, chase thee afar behind;
But if thou catch thy hope, turn back to me
And play the mother's part, kiss me, be kind.
    So will I pray that thou mayst have thy *Will,*
    If thou turn back and my loud crying still.

Disappointed as they were at the failure of their plans, there was nothing more that Francis and Essex could do about it except to remain silent and wait for a chance to try again. Francis commented bitterly that no man had ever experienced so exquisite a defeat. Also, he took the occasion to write a warning letter to Robert Cecil telling him that he knew of his ill will[23] and that when his fortune grew better, he would settle accounts. As Cecil well knew, if Francis were ever "set at liberty," his own day was over. The battle was still on.

Essex tried in the only way left to him to make it up to Francis. He knew in his heart that he had been the cause of the delay and anguish as well as the time lost, which could have been used more constructively and more lucratively by his deserving brother. He visited Francis in his rooms and tried to make amends.

> The Queen hath denied me yon place for you, and hath placed another. I know you are the least part in your own matter, but you fare ill because you have chosen me for your mean and dependence; you have spent your time and thoughts in my matters. I die if I do not somewhat towards your fortune: you shall not deny to accept a piece of land which I will bestow upon you.[24]

Essex deeded to his brother a valuable piece of property adjoining the estate at Twickenham. Both he and Francis knew the fairness of this, and yet Francis accepted it only on one condition:

> My Lord, I see I must be your homager and hold land of your gift: But do you know the manner of doing homage in law? Always it is with a saving of his faith to the king and his other lords: and therefore, my Lord, I can be no more yours than I was ... and if I grow to be a rich man, you will give me leave to give it back to some of your unrewarded followers.[25]

Francis *did* later grow to be a rich man, but it was only of short duration, and by that time Essex was gone. In the meanwhile, to maintain his integrity he would accept Essex's gift only if it was thoroughly understood that his first obligation would still be to the queen. He later sold the land (to raise money for his publishing enterprise, no doubt), realizing only a small portion of what the solicitor general's office would have given him. Once again, some misinformed historians comment on how generous Essex was to give Bacon the land and how greedy Francis was to accept it!

Chapter Ten

Try, Try, Try Again

Answer to the question, when a man should marry:
A young man not yet, an elder man not at all.

It must have seemed to Francis that "the world is
bent my deeds to cross"[1] after the devastating disappointment.
Delayed but not discouraged, he had already devised a new plan.
Defeat was no part of his nature. Elizabeth would not help him
rise to a position where he could acquire the funds necessary to
carry out his "great scheme"; therefore he must find another way.

For upper echelon Elizabethans there were only three paths to
fortune. The easy way to riches was to inherit them; it was not
socially acceptable for nobility to work for a living. Only the
other classes were permitted the privilege of providing for
themselves. Neither Francis's foster father nor his real father had
provided for his future—and certainly his mother had not. The
next course was to gain the favor of the Crown and thus obtain a
grant of property or some lucrative appointment or levy. Francis
had tried with all the fervor of his heart to obtain favor, as we
know, but only disgrace and accusations of being too ambitious
had come of it. The third way was not only perfectly honorable

but it was the norm in Elizabeth's realm—marry money. Family fortunes and titles were protected by arranged marriages; it was a way to increase one's estate.

Francis badly needed money for his plan, and he could see that his best hope was to marry wealth. With his hopes of someday wearing the Crown, he would be a good prospect for a wealthy young heiress's hand. The thought of marriage was probably not unpleasant in his eyes—he was not growing any younger and it might be nice to have the companionship of a young wife. He so often felt alone. There is no one I can talk to, he had said.[2] It had been almost twenty years since his unhappy affair with his lovely Juliet and he would never forget her. Still, their love was only a memory now and there was a most suitable candidate for his more mature attentions.

The young widow of Sir William Hatton had been Francis's friend from childhood. Pretty little Elizabeth Cecil was the daughter of Thomas Cecil, Burghley's son by his first marriage. Lord Burghley, always eager to advance his children through marriage, had chosen for Elizabeth an older man, Sir William Hatton, nephew and heir to the elegant bachelor Lord Chancellor Sir Christopher Hatton.

Elizabeth Cecil was apparently a true charmer, even as a child and then when she grew older. Francis was sixteen when she was born, but the sparkling grace and beauty of this little Cecil "cousin" had captivated him early. Daphne du Maurier says that he had flirted with her since her teen years.[3] She in her turn is said to have loved the courteous, friendly attentions of her gallant older "cousin." (Even if Francis had actually been a Bacon, there would have been no blood tie between them. She was related through Burghley's first wife, not the Cooke sisters.)

Francis and Elizabeth remained good friends during her marriage, and when she was left a widow at twenty, she must have seemed to him a most acceptable prospect. She was not only intelligent, witty, beautiful and high-spirited, she was also enormously wealthy.

In those times, young widows of good property were expected to remarry almost before laying aside their mourning veils, and there were abundant suitors for Elizabeth's hand. Her imposing Hatton House in Holborn, with its luxurious gardens and parks, was within easy walking distance of Gray's Inn. With perhaps a reserved hope, Francis made the short trek and presented himself as an old friend. But to the surprise of all of London, it was to Attorney General Coke that she became engaged.

Elizabeth was obviously not happy about her engagement. She refused to have it announced publicly and insisted that the marriage ceremony be held in secret. She allowed only her father and one witness to attend the ceremony, which took place late at night. She declared that she would not take Coke's name but would retain her name of Lady Hatton. The whole extraordinary affair was such a puzzle to onlookers that the gossip John Chamberlain wrote to Dudley Carleton:

> The seventh of this month, the Queen's Attorney married the Lady Hatton to the great admiration of all men, that after so many large and likely offers she should decline to a man of his quality, and the world will not believe that it was without a mystery.[4]

The mystery was, of course, that the Cecils all knew of the royal birth of Francis. Lord Burghley had recently died, and Robert, the youngest son, now secure in the queen's good graces, was the undisputed head of the house of Cecil. It had long been Robert's sworn mission to do harm to his Bacon cousin, as we know. For Francis to marry into the Cecil family would have defeated Robert's purposes; furthermore, he had no intention of allowing Francis to have access to his niece's fortune.

A marriage such as this could not possibly take place without the queen's permission. Therefore Essex entered into the fray on Bacon's behalf, thus ensuring once again that Francis's hopes would not be fulfilled. For if Essex wanted the marriage, the queen would thwart it.

Some may have been aware of the mystery involved; others may not. From the young bride's standpoint, one has to believe that she would have much preferred Francis, with all his wit, humor and charm, to Coke's irascible and "elderly" ways. Time indeed proved that this was so. Elizabeth Hatton not only refused to take the name of her new husband, at one point she even refused to allow him to enter Hatton House. She ignored him almost totally. The gossips had a festival.

Once again Francis had been defeated by the Cecil faction and their tool Sir Edward Coke. But this time there was no sign that he felt embittered by the defeat. Perhaps he understood the situation thoroughly and perhaps he was relieved not to have to bother with the extra burden of marriage. He was, however, still in the most dire of financial straits. The irony was that in spite of the success of his plays in the theaters, they were still eating up more money than they took in.

His plays *were* doing famously. Only a couple of years earlier, before the new Globe Theatre had been constructed from the materials of another playhouse, "the Theatre," there had been a typically Elizabethan quarrel over the old building. The Burbages had been leasing the land under it from one Giles Allen, but he was being difficult about renewing the lease. Fed up with the delay, the Burbages insisted that the building belonged to them and that they therefore had the right to demolish it. And to prove it, they made a raid on the old building with an armed posse. They tore it down and ferried the materials to Southwark on the

Detail of Visscher's panoramic view of London, 1616
The city of London is on the north (far) bank of the river. The Globe
Theatre is the multi-sided building just to the left of center on the south
bank. To its left is the Bear Garden.

other side of the Thames. There they proceeded to build the now
world-famous Globe Theatre out of the remains of the old
playhouse. It opened in 1599 with the play *Julius Caesar*.

In order to finance the project, ownership was divided into
shares, half of them retained by the Burbages, the other half issued
to five actors—William Shaksper, John Heminges, Augustine
Phillips, William Kemp and Thomas Pope. But we learn an intriguing detail from Orville Owen. He says that the owner of the
Globe was actually Anthony Bacon.[5] The Bacons' connection
with the playhouses was so purposely vague that to this day it is
still far from clear. One clue is the name *Globe*, a symbol popular
with Francis and his scriptorium, denoting the universal nature of
their intentions.

Also, we know that in 1594 Anthony bought a rundown old
house in Bishopsgate, an area disreputable due to its proximity to
the theater district. Theaters were later "thrust out of the city"
because of the undesirable atmosphere they created.[6] These Lady

Anne disliked with all her pious heart, and she tried to prevent her son from moving to such a place. They had no ministry there, she complained.[7] Anthony should not have moved away from Gray's Inn, where there was "good Christian company." Poor Lady Anne! How she suffered over what she conceived to have been her sons' immorality.

Anthony must have had a good reason for leaving his far more pleasant surroundings at Gray's Inn or his own estate to live in this "somewhat melancholy" place within easy reach of the Burbages' playhouses. Will Shaksper, too, lived in Bishopsgate for a while, but he eventually moved across the river to Southwark to be near the Globe, leaving behind him, according to official records, an unpaid bill of five shillings debt. The details of Anthony's interest in the Globe are vague, but glimpses of a connection keep popping up, such as the name Burbage appearing in Anthony's papers.[8]

A mysterious incident was reported by early biographer Nicholas Rowe concerning a gift of money that was supposedly given to Will Shaksper by the earl of Southampton. This young earl, Henry Wriothesley, was an intimate friend of Lord Essex. He followed Essex in almost slavish devotion through all the episodes of his life. When they were young, the two little earls had lost their respective fathers, and both had been brought up as wards of Burghley, spending much time together, no doubt, at Theobalds. When Southampton was about twenty years old, Shakespeare's two long narrative poems, *Venus and Adonis* (1593) and *The Rape of Lucrece* (1594), were printed with dedications to him. At that time, no one of such a low degree as an actor would dare to dedicate his works to someone of high degree, and yet this is what Shakespeare, or Shaksper—son of an illiterate glover, fresh out of the country—is supposed to have done.

Henry Wriothesley, earl of Southampton
Shakespeare's two long narrative poems, *Venus and Adonis* and *The Rape of Lucrece,* were dedicated to Southampton. He was a close friend and supporter of Essex, and it seems that he was involved in the financial support of Francis's literary endeavors: he was known at the time as a patron of the arts. Southampton turned against Francis in the end. It seems that he could never forget the part Francis played in Essex's downfall. Southampton himself was convicted of plotting against the queen and was imprisoned for a time in the Tower.

Stratfordians* have worked this into a claim of a connection to Southampton. The connection has been elaborated to the extent that now, strangely, many scholars believe that South-ampton was not only a patron to "Shakespeare" but also the "lovely youth" to whom he wrote his sonnets. Not a shred of evidence exists that the Stratford actor and the earl of South-ampton ever even met. The more realistic assessment is, as cipher devotees know by now, that it was Francis who had dedicated the poems to this younger friend, whom he had known for some time

---

* Stratfordians are those who believe that William Shakespeare was the real writer of the plays and poems released under his name.

and who had the advantage of a large income, something which Francis had been denied. Southampton was a valuable and, undoubtedly, generous member of the inner circle of the Essex-Francis-Anthony faction.

Still, we have the mystery of the gift of money supposedly given by Southampton to "Shakespeare." The gift is said to have been £1,000, a very large amount in Elizabethan terms. Be that as it may, if Southampton did give "Shakespeare" such a gift of money, there had to be a good reason for it, and apparently there was. Being a member of the "magic circle," Southampton is sure to have known who was writing the plays and all the secrecy that went with it, and this must have caused much hilarity among the young gallants in-the-know. While Southampton was in Ireland in 1599 soldiering with Essex, his wife, the former Elizabeth Vernon, tried to keep him cheerful with amusing letters from home. In one letter she added an intriguing postscript:

> All the news I can send you that I think will make you merry is that I read in a letter from London that Sir John Falstaff is, by his Mrs. Dame Pintpot made father of a godly Millers' Thumb, a boy that is all head and very little body. But this is a secret.[9]

We get the impression that in this tight little circle of high society, Falstaff is somehow a delicious joke but one that would be recognizable only by those in-the-know. As is apparent in the cipher, Shaksper is the model for Falstaff.[10]

The matter of the "Sir" before Falstaff's name recalls another odd situation that took place about this time in which Shaksper was involved, the strange case of the Shakespeare coat of arms. In 1596 John Shakspere (spelled without the middle e and the last a in this instance) made application to the College of Arms for a family coat of arms. Most authorities agree that it was his son, William, who wanted the family heraldic crest. But since he could not qualify for it, he pressed the senior Shaksper to apply for the grant. John had been a town official in Stratford and had a better chance at being accepted.

In October 1596, the College of Arms granted the request. Although heraldic documents usually yield a detailed account of the family genealogy, this particular one is vague about details, stating only that the petitioner's ancestors had been rewarded by Henry VII for "faithful and valiant service"—no details given. Once before, John Shaksper had requested a coat of arms, but it was denied him. This time it came.

The chief herald of the College of Arms, William Dethick, who made the final grant, was later criticized by other heralds for making the grants to unworthy, "base" persons; among the "base" persons listed was John Shaksper. It was hinted by other heralds that Dethick had acted from motives of greed, implying that he had accepted bribes for bestowing grants.

At the top of the document affirming the grant to Shaksper was written the chosen motto *Non Sanz Droict,* "not without right," a noble enough sounding choice—unless one reads it as it supposedly was first written on the parchment and then changed. As the story goes, a Baconian, in 1913, went to the Heralds College to examine the documents. He discovered that the motto had first been written with a comma after the *non*, thus reading *Non, Sanz Droict.* This gives a completely different meaning from the same motto without the punctuation. Were some of Shaksper's betters making a joke on an early draft? It seems quite possible.

By this time Ben Johnson was a loyal member of Bacon's team, one of his "good pens" and a secretary entrusted with translating some of Bacon's works into Latin. There seemed to have been much joking and satirical leg-pulling in their exchanges. Old Ben knew, of course, the real identity of "Shake-speare." A few years after the granting of the Shakespeare arms, a

NON SANZ DROICT

The Shakespeare coat of arms

"Comicall Satyre" was staged, a play by Ben Jonson called *Every Man Out of His Humour*. No Shakespeare commentator, orthodox or otherwise, can ignore this play because of the ludicrous episode in which the ridiculous Sogliardo gets a grant of coat of arms with the amazing motto *Not Without Mustard*.

Sogliardo is described as an "essential clown ... so enamored of the name of a Gentleman that he will have it, though he buys it.... He is in his kingdom when he can get himself into company where he may be well laughed at."[11] In act III we have:

> *Sogliardo:* By this parchment, gentlemen, I have been so toiled among the Harrots [Heralds] yonder, you will not believe. They do speak i' the strangest language, and give a man the hardest terms for his money that you ever knew.
>
> *Carlo:* But ha' you arms? Ha' you arms?
>
> *Sogliardo:* I' faith, I thank God I can write myself gentleman now. Here's my patent. It cost me thirty pound.... How you like the crest, sir?

Puntarvolo: I understand it not well. What is 't?

Sogliardo: Marry, sir, it is your boar without a head,
   rampant.

Puntarvolo: A Boar without a head. That's very rare.

Carlo: Ay, and rampant too. Troth, I commend the
   herald's wit. He hath deciphered him well: a swine
   without a head, without brain, wit, anything, indeed,
   ramping to gentility.[12]

The reader can decide for himself what or who the "Boar
without a head" might be.

These glimpses of the actor Will Shaksper are partly explained in the cipher discovered by Ignatius Donnelly and partly
in the Bi-literal Cipher. Donnelly could never explain the workings of the cipher that he discussed in his two enormous volumes
called *The Great Cryptogram*, though a few sleuths have claimed
to be able to follow his complicated directions for deciphering. It
may be that he missed the true method and came in by a "side
door." His process is complicated, but the concept is simple
gematria—an elaboration of deriving "root numbers," "modifiers"
and "multipliers" in a system that he explains minutely but not
clearly. (One with a good head for mathematics and detail might
find great pleasure in enlarging upon Donnelly's lead through this
labyrinth. As for me, I am content to let the congressman from
Minnesota work it out, while I marvel at the results of the
collaboration between encipherer and decipherer.)

Donnelly presents a fascinating view of Will Shaksper, but
there has not been, as far as I know, a corroboration of it from a
second source. However, it is close to the description given in the
Bi-literal Cipher.[13] If the picture is distressing to one who has
spent a lifetime of respect for William Shakespeare and his
gorgeous dramas, the conflict is easily understood. But as the
French cryptoanalyst Pierre Henrion has said, those who dismiss

ciphers as fantasy or child's play will live in ignorance, because truth sometimes comes from unexpected sources.

The key is to differentiate between the "Shakespeare" who was the poet—that brilliant, sensitive soul of genius—and the Shaksper who was the mask.

The episode of the supposed gift of £1,000 from Southampton to Shaksper, the apparently trumped-up coat of arms, plus the situation of Shaksper's owning a tenth share in a theater that seems to have been owned by Anthony Bacon—all this seems to reveal a recognizable pattern. The fortunes of Shaksper appear to grow in inverse ratio to the decline of the fortunes of the Bacons. They were growing desperate for money while Will of Stratford was becoming, if not rich, certainly prosperous according to the standards of his village. By 1597 he had bought New Place, one of the largest houses in Stratford, and he was planning to remodel it. He had acquired other properties and was beginning to do business in malt and money lending. When he had left his home village for London eight years earlier, he had not owned a farthing. He had done surprisingly well. It had all been so easy! The only thing required of him was that he remain silent and be quick-witted enough to "dissemble" if the wrong questions were asked. And yet, as "Greene-Bacon"* had intimated in *Groatsworth of Wit*, he had bragged that

> he is as well able to bombast out a blank verse as the best of you; and being an absolute *Johannes Factotum*, is in his own conceit the only Shake-scene in a country.

Shaksper had come to London straight from his somewhat shabby life in Warwickshire with no more than three or four years of country schooling. Supposedly, he already had written two poems in the classic style, *Venus and Adonis* and *Lucrece*.

---

* Refers to Robert Greene, another of Francis Bacon's masks.

After he arrived in London, he was given credit for having created enormously popular dramas, some based on stories not yet translated into English, such as *Timon of Athens* and *Othello*. These were foreign tales with plots that the playwright had borrowed and adapted for his own use. It was enough to make any Falstaff's head swell a bit.

The character of Falstaff was so clearly drawn that no fictitious character, with the possible exception of Hamlet, has ever seemed so real. Taking Prince Hal to represent the young Prince Francis and Falstaff as his mask Shaksper, we find a delightful contrast between true wit and a kind of low vulgar humor. The cipher tells that Will is

> full of his own most beastly desires.... But I must confess there was some humor in the villain; he hath a quick wit, and a great belly; and, indeed, I made use of him, with the assistance of my brother [Anthony], as the original model from which we draw the characters of Sir John Falstaff and Sir Toby.[14]

Sir Toby Belch is, of course, the ludicrous and bibulous master liar from *Twelfth Night* who tries to cover up his lowly beginning by putting on the airs of a gentleman.

This is the only reference in the cipher which mentions that Francis's brother (in this case Anthony, Donnelly tells us) collaborated with him on some of the plays. Both Bacons were known for their lively sense of humor, and it is delightful to think of them working together, surely with howls of laughter, creating the ridiculous characters of their plays. The cipher tells us that even then the comic Falstaff

> draws together, to the playhouse yards, such great musters of people, far beyond my hopes and expectation, that they took in at least twenty thousand marks. [Falstaff] pleases

Falstaff
One of the most intriguing characters in the Shakespeare plays is Falstaff. He is a drunkard, a thief and a coward—yet somehow likable for his jovial nature and free spirit. Donnelly's cipher reveals that the actor Will Shaksper was the original model for Falstaff and Sir Toby Belch.

her Majesty much more than anything else in these plays....

Then Francis indulges in a little well-deserved satisfaction at the popularity of his dramas:

> I heard that my Lord the German Minister told Says-ill [Cecil] that it was well worth coming all the long way to England to see this part of Sir John alone, in this play and *The Merry Wives of Windsor*. [He] swears up and down they cannot equal it in all Europe. He said: I tell thee, the man that could conceive such a part as this, and draw it so well, should be immortal.[15]

A fine compliment and an interesting evaluation on the part of a playgoer at the time. Now this "upstart crow beautified" by someone else's "feathers"[16] was beginning to cause problems and, according to Donnelly's cipher, he was demanding more compensation for his role of cover-up.

The history plays that include Falstaff *(Henry IV, Part 1* and *Henry IV, Part 2)* are concerned chiefly with history and kingship, subjects not of much interest to the average Elizabethan playgoer standing in the penny galleries. But the antics of Falstaff made up for all that—the public loved him. So did the queen. Elizabeth probably saw *Henry IV, Part 1* during the 1596–97 Christmas revels. Captivated by the fat knight, she told her cousin Lord Hunsdon, who was a patron of Shakespeare's company, the Chamberlain's Men, that she would like to see a play in which the old rogue was in love. Hunsdon quickly contacted Shakespeare, who set immediately to work to satisfy Her Majesty's demand. The comedy *The Merry Wives of Windsor* is the result.

Critics believe that the play was written in the amazingly short time of three weeks. There is little of a serious nature in the play, and it is the only one of the entire thirty-six that does not deal with aristocratic persons and themes but only with the middle and lower classes. Francis was probably doing his best to make it sound like something Will might have written—bawdy but not disgraceful, the kind of comic situation that Francis knew his mother would adore.

From all we know, Elizabeth was delighted with the farce, but she was also growing a bit suspicious. In the Donnelly cipher we learn that Francis received the devastating news that the queen was asking questions about this man "Shakespeare," the supposed author of the plays. More accurately, one might say that Cecil had become suspicious and was trying to convince Her Majesty that Francis was, in truth, the writer:

On hearing this heavy news I was overwhelmed with a flood

of fears and shame. I saw plainly all the perils of my situation. I knew very well that if Shak'st-spur was apprehended, he will be ... as tallow in the hands of that crafty fox, my cousin Seas-ill [Cecil]. It was ten to one the whorson knave will tell in self-defense and for his own security that the play of *Measure for Measure* ... that noble composition, the play of *King Richard the Second* [were mine].[17]

The first play, with its flavor of religious satire, and the second, dangerously close to political rebellion, were plays that Francis especially wanted to avoid any connection with. For if it became known that he was the author, he feared that "All my hopes of rising to high office in this commonwealth were blasted."[18] It would mean not only the end of his career but perhaps the end of his life.

Her Grace was furious, with that fury that was so striking a part of her nature. She sent out "well-horsed, unarmed posts" to find Will. They raided the playhouses and theaters on both sides of the river. In 1597, around the same time, all the theaters in London were closed down by order of the Privy Council after a showing of *The Isle of Dogs*, a political satire, supposedly by Thomas Nashe and Ben Jonson, which had been playing at the Swan. It was described as "seditious and slanderous." Since we know who Jonson was working for and that Bacon collaborated on the works of Nashe, it is not out of line to assume that the furor over the closing of the theaters and the search for "Shakespeare" was all of a piece—a disturbing and hazardous time for actors and playwrights alike.

Cecil was highly suspicious, says the cipher, and he didn't believe that the actor from the Globe had either the intelligence or the education to have written the plays. (Cecil was on the right track.) He sent word to the Bishop of Worcester, who had Stratford under his jurisdiction, and asked for information about Will.

The Bishop's report on Shaksper was far from complimentary and cast more doubt on his parishioner's capabilities. In the Donnelly cipher, Cecil reports:

> I ventured to tell him [the Bishop] my suspicion that Master Shak'st-spur is not himself capable enough, and hath not knowledge enough, to have writ the much admired plays.... It is rumored that every one of them was prepared under his name by some gentleman.[19]

Cecil's conclusion:

> More-low [Marlow] or Shak'st-spur never writ a word of them. It is plain he is stuffing our ears with false reports and lies this many a year. He is a poor, dull, ill-spirited, greedy creature, and but a veil for some one else.... I have a suspicion that my kinsman's servant, young Harry Percy, was the man to whom he gave every night the half of what he took through the day at the gate.[20]

The Bishop told Cecil that Will no longer lived in poverty:

> His coffers are full. They divide the money into three fair and equal divisions.... His own part is five hundred marks. He hath bought a goodly estate called New Place.... His pretty daughter, to whom he is much endeared, a sweet visage.... It is the earnest desire of his heart to make her a lady and advance himself among the file of the quality.[21]

This is a description of Susanna, Will's oldest daughter, who seems to have been head and shoulders above the rest of the family in character and poise. Will was proud of Susanna and left most of his possessions to her in his will. The younger daughter, Judith, did not rate as high with her father.

> His Lordship [the Bishop] advised that the best thing we could do is to make him [Shaksper] a prisoner,... bind him

with iron, and bring him before the Council; and it is more than likely the knave would speak the truth, and tell who writ it.[22]

Never had things been more precarious for Francis—it looked like the game he had been playing for so long was up. Cecil was on his track and closing in. Francis would have no defense if Will Shaksper chose to expose him. Always before he had managed to somehow pull himself out of the tight spots and keep going, but this would be a different matter. He doubted that anything could save him now.

Surprisingly enough, it was Elizabeth herself who saved the day for her son. When Cecil went to her to report on his suspicions and to make his accusations against Francis, Elizabeth accused Cecil, along with his now deceased father, of being jealous of their kinsman and trying to undermine whatever he did. They were always trying to entrap him, she stormed, and she didn't for a minute believe that anyone as educated and as honorable as Francis Bacon would stoop so low as to consort with low-life theater people such as an actor from the Globe.

Whether Elizabeth was suspicious that her son was only degrading himself by writing plays, we cannot know. Whatever her state of mind, it was good fortune for Francis. His mother had given him breathing space and time to get Shaksper out of the way of their enemies.

Chapter Eleven

Trouble from Stratford

*Glorious [boastful] men are the scorn of wise men,
the admiration of fools, the idols of parasites,
and the slaves of their own vaunts [glorification].*

The immediate danger was past, but Francis and his cohorts wouldn't be safe until Shaksper was out of the country. Harry Percy, a much appreciated and loyal defender of Francis, was given the job of locating the troublesome Will and getting him out of harm's way and beyond reach of the queen's fury.

The scene now revealed by the Donnelly cipher is an amazing one. We are given a peek into the household of the Shaksper family in their village home such as has never before been seen. The view will not appeal to those who refuse to see that Shakespeare and Shaksper were not the same man.

Percy finds Will at his house, New Place, in Stratford. He is ill, ravished by disease, and looking much older than his thirty-three years. In haste Percy explains to him all that has happened and tells him that he must leave the country at once. He must go into hiding until it all blows over. But Will feels secure as long as he can expose Bacon if a showdown comes, and he refuses to go. His wife, Anne, weeps and moans and throws herself around his neck, babbling incoherently.

The only sensible person in the house is the daughter Susanna, who appears to be intelligent, calm and reasonable. She persuades her father that it would be the better part of wisdom to follow Percy's advice. He must understand that if it should be learned that he falsely claimed the authorship of the plays, not only would Bacon be in trouble but so would the entire Shaksper family. There could be an instant end to their sizable income and, even worse, Will could be arrested for false claims and perhaps even accused of treason.

It is fascinating to see that the cipher speaks of Susanna so highly and expresses surprise that such a fair one as she could have been reared in a household such as the Shakspers'. History seems to agree since she later married Dr. John Hall, a prosperous university-educated physician who became one of the leading citizens of the town.

Susanna wins the argument and Percy leads him, under cover of darkness, to the coast, where a boat is waiting to take him out to sea.[1] Where he was taken is not stated in the cipher, but apparently the ruse worked. Francis was safe again, at least for the time being, and Will was eventually returned to his home.

Momentarily saved from the danger of Cecil's spying (as Donnelly has described it),[2] there was a still greater danger at home. We now return to events that are recognized historically, at least in part. The danger had to do with Essex, who was becoming more troublesome each day. Francis was getting exasperated with the erratic behavior of this unstable brother. Was he becoming unbalanced to the point of insanity? Francis was worried.

Essex had again failed in his final appeal to place Francis in the office of solicitor general. Francis then wrote to Elizabeth's lord keeper, Sir John Puckering, asking for his help, coming as close as he dared to actually speaking of his royal birth. In his letter he says:

> For if it please your Lordship but to call to mind from whom I am descended, and by whom, next to God, her Majesty, and your own virtue, your Lordship is ascended [meaning in both cases, of course, the queen], I know you will have a compunction of mind to do me any wrong.[3]

But no one could help Francis if Her Majesty did not will it. At this moment it was not her will, although she had taken Francis back into her good grace. It was Essex who was currently the "bad boy." Whatever Essex wanted he was not to have, no matter how unjust it was to Francis.

Of course, Essex was furious and Francis was discouraged. It had been a long struggle, and the queen had won hands down—two and half years of futility. It had been particularly infuriating because they could see that Elizabeth had never intended to enter into a battle with them; she had just engaged in her usual delay tactics, refusing to make a decision out of irritation with Essex and distrust of Francis. Everyone but Her Majesty had suffered. There was nothing for Francis to do but to get on with the work to which he had devoted his life. As long as his mind was occupied, he could forget. Essex realized only too well that he had been severely chastised, and the loss of prestige shattered his already injured ego. He knew that his sponsorship of his friend (and brother) had done Francis more harm than good. He was sorry, but he seemed to be incapable of changing his ways.

All pretense of friendship between the Essex circle and the Cecils was now cast aside; only the thinnest gossamer of civility veiled the animosity between them. In spite of Francis's efforts to maintain a balance of normalcy, open warfare had been declared. Even Lady Anne, watching from her home at Gorhambury, loyally entered once more into the fray. She wrote to Anthony that she was convinced that the earl had "marred all with violent courses"[4] and she was worried about Francis. (Dodd agrees with her assessment and adds that the queen might have even denied Francis for the perverse pleasure of contradicting Essex. "The more she hung back the more he pressed."[5]) Francis had been caught in the middle.

Only a short time earlier, the queen had remarked to a friend that Francis "begins to frame very well," an oddly maternal phrase to have used in speaking of the lord keeper's son. But Francis had been encouraged. The queen was beginning to depend more and more on his wise counsel. Perhaps she would even have begun to acknowledge him openly if she had not been so deeply involved in the love-hate relationship with her younger son.

"Wronged, yet not daring to complain," Francis managed to muster up enough equanimity to bear the humiliation with a certain amount of grace. Not so Essex. He reacted with his usual uncontrolled show of self-will. He stamped, he shouted, he swore, he threatened all manner of dire consequences. The queen was not to be moved; she still treated him like a wayward child. Once, he fumed, she even "bade me go to bed, if I would talk of nothing else."[6] The humiliation burned within his soul until both his physical and his mental conditions became seriously eroded.

As for Francis, the prolonged strain had been damaging to his delicate constitution. He had taken to his bed for long periods of rest after Coke was appointed attorney general, but he seemed more settled with this second disappointment. Now, if ever, was the time for him to rely on the compassionate advice of his celestial vision: "Some men become great by advancement ... some achieve greatness by reason of their wit.... Take the current when it serves."[7]

To Francis, it appeared that Essex was aiming for the throne. Nothing so bold was spoken outright, but Francis could see the trend of his thought:

> But at times he maketh a great show, [even] stranger to our heart than the cold ungracious manner.[8]

Essex was sick with jealousy, ambition and frustration. Perhaps it wasn't the earl's fault; perhaps it was just a trick of character inherited from his stormy parents. But unless he could be brought to a more reasonable state of mind, nothing but tragedy could follow. Robert was beginning to show a marked tendency toward the manic-depressive state that characterized the last days of his life. Instead of adopting the difficult course of tact urged by Francis, he forged headlong toward trouble, retreating periodically into a somber world of sickness and depression. Francis admitted to a foreboding sense of disaster.

The loss of Elizabeth's favor spurred on Robert's longing for glory. When he wasn't sulking in solitude, he was champing at this bit like a young stallion straining for action. On one occasion the queen was heard to say: "Someone or other should take him down and [teach] him better manners."[9] Like mother, like son!

In the spring of 1596 came Robert's hope for proving his mettle again. The hated Spaniards had taken Calais, the closest port across the Channel, which the English could ill afford to have in the hands of an enemy. When it became "bruited" about that Philip of Spain intended to ship aid to the Irish, assisting them against England, the queen's usual reluctance to engage in open warfare could no longer be excused. Essex saw his chance. He blustered and implored and even threatened to withdraw to the country and "become a monk upon an hour's warning"[10] if Elizabeth would not agree to a plan to attack Spain and head off the threat from Ireland.

The queen was forced by circumstances to address herself to the desperate situation. She appointed Essex along with Lord Admiral Howard as joint commanders of a force to attack Cadiz, which was in Spain itself. Sir Walter Raleigh (whom Essex detested, probably because of his popularity with the queen) was given subordinate command. As it turned out, in spite of intense friction between the commanders, the expedition was crowned with success—due more to Raleigh's experience and judgment in attacking by sea, it was said, than any other single factor.

Essex had his chance, leading the land attack under his own banner. He carried out the charge with great courage and bravado, and the humane treatment he ordered for his captives earned him the praise of conquerors and conquered alike. At his orders, priests and churches were spared, three thousand nuns were given safe-conduct and looting was forbidden. This was Essex at his best, carrying out his duties in a tradition of chivalry and courtesy which did him great honor. The lord admiral even wrote back to Burghley: "I assure you, there is not a braver man in the world than the Earl."[11] When Essex was good, he was very, very good. Elizabeth's maternal pride, no doubt, was touched to the core, but only for a moment.

When Essex returned to England, it was as the triumphant hero. No warrior had ever paced a horse through London more gloriously. Tumultuous applause and unfeigned adoration welcomed him everywhere. If Francis, whose choice had been to serve his country quietly from behind a screen of anonymity, felt a twinge of envy at his brother's phenomenal success, it would have been only momentary we can be sure.

Essex expected the queen to rejoice in the victorious return of her conquering son. But Elizabeth never did the expected, and she didn't do it now. She soon threw a blanket of indifference and disdain over the entire triumphal return. And she immediately criticized Essex because the bounty looted from the Spaniards had not covered the cost of the campaign. Besides, why hadn't they captured the Spanish treasure ships returning from the West Indies?

Essex was shocked by the coolness of his reception, and Francis was wise enough to sense what lay at the bottom of it. The earl, a virile and handsome young male of bravery and valor, had become an idol to Elizabeth's subjects, and Elizabeth did not like sharing the limelight. A tired and aging female could not endure the competition.

Francis had already anticipated the problem. It was always dangerous to put the queen in the shadow, especially if you were young and masculine and you had the backing of the military behind you. It was the exact volatile mixture that Elizabeth most dreaded. Unlike Francis, Robert had not managed to convince the queen of his total loyalty to the Crown, whomsoever's head it might rest upon. She had a suspicion that he desperately wanted to wear the Crown on his own head.

Francis repeatedly warned Robert to trim his sail to avoid the storm that was brewing. Everyone at court knew what was going on, and they were watching warily. The two Cecils' usual game plan of playing both ends toward the middle was a difficult one to maintain, but they continued the expedient of urging Robert into dangerous military adventures and then sitting innocently on the sidelines hoping against hope that he would either get himself killed or at least get himself into such financial-political difficulties at home that there would be no extricating himself. Only by eliminating both Robert and Francis could the Cecils maintain their hold on power. The ambassador from France noted: "If he

[Essex] comes back victorious, they [the Cecils] take occasion thereby to make him suspected by the Queen, and if nothing is accomplished, then to ruin him."[12]

Francis and the Cecils knew how to stay in the queen's good graces through tact and diplomacy. Essex did not. The older brother wrote a long letter to Robert. Change your course, warned the letter. You have the queen's affections and you know it, you are popular to the point of idolatry with the people and, lastly, you are a man of a military mind. "I demand whether there can be a more dangerous image than this represented to any monarch living?"[13]

Francis implored Essex to change this picture of himself in the queen's mind, to do whatever was necessary to allay her suspicions, to take all occasions with the queen to speak against popularity and its pursuit. Furthermore, he warned, Essex must change his military image immediately. He advised, in effect: Dissemble, if you must, but make the queen believe that your only care is to please her. Enjoy yourself with courtly activities; and most of all, put all military ambition behind you, for Her Majesty loveth peace. Content yourself with seeking the place of the lord privy seal, and appease the queen with compliments and sweet words.

It was excellent advice. Every courtier at Elizabeth's court knew the absolute necessity of prefacing each and every petition to her with the most extravagant praises they could dream up. Her beauty, her charm, her feminine virtues—all must be mentioned and exaggerated. Essex would neglect this policy to his own detriment. It would be wise, said Bacon, if you would pattern your own behavior with the queen after that so successfully used by Lord Leicester (of course he did not have to remind Robert of his relationship to Elizabeth's other "Robin"). "For I do not know a readier mean to make Her Majesty think you are on the right way."[14] Supreme tact and flattery—there was no other way.

If Essex had followed this advice, he might have avoided calamity, but perhaps it was already too late. The knowledge that he was princely in truth, while at court his standing was only that of a courtier, warmed into life and action the ambitions that were his inherited instincts. How far he ventured in pursuing his royal prerogatives history plainly shows.

Only Francis could fully understand the dilemma, and only the cipher story can explain the unexplainable. All the same temptations were doubly applicable to himself—he was, after all, the oldest son—but he managed to endure, whereas Essex could not. Robert did, however, follow Francis's advice as far as writing adoring letters was concerned. He could do that as well as Leicester ever had.

All went well for a time. Essex remained at court and occupied himself with flattering the queen and flirting shamelessly with the ladies. His flirtations caused such gossip that poor pious Lady Anne Bacon felt called upon to admonish him personally, which she proceeded to do in a letter, just as she did so frequently with her own sons. To the earl's credit, he wrote to Lady Bacon that she need not worry on his behalf, for the things that were said about him were only false reports made by his enemies.

For a while, things seemed to be on even keel, even though Elizabeth showed unmistakable signs of being jealous of the attention her dear Robin was paying to other ladies. But as time went on, the uneasy relationship between queen and favorite, mother and son, became strained again. Then came that tragic explosion which history books relate but few understand. During a quarrel over the issue of the appointment of a deputy to Ireland, Essex did the unthinkable. Overcome with irritation over the queen's refusal to do as he wished, he whirled around on his heel, turning his back on her sovereign person, preparing to stride from the room.

Turning one's back on a ruling monarch is strictly forbidden in any royal court; in Elizabeth's it was little short of treason. It was too much for her to bear. The queen let loose a volley of vivid oaths and soundly boxed his ears. Essex went berserk. He reached for his sword, turned on the queen and shouted that he would not have borne such an insult even from her father. In a state almost of shock, the daughter of Henry VIII stood and glared at this grandson of Henry VIII while the earl of Nottingham frantically rushed to subdue him.

It was an appalling scene, and the entire court waited in breathless suspense to see what the queen would do. Would Essex's head join those of other traitors, stuck on pikes high above London Bridge? Or would he merely be sent to the Tower? He had most certainly committed treason in grasping a sword, threatening the queen. How much would she stand for?

The response from the offended queen shocked the court— Elizabeth did absolutely nothing! And thereafter, she calmly went about her business at court, allowing Essex to retire to his estate in the country at his will. Whether or not Francis had a hand in persuading her to act with compassion, we can't know for sure. There can be little doubt, however, that Essex was the most relieved man in London.

As the months wore on, old Burghley, increasingly worn out by the secret as well as the public affairs of state and depressed by problems he could not seem to solve, slipped quietly out of the picture. Elizabeth was devastated by the loss of her old minister. They had worked together for a long time (forty years, since her accession in 1558), and in spite of endless differences, they had somehow managed to weather the storms. At this time, England had never been in a better position to take her place in world affairs. Regardless of Elizabeth's personal life, she was well respected abroad, the self-confident "Gloriana" of her island kingdom "set in the silver sea." In spite of Burghley's ambition for his son, he had worked diligently for the good of his queen. Together they had come far, and Her Majesty shed bitter tears at the end as she sat by the old man's bedside feeding him broth with her own hand.

While the trouble between Elizabeth and Essex was momentarily at a low boil, Francis was busying himself with the first publication to be printed under his own name—an amazing situation since he had been writing and publishing for many years (albeit anonymously). When his first acknowledged works came out in 1597, he was thirty-six years old! This man of obvious genius who had taken "all knowledge to be my province," who had declared that his greatest desire was to retire to the country and "become [some] sorry book-maker"—this dedicated and brilliant writer had supposedly written nothing worth publishing during the prime years of his life. What had he been doing with his scriptorium all this time? Only his secret writing explains it.

The book he now published was a small volume containing the first ten of his essays (others would be added in later editions). The essays were dedicated to Mr. Anthony Bacon, his "loving and beloved brother," and they were like the "new half-pence, which though the silver were good, yet the pieces were small."[15] The essays were immediately popular—pithy, simply stated, brilliantly practical. They are the observations of a man who has thought deeply on a wide array of human affairs and is able to condense his thoughts and convey them. "He talks," it was said, "in language which everybody understands." Richard William Church observed that "he writes as a looker-on at the game of human affairs, who … sees more of it than the gamesters themselves, and is able to give wiser and faithful counsel, not without a touch of kindly irony at the mistakes which he observes."[16]

If only Essex had paid more attention to his brother's understanding of human nature, history might have been quite different. In "Of Honour and Reputation," Francis gives the perfect formula for avoiding envy and jealousy toward oneself. It was something he had learned to put into practice as often as possible:

> Envy, which is the canker of honour, is best extinguished by declaring a man's self in his ends, rather to seek merit than fame; and by attributing a man's successes rather to divine Providence and felicity, than to his own virtue or policy.[17]

Furthermore, he implies you can tell how far you may go in dealing with a man by watching the look of envy in his eye.[18]

Francis had used these tactics to the utmost in an effort to head off the inevitable final battle between Essex and the queen. But once again Essex laid bare his streak of Tudor rashness. It was as though victorious in one battle, he couldn't resist the temptation to take on another one. Essex managed to persuade the queen that he was just the man who could subdue the rebellious Irish Tyrone, the wily and unconventional warlord whom no one else had yet been able to handle. To his amazement, the queen gave in without too much argument and named him lord deputy of Ireland. "By God I will beat Tyrone in the field; for nothing worthy [of] her Majesty's honour hath yet been achieved."[19]

Obtaining this new position would prove to be a hollow victory. Only too soon did Essex begin to realize that his prolonged stay in Ireland would play directly into the hands of his rivals. It would remove him from the affairs at court and keep him occupied far from home, while those he trusted so little could manipulate matters without his interference. The best scenario from Cecil's standpoint would be that he would never return. Robert was now regretting his rashness in demanding the post, but there was nothing that he could do now except go.

Great fanfare and excitement flared up in London when the people's darling was finally prepared to sail with his troops and his horses to the wild land of Ireland. The soldiers of Tyrone were only half civilized, it was said; they wore animal skins for clothes, fought from behind trees like savages, and never cut their hair. Certainly the gallant and elegant, the handsomely equipped hero, the earl of Essex, would be more than a match for them.

What did Francis have to say about his brother's total disregard of his advice and his ignoring the admonition to refrain from seeming to be surrounded by military might? Typically, now that he knew that it was too late to change matters, he wrote Essex a "quiet, encouraging letter." He later admitted, however, that he did "as plainly see his overthrow chained by destiny ... to that journey"[20] as it was possible for one man to predict another man's future. Bacon's future depended so much on that of the earl, it must have taken all his hard-won fortitude to keep his own philosophical calm.

Chapter Twelve

Essex, Bacon and Tragedy

He that is too much in anything ...
maketh himself cheap.

Essex's departure for Ireland may have started with fair weather and the most gracious smiles of Her Grace, the queen. But as he and his troops were processioning through Islington on the way to their ships, a storm cloud blew over, the skies turned dark and foreboding, and the cheering crowds grew suddenly quiet. This, they said, was a bad omen—perhaps it foreshadowed disaster for the venture. It was certainly cause for apprehension. The hopes of all had been soaring high. The whole nation was convinced that the glorious Essex could not fail. "Shakespeare" expressed as much in *Henry V:*

> Were now the general of our gracious empress,
> (As in good time he may) from Ireland coming.
> Bringing rebellion broached on his sword,
> How many would the peaceful city quit
> To welcome him!
>
> *act V, chorus*

The amnesty between Elizabeth and Robert was destined for a short life. Once her Robin was out of sight, the aging queen began to fret impatiently, torn between concern for the well-being of her country and her neurotic fixation on Essex. Why had she let him leave her side? Had it been a mistake to give him power and weapons without giving him security for the future?

No sooner had her darling's feet left English soil than she started looking for good news to come out of Ireland. Here was the English counterpart of Shakespeare's Cleopatra—the fretful, restless, willful queen forced to endure the almost unbearable suspense of a lonely throne. Cleopatra received no word from her precious Antony, only recently returned to Rome. Her Egyptian anxiety was mirrored in that of Elizabeth of England. Was the character and personality of Cleopatra in *Antony and Cleopatra* patterned after the fiery Elizabeth herself? Some commentators have suggested that it was.

Day by day the fretful queen searched for something to help pass the time away—she could think of nothing but Robert. It was more than the impatience of a mother longing to hear from her recalcitrant son; it was an obsession amounting to mono-mania. Like Cleopatra, Elizabeth wanted to talk about nothing else but the absent lord:

> Where think'st thou he is now? Stands he, or sits he?
> Or does he walk? Or is he on his horse?
> O happy horse, to bear the weight of Antony!
> Do bravely, horse, for wot'st thou whom thou mov'st?
> The demi-Atlas of this earth, the arm
> And burgonet of men. He's speaking now,
> Or murmuring "Where's my serpent of old Nile?"
> (For so he calls me.)
>
> *act I, sc. 5*

A mere change of the Nile to the Thames would tell the story of Elizabeth.

Fret as she would, the time did pass and news did seep through. There were reports of failure and delay, excuses in abundance, promises for better results in the future. Little else. It soon became painfully clear that there was no other news to report. Nothing had been done, no progress, no victories. Whatever was going on, it was obviously not to the benefit of England.

Elizabeth grew increasingly impatient and then angry with the curiously inept behavior of Essex. There was a limit to what she would take from him. Why was there no news of victory over the Irish chieftain Hugh O'Neill—the half-savage, half-gentleman earl of Tyrone, with his intolerable arrogance in the face of British demands? Camden wrote that Tyrone was a young man whose "understanding was very great, his soul large and fit for the weightiest business. He had much knowledge in military affairs, and a proud dissembling heart."[1]

Tyrone was a formidable enemy, but Essex should have been a good match for him. He had been given men, money and the authority he had so imperiously demanded. All had been entrusted into his hands. Vast resources, seldom before granted, were at his disposal. He had all that it should have taken for a success, and more. And England had every right to expect victory, but it was not forthcoming.

The queen wrote and the Privy Council wrote and they all demanded explanations, and yet nothing was explained. Instead, Essex gave excuses and sent fervent letters begging to be reinstated in the grace he had once known. And yet, if he had only settled down to accomplish his mission, he would have found that one good victory would have done far more than a dozen letters. But in Robert's paranoid state of mind, concentration on battle plans was beyond him.

Matters in Ireland grew daily more desperate. Lack of leadership destroyed the morale of the troops. Wasted money left them improperly fed and cared for. Essex loved the glory of war, but he was a poor man to be in charge of troops. His own brother, watching apprehensively back in London, knew this only too well. Something had to be done, and that in haste.

The queen pulled Francis aside one day shortly before receiving more letters from Ireland. She berated Essex, "showed a passionate distaste of my Lord's proceedings in Ireland ... and was pleased ... to fall into the like speech with me." He urged her to recall Essex, to let him remain with her as "society to yourself, and for an honour and ornament to your attendance and Court.... For to discontent him as you do, and yet to put arms and powder into his hands, may be a kind of temptation to make him prove cumbersome and unruly."[2]

But it was of no use; Robert's excuses were intolerable. Elizabeth often acted foolishly, but history tells us she was far from being a fool. She was not taken in by Robert's pleadings. As his letters grew more pathetic, her answers grew more demanding. She castigated him ruthlessly for his negligent behavior, for his failure to move forcibly against the enemy, for putting Southampton in command of the cavalry against her express wishes.

Most aggravating of all were the rumors that Lord Robert was daily creating new knights from the ranks of those loyal to himself—170 new knights already, more than a quarter of the number in her entire realm at that time. Such a policy was definitely anathema to the queen, and Essex knew it. Too many knighthoods would dilute their value. Keep favors few and difficult of attainment; it was a policy that had worked. The smaller the band of elite at her command, the more efficient her government. Was Essex building a force of those who would be loyal to himself rather than to the queen? It was so according to his brother's secret diary,[3] and it was a dangerous course, as he had warned.

Essex's daily actions became those of a man beleaguered and panicked beyond rationality. One minute he was depressed and melancholy, sulking in his tent. The next, he was fuming in desperation over the injustices he imagined were being carried on during his absence.

More than one commentator has suggested that the cowardly behavior of Achilles in *Troilus and Cressida* (that lion of "proud heart," the warrior sulking in his tent with "melancholy" rather than going out to fight the Trojans) was an echo of Essex in Ireland. It was one of the plays of tragedy first published after both Essex and Elizabeth were gone. It would have been dangerous to publish it sooner, since it showed some of the more wanton traits of Cressida as paralleling too closely the ambivalent personality of the queen and reminded audiences of the tragic downfall of Essex.

On September 7, 1599 (the queen's sixty-sixth birthday), Elizabeth's Lord Lieutenant Robert rallied enough to meet with rebel chief Tyrone, a strange rendezvous that has always baffled historians. Tyrone had requested that the meeting be private between Essex and himself. The two chiefs met on horseback at the ford on the river at Bellaclynth. What might have had the potential to be a great event turned into a pathetic defeat for Essex. Out of earshot of the men ranged on either side of the river, Essex committed what amounted to an act of treason to his queen and his country—he chose the dangerous course of compromise. It led him to disaster.

For nearly an hour, the two men sat in their saddles and talked. Essex agreed to terms that meant almost total surrender of the English forces. Author Robert Lacey considers the unwitnessed conversation between Essex and the Irish rebel a desperate act of treason. "He was," wrote Lacey, "at worst a traitor, at best a fool."[4]

When news got back to London about this latest debacle, Her Majesty was beside herself with fury. Essex had done all the things that Francis had warned him not to do. For Francis, all that was left to say to Robert was that he was "sorry that your Lordship should fly with waxen wings, doubting Icarus' fortune."[5] Essex had indeed tried to fly too close to the sun. He had made himself a military threat to the queen, ignored her commands and wasted her arms, her money and her men.

It all happened as Francis had foreseen. In London the earl was being accused of planning to make himself king of Ireland with the assistance of Tyrone and even of aspiring to invade England with a troop of wild Irish fighters—plotting to dethrone the queen.

Close to collapse and on the brink of mental imbalance, Essex committed the final desperate act that would end in his own destruction as well as that of the queen. For Francis it meant the end of his last hope to succession. Psychologically, Essex had reached the point of no return. Only the cipher story makes the desperation of Essex understandable. This woman—his mother, his queen, who had the power of life and death over him—"did meditate naming [him] successor."[6] Would she at last acknowledge their relationship when he returned from Ireland? Would she acknowledge Francis too? To acknowledge Francis would be to name him successor to the throne. But she had promoted his hated rival Cecil ahead of them both. It was too much for Robert to bear.

In a wild mood of desperation, he summoned a small group of the faithful together in Ireland on September 24. Leaving troops and responsibilities behind, they set sail for England. Four days later they were riding into London.

Few authorities agree about the motives of Essex in this unheralded return. Perhaps the earl himself didn't know. It seems that he felt only the need to reach his tormentor and throw himself at her feet. The scene that now follows has intrigued every one of Elizabeth's biographers.

The queen was not at her palace in London when Essex arrived, exhausted from his furious ride from the coast. She had moved to her palace at Nonsuch, ten miles away. Momentarily thwarted, the earl wavered for an instant—to go or not to go? He rallied shortly, ferried across the Thames and tore on to Nonsuch, his horse sweating and heaving beneath him, his sword lurching at his side. Once there, muddied and disheveled, he rushed into the palace, brushing aside guards and ladies-in-waiting.

It was ten in the morning and the queen had not yet made her appearance. Not to be deterred, Essex tore up the stairs into the queen's privy chamber and on to that holy sanctuary, the royal bedchamber. Essex threw himself at the feet of Her Royal Highness, who was clad only in her dressing gown.

The queen looked with astonishment at this exasperating young man whom she had often called her Wild Horse. The elaborate wig had not yet been placed on the wispy gray hairs of her head, the white pasty face had not yet been adorned with its coat of paint, and she looked old and gray and alarmed. At first with amazement and then with tenderness, she gazed at the young man gasping for breath at her feet.

The serving ladies stood by, aghast at Robert's boldness, but Her Majesty was pleased. Once she found her voice, it was clear that she was delighted. This adored young man had been so eager to see her that he had let nothing stand in his way. He had come all the way from Ireland just to throw himself before her. It was the kind of gesture she liked well—Tudor dash and brashness.

Abnormal affection or not, here was a son after her own heart. Sounding like a good mother, Elizabeth told Essex, perhaps with a touch of tender amusement, to get up and go change his clothes while she finished her dressing. Later he could return and have a private audience with her.

After dinner they both retired with the members of the Privy Council to a private room for discussion. Essex was unable to explain his actions satisfactorily, and exactly thirteen hours after his arrival, the Lord Lieutenant of Ireland was under house arrest, commanded to keep to his quarters. Elizabeth was, at last, carrying out her determination to break his will.

One can imagine Francis's consternation at hearing the news. He immediately demanded, and received, an interview with the earl in his confinement at Nonsuch. He did his best to gently advise Robert, but as he later wrote, "He spake very few words and shaked his head sometimes, as if he thought I was in the wrong."[7]

Francis poured out his feelings of resentment in secret in his cipher. Was Robert's rashness going to undo all the harmony that he had so patiently tried to build? "Like his mother in temper," he wrote, "he [Essex] could break, but never even slightly bend."[8]

Elizabeth, who kept the foreign ambassadors informed of her actions, assured the French envoy that the English policy toward Tyrone, far from being her idea, was that of "Monsieur d'Essex." And, she declared hotly, even if it had been her own son, she would have put him in "the highest Tower in England." Essex was shortly sent to York House for confinement.

Francis did everything in his power to secure his release and his forgiveness by the queen (although some thought he had abandoned the earl and even poisoned the queen's attitude about him[9]). He reminded her that she had promised to try to reform Essex, not to ruin him. He even used his best weapons, letters of reconciliation to Her Majesty, which Essex sent to the queen as his own.

To the earl he wrote: "I desire your Lordship also to think that though I confess I love some things much better than I love your Lordship—[such] as the queen's service, her quiet and contentment, her honour, her favour, the good of my country, and the like—yet I love few persons better than yourself."[10] He hopes his younger brother will understand that as much as he loves him, he loves his queen and country more. Robert certainly does understand, but in his mood of melancholy and frustration he is not thinking much of anyone but himself.

Francis tried every persuasion with the queen. "You must distinguish," he wrote her, "my Lord's desire to do you service, as that which he thinks he was born for." It could not have been said more plainly—Robert feels that he is born for "special" service to Her Majesty. "Speak for yourself: For the Earl, not a word," the queen tells Francis.

The queen was so annoyed at Bacon's continuous pleadings on behalf of Robert that she began to look coldly again at Francis too. He had been pleading the cause of Essex at his own peril. Nevertheless, she did allow Essex to leave York House and continue his confinement in his own home at Essex House. His family and friends had been removed from the estate, and even his wife, who six months earlier had given birth to their daughter Frances, had to seek permission to visit him.

Elizabeth decided to subdue the earl farther by cutting off his profits from the "sweet wines." His ten-year lease was not renewed; henceforth, the revenue would revert to the Crown. This was the last straw! The queen's godson John Harington leaves us a picture of Essex's state-of-mind when he received this news.

He shifteth from sorrow and repentance to rage and rebellion so suddenly as well proveth him devoid of good reason or right mind.... He uttered strange words, bordering on such strange designs that made me hasten forth and leave his presence.... His speeches of the Queen becometh no man who hath *mens sana in corpore sano....* The Queen well knoweth how to humble the haughty spirit, the haughty spirit knoweth not how to yield.[11]

More insanely still, on one occasion Essex said of the queen that Her Majesty's conditions "are as crooked as her carcase." The remark did, of course, make its way back to the queen, and some think that it was the final blow for which she never forgave him.

Allowing Robert to return to Essex House was a mistake. Although he was under orders to keep to the premises, there was nothing to keep his friends and followers from coming to him. An air of excitement pervaded the city; wild rumors were repeated everywhere. Something was sure to explode, triggered by the volatile energy of the earl's devoted followers gathering around.

And explode it did. On Saturday afternoon, February 7, 1601, Sir Gilly Merrick, one of the staunchest supporters of the earl, went across the river to arrange with the players at the Globe Theatre the staging of Shakespeare's play *Richard II*. The actors complained that it was an old play, that it had been performed many times and would not draw an audience. Forty shillings was enough to persuade the players to put on the performance one more time. The play depicted the dethroning of the monarch Richard and was thus considered subversive. "I am Richard II. Know ye not that?" roared Her Majesty at a later time.

The rest of the story of Robert Tudor Devereux is a heartbreak. The Privy Council, aware of danger brewing, doubled the guard at Whitehall the next day and sent four high dignitaries to investigate the extraordinary gathering in the courtyard of Essex

House. The earl invited them into his library. His angry followers locked the deputy councilors in the house and forced Essex outside. The die was cast. Essex strode out of the open gates toward the city and down the Strand, trailed by three hundred frenzied followers. The story is well-known.

Although the queen's subjects adored the gallant Essex, they were loyal to the queen. It was one thing to bravely flaunt authority—quite another to actually aim for the Crown. When Essex passed through the streets, flushed and perspiring, calling out, "For the queen! For the queen! A plot is laid for my life!" the people stayed in their houses and let him pass in silence. The great outpouring of support he had expected was not happening. He had gambled on the crowd's loyalty, and he had lost. The rebellion was a flop! In stupefied desperation he turned back, but he found that the streets had been blocked by chains. Turning to the river, he took a boat and entered Essex House by the water gate.

The queen's councilors had been released by now. Essex quickly went to the fireplace in his chamber, burned his diary and some papers contained in two iron chests, then prepared to submit to arrest. It is always mentioned with curiosity that he took from around his neck a little black pouch that he always wore. This was also burned with its contents. Speculating, historians have decided that it must have been a letter from James of Scotland concerning the succession. Certainly Essex would not have worn this "always," nor would it have been the cause of his trouble. Something more personal was surely involved. For those who know of Essex's real relationship to the queen, it seems more likely that he carried around his neck some evidence that linked him to his royal birth. Francis does not tell us, and of course we can't be sure.

The trial of Robert Earl of Essex and his devoted co-

conspirator, the earl of Southampton, was set for February 18 at
Westminster Hall. It was, Francis said in cipher, a "sad, awful
story ... my brother's cruel, foul ending."[12] He does not gloss over
the earl's guilt in his cipher story:

> His plan was nothing less than a mad design to take
> possession of the Court: his assistants, Davers, Davis, and
> Blount, being well known, might enter unchallenged with a
> sufficient number of aides. At a given sign they were to seize
> the halberds of the guard ... whilst Essex should enter the
> presence chamber and virtually get possession of the Queen,
> under the pretense of complaining that certain of her
> advisers and informers were his mortal enemies.... Then
> was Parliament to be called to make concessions, and the
> city itself to be under his [Essex's] control.
>
> This plan, known perfectly to Southampton, the chief of
> his friends,... suited that adventurous assistant well, but it
> failed in execution, as we know....
>
> Had [Robert's plan] not met the overturn deserved,
> the younger of the sons would inherit ere the elder. By law,
> this could occur only when the rightful, or, as we name
> him in our country, heir-apparent, hath waived his rights. As
> I was known, not as his brother only, but as the Queen's
> first-born, such plots should at best naturally await my full
> knowledge and consent. But puffed up thus with show of
> military glory, an entrance to power, whose signs ... so
> worked on his inflamed fantasy, as to have far more value
> than royal sword.
>
> This was much aggravated in our minds by some
> private assurances that had so deceived us, that we saw not
> a sign of danger, but trusted his word,... expecting right and
> honest trustworthiness of Robert as a gentleman ... by that
> royal blood that is our heirship....
>
> It shall thus, perchance, somewhat content my heart at
> that far-off day that those who dwell on the Globe may fully

learn how great is the wrong turbulent Robert did by thus
endangering as well [as himself] a worthy and devoted
friend and a loving brother....

Remorse doth make my grief so bitter, for my very life
did hang on that thread, and by the truth my brother was
attaint [guilty].[13]

Francis knew his brother well but not well enough to suspect
him of such a double cross. The story of the remaining days of
Prince Robert Tudor's life and the trial are almost too painful to
record—tragic for Essex but even more so for Francis. His destiny
was to live on and to try somehow to tie up the shattered ends of
the event that had been set in motion by his uncontrollable
brother. Francis's hurt was deep and justifiable, and he poured
out his ache in his cipher:

I write mildly of so terrible events, so galling memories of
fifteen such woeful, ay, such dreadful days. 'Tis limned in
fire, in gloom of the night or day, O Essex, thy murder. [I]
hear Robert's voice, so entreatingly,... haunting all dreams,
greeting every day that doth dawn on our home.[14]

Elizabeth's revenge on her two sons was unbelievably cruel—
at the trial she forced Francis to act as a prosecutor on behalf of
the Crown.[15] It was his life or Essex's. There was simply no way
he could refuse. It was a heartless punishment of Francis for
something he had not been guilty of doing. The dilemma was
unsolvable, said Francis, and he contemplated taking his own life
to avoid appearing at the trial. But self-destruction could never be
an alternative for him.[16] He could not avoid the trial.

Bacon admonished Robert "to confess not justify," knowing,
no doubt, that their mother would give in if he showed humility
and remorse. But it was not to be. Essex continued to try to
explain away his doings. It was useless. When the trial was over,

Essex and Southampton were found guilty.

Never was there a scene in fiction to compare in dramatic intensity with the disaster of Robert Dudley Devereux, Lord Essex. He was led from the jury room with the blade of the guard's axe pointed toward him and, along with Southampton, transported to the Tower. (The younger earl was spared and later pardoned.) Once the prison door was shut, all chances of Essex being heard were canceled out.

Francis tells us that the earl desired a private execution,[17] and this was arranged. He would be beheaded within the walls of the Tower. Others thought that what Essex wanted most was a public execution, perhaps to rouse the populace on his behalf or to have a last chance to cry out his true birthright. When Henri of Navarre (Marguerite's ex-husband and now King of France) was told that Essex had asked for a private execution, he burst out: "Nay, rather the clean contrary, for he desired nothing more than to die in public."[18] Henri knew the story of the queen and her sons.

One may wonder why when Essex was on trial, he didn't claim his royal relationship to the queen. The answer is that any such accusation would have immediately been declared treasonous, although half the assembly probably already knew the truth anyway. There would have been no hope for acquittal. As it was, there was still the possibility of a grant of pardon from the queen, which would never be forthcoming if Essex should speak on his own behalf. At the end of the trial, he had said that prior to his execution he would make something known that should be acceptable to Her Majesty. What this might have been nobody knows.

In his last days, Essex requested a chaplain for confession. Rev. Abdy Ashton, his own preacher, and three others were chosen by the Privy Council to hear him. At the time, these divines were

Robert Devereux, earl of Essex
Robert was born, the second son of Elizabeth and Leicester. Unlike Francis, he secured the favor of the queen and won fame and fortune during his life. However, his quest for recognition would be his downfall. Francis's advice foreshadowed his unfortunate end: "I was ever sorry that your Lordship should fly with waxen wings, doubting Icarus' fortune."

sharply criticized as being mere tools of the government. Ashton was said to be base, fearful and mercenary. The most pressing instructions had previously been given to the divines to urge the condemned man to admit his offenses.[19] It was a sad and bitter end for Essex, who was even deprived of the comfort of a genuinely spiritual confessor. Cecil and others went to the cell to hear Robert's confession and afterward claimed that they had four pages of confession from the inmate himself.

Dodd says: "The truth is that Essex has been pulled down by vicious enemies. The public knew it. The Government therefore resolved to persuade him or to trick him into a 'confession' that he had committed treason and richly deserved death."[20] It was the desire of his jealous enemies to deprive the earl, in the memory of the English people, of all honor and nobility—to show him not as a martyr, not as a popular hero, but as a man faithless to his friends, a traitor to his sovereign, a braggart who quailed in fear before his last enemy, death.

Prisoners who were not of royal blood met their fate on Tower Hill; for royalty and some nobility, Tower Green was used. Essex was executed on Tower Green. Dressed all in black with a scarlet vest, he stood tall on the scaffold. "So—tall, splendid, bareheaded, with his fair hair about his shoulders—he stood before the world for the last time," wrote Lytton Strachey.[21] The headsman's axe struck while Essex was repeating the fifty-first Psalm. "God save the Queen," shouted the executioner when it was over, and he had to fight his way home to escape the mobs, angry at the death of their hero.

The queen had subdued her thoroughbred at last.

> Is not my dearest brother slaughtered?
> And is not my dear Lord dead?
> O Essex! Essex! Essex! the best friend I had!
> O courteous Essex! honest gentleman!
> That ever I should live to see thee dead![22]

> Bring me a father that so loved his child
> As I loved Essex.[23]

There was never a more heartbroken lament than that of Francis's cipher cry. He leaves an echo of it in *Hamlet*:

> Now cracks a noble heart. Goodnight, sweet prince,
> And flights of angels sing thee to thy rest.
>
> *act V, sc. 2*

Chapter Thirteen

Tudors Out

Revenge triumphs over death,
love slights it, honour aspireth to it,
grief flieth to it, fear preoccupateth [anticipates] it.

In March 1603, Francis realized that his
mother, the queen of England, was dying. For ten days she lay at
Richmond Palace, weak and suffering from the symptoms of a
"bad cold." She rested, but not on a bed like ordinary mortals;
rather she sat on cushions piled high on the floor by worried
attendants. She would not go to her bed, she would not take
medication or nourishment. When pressed by her ladies to let
them help her, she retorted that she knew her constitution better
than they did and that she would be left alone.

The Privy Council urged the earl of Nottingham, one of her
highest nobles, to cajole her into going to bed. "If you were in the
habit of seeing such things in your bed as I see," she whimpered,
"you would not press me to go there." Her deathbed dreams
were not pleasant to remember. Not even Robert Cecil had any
influence over her now, but he tried. "Madam," he said, "to
content the people, you *must* go to bed." "Little man, little man,"

she replied in scorn, "the word *must* is not to be used to princes. If your father had lived ye durst not have said so much."[1]

It had been two years since the earl of Essex had died on Tower Green. When the messenger had come to Elizabeth bearing the news of the earl's execution, he had found her sitting quietly playing the virginals,* ostensibly unmoved by the news. Calmly she had played on in a kind of stuporous serenity that she had somehow managed to achieve. Although noticeably not her former self, it was still a marvel that she bore up so well during the days and months that followed. But this passionless tranquility was due to come to a sudden end. She began to complain, in a dreary tone, that she no longer wished to live. Her health, as if affected by her wish, started to deteriorate alarmingly.

The downhill trend coincided exactly with the death of her cousin, the countess of Nottingham, but it was certainly not caused by grief over the loss of the countess, whom she may not have liked much anyway. The sudden collapse of Her Majesty's mental and physical health came about, so it is said, from another cause entirely—the deathbed confession made by the countess. The story of this confession and the consequent sad decline of Elizabeth as recorded by Francis in cipher[2] was not to be decoded until nearly three hundred years later, but this was not the first public account.

It was first referenced in a play written around 1620. Later, a book entitled *The Secret History of the Most Renowned Queen Elizabeth and the Earl of Essex, by a Person of Quality,* published in 1695, again told the story, which had been spread by rumor for many years. Another account, reprinted in Strickland's *Life of Queen Elizabeth,*[3] was given by the grandneice of Robert Carey, who attended the queen during her final days.

---

* virginals: An Elizabethan keyboard instrument, like a spinet or early harpsichord.

Queen Elizabeth in her later years
by Marc Garrard, the Elder
After the death of Essex, it seemed that the queen was never the same. In her pride—and urged by Cecil and his supporters—she would not spare his life. In her sorrow over the death of her favorite son, it seemed that there was no longer any joy in life.

The story relates that when the countess of Nottingham was dying, she entreated the queen to visit her, for she had something to reveal before she could die in peace. When the queen arrived, Lady Nottingham told her that when the earl of Essex was lying under sentence of death, he was desirous to ask Her Majesty's mercy, and to do so in a manner that she had prescribed during the height of his favor. Being doubtful of those about him and unwilling to trust any of them, he called a boy with a pleasing appearance who was passing beneath his window. He engaged the youth to carry a ring, which he threw down to him, to Lady Scrope (a sister of Lady Nottingham who was also in attendance on the queen) with the message that he begged her to present it to Her Majesty.

By mistake, the boy took it to Lady Nottingham, who showed it to her husband to get his advice. Nottingham was part of the Cecil faction and an enemy of Essex. He forbade his wife to show it to the queen or to return any answer to the message, and he told her to keep the ring. Lady Nottingham, having made this confession to the queen, entreated her forgiveness. In a rage Elizabeth exclaimed, "God may forgive you, Madam, but I never can." She left the room in great emotion and was so agitated and distressed that she refused to go to bed, nor would she take any sustenance for a long time.

This story is essentially the same as the one told by Francis in cipher. He states that he knew of the promise made by Elizabeth to Essex and, trusting that he would send her the ring, never once dreamed that the execution would actually take place. He writes:

> It must be acknowledged that the crime for which he [Essex] suffered could not [in] any wise be palliated by his past services or bravery, but, had a signet-ring that he did desire to present, reached Elizabeth, Robert, the son madly loved, might have received a royal remitment, inasmuch as it was her well known seal and token.... It came not, for good reason, to Her Majesty's eyes. Dreadful was her passion of anger and her bootless sorrow of heart on finding that our proud hero had so stoopt, and was not met. As he had been led to believe he had but to send the ring to her, and the same would at a moment's warning bring rescue or relief, he relied vainly, alas! on this promised aid. A bitter grief it was, not the less because he was far dearer, as you know, though but a younger child, than one as worthy [of] her love who is the heir.[4]

Some historians deny the truth of the story about the ring. It is too romantic, too convenient, too dramatic to be true, they say. But according to several most fastidious historians, it is highly believable.[5] There are even descriptions of the ring. Some say that it was gold and blue enamel with the head of Elizabeth carved in relief on a sardonyx stone. Others believe that it was a diamond in a gold setting with black enamel on the sides and back.[6]

From the moment of Lady Nottingham's confession, Elizabeth grew melancholy. She found sleep impossible. Was the terrible anguish of the distraught Lady Macbeth patterned after Elizabeth in her final desperate hours? The lady of the play *(Macbeth)* is suffering from immense remorse at the terrible murder she has persuaded her husband to commit, the slaying of the Scottish King Duncan. In her restlessness, she sleepwalks and talks and wrings her hands. The famous scene shows her trying in vain to wipe away the imagined spot of blood that stains her white fingers. Just as the doctor and the gentlewoman in the play watch Lady Macbeth, so Elizabeth's favorite chaplain, Dr. Parry, watches over her while she sleeps. Thus goes the well-known scene of the play:

> *Doctor:* What is it she does now? Look, how she rubs her hands.
> *Gentlewoman:* It is an accustomed action with her, to seem thus washing her hands: I have known her continue in this a quarter of an hour.
> *Lady Macbeth:* Yet here's a spot.
> *Doctor:* Hark! she speaks. I will set down what comes from her, to satisfy my remembrance the more strongly.
> *Lady Macbeth:* Out, damned spot! Out, I say! One: two: why, then 'tis time to do't. Hell is murky.... What, will these hands ne'er be clean?
>
> *act V, sc. 1*

Lady Macbeth
engraving by John Raphael Smith
After hearing the deathbed confession of Lady Nottingham, the queen
seems to have lapsed into profound guilt over the death of Essex. Her
state of mind is reflected in the anguish and the madness of Lady Macbeth
in the Shakespeare play.

Lady Macbeth suffered remorse, just as Elizabeth did.[7] (It was
about three years after Elizabeth's death that the play was first
performed.)

Now Elizabeth's oncoming death was certain. Her subjects
waited outside the palace in silence to hear the final word, and an
air of controlled excitement pervaded the nation, just as it had
at Mary's death forty-five years earlier. In all those years, no
successor had been named. What would she do now that she
could no longer put it off? She must not choose a woman—
on that the people were determined. They had had enough of
females on the throne. Would it be James of Scotland, the son of
Mary Queen of Scots? This seemed to be the most likely choice,
and he was certainly the one that Cecil and the Privy Council
were pulling for. If she should suddenly acknowledge a son of her
own flesh, it would be disastrous for those now in power.

Everyone was on edge.

In Strickland's *Life of Queen Elizabeth*, an account of Elizabeth's final moments is reported by Lady Southwell, who witnessed the death scene:

> Being given over by all and at the last gasp, keeping still her sense in everything, and giving apt answers, though she spoke but seldom,... the council required admittance, and she wished to wash (gargle) her throat, that she might answer freely to what they demanded, which was to know whom she would have for king.... Her throat troubling her much, they desired her to hold up her finger when they named who she liked; whereupon they named the King of France (this was to try her intellect)—she never stirred; the King of Scotland—she made no sign; then they named Lord Beauchamp. This was the heir of Seymour, whose rights were derived from his mother, Lady Katharine Grey, one of the most unfortunate of Elizabeth's victims. Anger awakened the failing mind of the expiring queen, she roused herself at the name of the injured person, whom she could not forgive, and said fiercely, "I will have no rascal's son in my seat, but one worthy to be a king.".... The interested courtiers sat watching the twitchings of her hands, and the tossing of the arms of the dying Elizabeth, interpreting them into signs of royalty for the expectant heir. In her last struggles, the clasping of her convulsed hands over her brow is seriously set forth as her symbolical intimation that her successor was to be a crowned king![8]

The Privy Councillors immediately seized on this gesture to indicate James VI of Scotland, a crowned king, in spite of the fact that earlier he had been dismissed by Elizabeth with silence. "By what logic" these gestures were considered a serious sign of "her pleasure" only they could explain, says Strickland,[9] one of the leading orthodox authorities on the queens of England.

On such a slender thread did the fate of Francis hang. Had she mentioned his name? It has been suggested that by her reference to "a rascal's son," she meant the son of Lord Leicester. And yet, she loved that man. Would she have called him a rascal? The father of James, Lord Darnley, was as much of a rascal as Leicester. Did her gesture of a crown indicate her own royal son? Did Cecil and his cohorts deliberately conceal the fact? Or did she uphold, to the end, her oath made to him as a child that he would never inherit the kingdom?[10] Or did she relent at last, recognizing the superior qualities of this brilliant son of hers, and name him, only to have it ignored by the handful of men present? It is another one of those enigmas of the Elizabethan reign to which we will never have definite answer.

When the death of a monarch takes place, it has often been the custom throughout the ages for the body of that monarch to be "embalmed," according to the methods of the time, to preserve it as long as possible. With Elizabeth Regina, queen of England, this was not done (although some sources disagree). Alfred Dodd quotes a report by Piers Compton on the strangeness of the situation:

> No male touch laid aside her drapery when she was dead to carry out the dissection and embalming that preceded a royal funeral in those times. The duty of preparing for burial fell to her ladies, and if one of them was overcurious we have no record of her discovery.[11]

A few hours after Elizabeth was proclaimed dead, the Accession Council assembled and drew up the proclamation for James of Scotland. A train of lords and ministers immediately formed a cavalcade to march to London to proclaim the news. They found the gate to the city locked and barred against them. Only with adequate assurances that it was actually the king of Scotland who had been named would they unlock the gates. They were certainly remembering the fiasco of Essex and wanted to avoid further trouble. The same thing happened at the Tower. It was obvious that there was great doubt about who had been named, and the officials only accepted the proclamation after much delay and hesitation.

For five weeks the queen's body lay in state in a coffin draped in black velvet surrounded by black ostrich plumes. Her funeral procession, on April 28, 1603, included one thousand people accompanying the coffin through the streets to Westminster Abbey. After the funeral, her body was laid to rest in the Abbey, in the vault of her grandfather, Henry VII (later moved, in 1606, to a marble monument in the Abbey, where it resides to this day). The "virgin" queen's dark secret was now safe.

Francis Bacon, whose "birthright hath, like Esau's, been given to another,"[12] does not tell us where he was or how the news was broken to him that the Tudor reign was over and the Privy Council had decided that Elizabeth had chosen the Stuart son of her enemy, Mary Queen of Scots, for her successor. Allegedly the queen once said that she thought James was a fool. Was he the one she chose as being worthy to wear a crown or was it Francis? Whatever Francis may have thought or felt, he kept it to himself, except in his cipher:

> I, last of my house, ruled by a tyrannical mother, feel the injustice under which youth's best days gave way to manhood's more hidden period. Disinheritance ... punished by Her Majesty's cutting off a scion, the only branch to perpetuate either our royalty or name. So greatness of our kingdom was no more due to Tudors, our sole memorial being a number of wise laws, mastery of the sea, and likewise quietness of all the border lands.[13]

Naturally one asks why Francis didn't assert his claim to the succession once Elizabeth was gone, and there were many reasons.

Primary was the fact that it would have caused a bitter struggle between opposing factions that could have resulted in a civil war (many blamed him for turning the queen against Essex). And it was his policy to keep the peace if possible. The original records that would prove the royal marriage and birth had long before been lost or destroyed, so the cipher tells us (destroyed by the Cecils?). Burghley, Essex, Leicester, Norfolk, Sir Nicholas, Lord Pembroke (at whose house the marriage had taken place) and most of the others—all whom he might have been able to call as witnesses—were gone. Also, there was the matter of Francis's literary efforts and his mystical group, which were becoming more important day by day.

The truth was that Prince Francis was beginning to realize that his service to his country was greater when he worked in private than it would have been in carrying on the responsibilities of kingship. He could see that the Scottish king could bring at least one gift to England—a dream long cherished by Bacon—the uniting of Scotland and England. Now for the first time it would be Great Britain, a truly United Kingdom. So Francis Tudor remained silent: "Of myself I am silent." He would look to the future: "Far beyond our small Isle, our vision prophetic doth see a realm, outstretched wider and yet wider as time shall elapse, in truth augmented beyond our belief in number, in extent of dominion, in sway of the Imperial Scepter."[14]

In Shakespeare's sonnet 107, the reference to the "mortal moon" is one of the many symbols in Shakespeare's works for which scholars are not able to agree on a meaning. Some think it refers to the defeat of the Spanish Armada, whose battle formation was a crescent shape. How much more sense it makes when read as referring to the death of the old queen—the moon queen:

> Not mine own fears, nor the prophetic soul
> Of the wide world dreaming on things to come

> Can yet the lease of my true love control,
> Supposed as forfeit to a confined doom.
> The mortal moon hath her eclipse endured,
> And the sad augurs mock their own presage,
> Incertainties now crown themselves assured,
> And peace proclaims olives of endless age....
>   And thou in this shalt find thy monument,
>   When tyrants' crests and tombs of brass are spent.

The "mortal moon" would seem to indicate Elizabeth, who was frequently called Cynthia (moon goddess) by Bacon as Spenser. She is now gone—"hath her eclipse endured." "Incertainties now crown themselves assured"—things hitherto unresolved are now defined.

Francis knows now that he will not be named successor. But the olive branch of peace will bring an end to all warring after the throne. With the new reign of James comes the uniting of the two kingdoms, and peace and hope of peace for the future. For Francis there will be no throne, but the "monument" of his poetry will outlast all the tombs of tyrants or kings.

Where Francis spent the hours when Cecil was triumphantly proclaiming the new king of England and Scotland, we do not know. Most likely he remained in seclusion with his followers at Twickenham. Or perhaps he preferred to be alone, where he could meditate on the irony of a fate that decreed he should remain the uncrowned king, while a man of far less ability was wending his way down from Scotland to sit on the throne that should have belonged to him. Did he hope that his decision to allow another man to usurp his throne would end his troubles? For Francis, called by some the most remarkable man of whom any age can boast, the greatest humiliation of his career was still to come—a full eighteen years in the future.

Someone seems to be missing from this busy group of activists at this time. Where was Francis's other "brother," Anthony? Little is heard of him, which would have suited Anthony well, for he shunned publicity in any form. He was content to serve behind the scenes in the shadow of Francis and Essex, both of whom he loved and admired with all the loyalty of his warm heart. Curiously, he was scarcely mentioned in connection with the Essex conspiracy. Was Francis able to protect him from prosecution, or had he been wise enough to follow his "brother's" example and stay clear of participation in the treasonous matter at Essex House? We can't know for sure.

All correspondence that Anthony Bacon may have had with anyone after 1598 has somehow disappeared. It may be, assume historians, that his letters were purposely destroyed in order to free him from all connection with the subversive activities going on at Essex House, which he left in March 1600. It is puzzling, though, says Dame du Maurier, that even his personal letters from this period should also disappear—correspondence written by the same man, Anthony Bacon, who left a voluminous pile of letters that were later presented to the Lambeth Palace Library.

Everything is puzzling about Anthony, including his death. When and how did he die? Where did he die? A book of pedigrees of Suffolk county families says that he died at Essex House. Du Maurier and others think that this is most unlikely. No record says he ever returned to the earl's mansion after leaving it.

The only contemporary mention of Anthony's death comes from a letter written by the gossip John Chamberlain to Dudley Carleton in 1601: "Anthony Bacon died not long since, but so far in debt that I think his brother is the little better by him."[15] This is a very sketchy notice for a man who spent his entire life in the diplomatic service of the queen.

With the enlarged edition of his essays in 1612, Francis

mentions having dedicated the first edition to "my dear brother Master Anthony Bacon, who is with God." He would never be forgotten by Francis, but why so little contemporary notice of his disappearance?

What we do know, because of Dame du Maurier's thorough delving into the records of the time, is that a registry entry for May 17, 1601, at St. Olave's Church near Bishopgate says: "Mr. Anthony Bacon buried in the chamber within the vault."[16]

Chapter Fourteen

Stuarts In

Princes are like to heavenly bodies,
which cause good or evil times.

From this point we take up the story of Francis Bacon without the aid of the Word Cipher. The tragedy of Essex also ends this, Bacon's favorite cipher. He does continue, however, with frequent entries in the Bi-literal Cipher, as decoded by Mrs. Gallup.

The change of a sovereign is an exciting time for a monarchy, and the British people reacted strongly to the incoming James VI of Scotland, who would now also be James I of England. Some were filled with hope, others with apprehension, but few with indifference. Even before the death knell sounded for the old queen, some of the courtiers had streamed north on the broad road leading from London to Edinburgh. It was a kind of spring-time sport, notes Bowen, this continual trying by men of good quality for placement with the king.[1]

Francis revealed his momentary relief in a letter to his friend Tobie Matthew, a few weeks after James was selected. Now that the decision had been finally and irrevocably made, it was out of his hands. It was only natural to breathe a sigh of relief: "The canvassing world is gone and the deserving world is come. And withal I find myself as one awaked out of sleep, which I have not been this long time."[2]

Awaked out of a nightmare would perhaps have been a better description of Francis's state of mind. He felt that he could now stop his striving for "place" suitable for an uncrowned king and do what he could to earn a role in James's kingdom. His usual consolation came to his aid now—his pen was his scepter; let the "gold circle" rest where it may.

It was a time for a complete revision of his life. The last of the Tudors, he was not to be officially acknowledged. The bizarre story of Elizabeth and her tragic family was at an end, and only Francis remained to tell the tale. He did intend to tell it but it would have to be in secret, buried in a "crypt of words," and he was not certain that it would ever be revealed. What lay in the future for this uncrowned king?

Questionable though his title may have been, it was James VI of Scotland who was now king of England. And Francis was the first to admit that only the monarch who went through the sacred rite of coronation could be called a king. He would only be a subject, but he intended to be the best subject of the land, just as he was with Elizabeth.

James took his royal time wending his way south through his new kingdom, passing on his way through St. Albans, the Bacons' territory, and making a stop at the Cecils' elaborate establishment, Theobalds. The new king became so enamored of this elegant estate that Robert felt compelled, probably reluctantly, to offer it to His Grace. It was accepted eagerly and Robert had to try to be content with his consolation prize, Hatfield, the girlhood home of Princess Elizabeth. But he had achieved what he had aimed for, the good graces of the new king.

James I, by Daniel Mytens (1621)
On Elizabeth's death, her councilors named James VI of Scotland the
successor to her throne. He was the only child of Mary Queen of Scots and
her husband Henry Stuart, better known as Lord Darnley. The new king
became James I of England, and his succession effectively united the
kingdoms of England and Scotland. Robert Cecil had been secretly in
contact with him before Elizabeth's death.

James arrived in England accompanied by hordes of Scottish
noblemen, who, in the eyes of the English, were uncouth, uneducated, unmannerly and much to be scorned for their thick accents
and crude country manners. The British aversion to foreigners
was well known, and the Scots, although not quite foreign, were
distant enough to be snubbed. Bacon was too much a man of
universal vision to be a victim of such insularity, as we see from
his essay "Of Goodness": "If a man be gracious and courteous to
strangers, it shows he is a citizen of the world."[3]

James felt himself to be more than adequate to his new job. Having been reared in the expectancy of being a king and infused with an overabundance of self-importance from childhood, he relished his exalted new position. At last the nation would be called "Great Britain"[4] and his claim to be the most recent descendant of King Arthur of Camelot would be established.

James's succession took place 289 years after the fierce battle of Bannockburn had divided the two nations. He had always desired their union. Now Bacon wrote to James suggesting he style himself King of England, France and Scotland, called Great Britain. James loved the idea and drew up a proclamation to that effect—not, of course, giving Bacon any credit.

But James was no King Arthur. He certainly did not look like a king according to contemporary reports:

> He was of middle stature, more corpulent through his clothes than in his body, yet fat enough, his clothes being ever made large and easy, the doublets quilted for stiletto proof, his breeches in great pleats and full stuffed. He was naturally of a timorous disposition,... his eyes, ever large, ever rolling after any stranger ... [so that] many for shame have left the room.[5]

The childhood of the Scottish prince would be a horror to a child psychologist of today. He was taken away from his mother as an infant when she was forced to abdicate, being accused of the murder of her husband, Lord Darnley. The child was proclaimed king of Scotland, James VI, at just thirteen months old. Brought up in a chilly castle by guardians, the earl and countess of Marr, he grew into a somewhat insecure youth.

Apparently there was little of refinement to be found at the court of Scotland. To the Scots, England was a land of dreams. To the English, Scotland was a land of buffoons. When the royal entourage arrived in London, shouting noisily in their harsh accents and laughing uproariously at their own ribald jokes, they were scorned by the British aristocracy, who considered themselves superior in every way.

James's main attributes were an excellent classical education, drilled into him by a harsh tutor; a love of peace, strengthened by his own personal cowardice; and a certain crafty wit, such that historians have called him "the wisest fool in Christendom." Perhaps referring to James, Bacon was to say that "Nothing doth more hurt in a state than that cunning men pass for wise."[6]

Francis was not one of those who rushed forward to greet James on his approach to London. He stayed put in Twickenham, no doubt engulfed in his own private thoughts. But he did send a message to the new king via his friend Sir John Davies, one of the many who had set out to greet the great entourage. His message to fellow barrister Davies bears an important reference, often quoted, concerning Bacon's secret life as a poet.

> Mr. Davies,
>   Though you went on the sudden ... I commend myself to your love and to the well using of my name, as well in repressing and answering for me, if there be any biting or nibbling at it.... So, desiring you to be good to concealed poets, I continue,
>
> Your very assured,
Fr. Bacon[7]

Davies was one of the poets of Bacon's inner circle, one of his "pens," and Francis was depending on him to be tactful in mentioning his name to James. This same Davies had earlier written a poem honoring six great poets—Homer, Dante, Chaucer, Spenser, Daniel and an unnamed sixth poet, his "sweet companion" who "under a shadow sings." Who could it have been but Bacon?

So Francis bides his time and does what he can to be of service to the king and gain an influential place in the government. But his progress would be slow. "Nothing can account for Francis Bacon's strange failure for so long a time to reach his due place in the public service," says R. W. Church, "but the secret hostility, whatever may have been the cause, of Cecil."[8]

Church did not see to the root of the trouble—that Cecil was, and always had been, jealous of Francis and afraid for his own position at court if Francis should get into power. I am "as a hawk" that cannot fly, being "tied to another's fist," Bacon had cried,[9] referring to Cecil. Was he still to be at the mercy of Cecil's hostility now that he had given up his claim to the throne? It was to Cecil's distinct advantage to see to it that Bacon was not yet untethered by his sovereign, and he did all that he could to prevent it.

Another biographer observed that Cecil "seemed to have possessed some secret concerning Bacon [which was] discreditable to him, which he imparted to King James, and this hindered his advancement after the death of the Queen."[10] Cecil was apparently using the same tactics with James that had worked so well with Elizabeth.[11] He had only to convince James that Francis would stop at nothing to get his birthright and seize the throne at the least provocation. It would be some time before Francis could calm the fears of James and convince him of his good intentions. James need not have worried. Francis had already made his decision not to contend for the right to the Crown (although many of his friends may have wished him to do so, and he might have had a good chance of winning).

As Francis considered the incoming monarch and his own circumstances, he saw two paths open to him. He could either retire to his country home and devote the rest of his life to his writings and to his literary and esoteric studies, or he could try once again, as the uncrowned king of his vision, to help the advancement of his country. For Francis there was no question—his responsibility to his country was engraved on his heart; it came first. He must stay in public life and be of as much service as possible to the new king. As he had written some time earlier:

> Believing that I was born for the service of mankind and regarding the care of the commonwealth as a kind of common property which like the air and the water belongs to everybody, I set myself to consider in what way mankind might be best served, and what service I was myself best fitted by nature to perform.... I was not without hope ... that if I came to hold office in the state, I might get something done for the good of men's souls.[12]

Francis was a modest man; still, subservience did not come easily to him. He felt himself to be as royal and as deserving as any man alive, and he was never a victim of false humility. But the goal was great, and it was worth any amount of sacrifice to please James so that the enlightenment of the people might continue. It cost Francis much regret to voluntarily reject the prospect of a quietly peaceful life as a scholar, but he forced himself to get back into the fray of the political drama. A letter to James was written at once to assure the new king of his good intent.

If James knew Francis's secret heritage, he would be gladdened and likely relieved to have his support. In no way would Francis interfere with the new king; he wished only to be allowed to serve his country honorably. In an amazing letter, sent with his friend Tobie Matthew (when he traveled to greet the king with the other courtiers), Francis wrote quite openly (that is, to those who knew the secret) of the access "which I enjoyed with my late dear Sovereign Mistress; a Prince, happy in all things, but most happy in such a successor."

He goes on to offer himself to the king's service:

I think there is no subject of your Majesty's who loveth this island, and is not hollow and unworthy, whose heart is not set on fire, not only to bring you peace-offerings to make you propitious, but to sacrifice himself a burnt-offering to your Majesty's service: amongst which number no man's fire shall be more pure and fervent than mine.[13]

James surely would not miss these references to "Prince," "burnt-offering" and "sacrifice," but he did not respond to Bacon's letter. When he issued a list of those who were "in office at the Queen's death" that he intended to keep on in their former positions, only Bacon's name was excluded. After a time, the Privy Council spotted the omission and confirmed with the king their desire to retain Bacon as learned counsel. Had the omission been accidental or deliberate? We can only wonder, but we do know that Robert Cecil was now His Majesty's secretary of state.

It was to this surrogate king that Bacon was forced to appeal when he decided to request the honor of knighthood. And who was the channel to whom he must direct his appeal? Of course, this new king's new secretary, Robert Cecil. Knighthood was to be the first title that this prince of the realm was granted in the long forty-two years of his life. Many times he had stood aside in silence while the queen bestowed on his friends, relatives and others much less deserving than himself the Order of the Garter—the highest and most coveted order of chivalry in the land. It was Francis's ancestor Edward III who in 1348 had originated the order, inspired, it was said, by the idea of the Arthurian Round Table. But the Garter was never bestowed on Edward's descendant Francis. It was, however, in 1608, granted to Robert Cecil.

The one thing that Francis did ask for in his petition was the favor of a private knighting ceremony, but Cecil refused to grant it. It would be a public ceremony with the other new knights. One can imagine just how much "honor" Bacon considered such a knighting to be, but gamely, as always, he did what had to be done.

In May 1603, Robert Cecil was created Baron Cecil of Essendon (later to be made a viscount and then earl of Salisbury). About the same time, Attorney General Edward Coke, Bacon's second worst enemy, was one of six given a knighthood. Two months later, July 23, 1603, prior to the coronation of James, Francis Bacon, poet-philosopher-prince, standing in the pouring rain in the garden at Whitehall along with three hundred others of varying degrees, was given "this almost prostituted title of knighthood."[14]

For Francis it would be another four years before he gained a crown office, that of solicitor general. Advancement would be slow as long as Robert Cecil was alive and Edward Coke held the position of attorney general. Francis accepted this. If heaven intended no interference, he wrote in his cipher,[15] for the time being he would have to be content with that.

For many years, the plan for the education of the common man had been building brick by brick in Francis's mind. Now, in earnest, he took the opportunity to put his plans on paper. In 1605 he published his first major book, *The Advancement of Learning.* Here was the great production that contained the essence of his inner life and his long-frustrated plans for mankind.

A sensitive glance between the lines of the dedication of *Advancement,* "To the King," reveals much to the informed reader. The book is a gift to James—for "there belongeth to kings from their servants both tribute of duty and presents of affection." Bacon was careful to reassure James repeatedly that he had nothing to fear from him concerning the governing of the nation. He even spoke of Elizabeth's unmarried state. He could not have

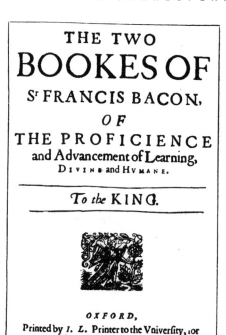

Title page of the 1633 edition of *The Advancement of Learning*
In this, the first major work published under his own name, Francis began
in earnest the great work of setting forth a new philosophy of science and
a new system of knowledge. Rather than purely intellectual analysis and
blind obedience to authorities such as Aristotle and the Bible, he proposed
a new method based on the observation of nature. What seems so simple
today was a revelation in an age when Galileo was persecuted for daring
to trust his own observations above the beliefs of the ancients.

made a clearer statement to James of his intention of giving up all
claims to his rightful inheritance from her.

These assurances were but a small part of his plan for the
Advancement. Some years later, Bacon spoke of the work that he
had begun with *The Advancement of Learning*: "First of all we
must prepare a *Natural and Experimental History*, sufficient and
good; and this is the foundation of all; for we are not to imagine
or suppose, but to discover, what nature does or may be made to
do."[16] Such an idea, writes Loren Eiseley in *The Man Who Saw*

through Time, is "the very essence of science as we know it today." Bacon was singlehandedly at work to chain "the imagination to reality, but at the same time ... free [it] to explore the dark crooks and crannies of nature."[17]

Bacon's aim was all-encompassing—he would attempt to catalogue existing knowledge to use in his scientific observations of the world around him. His innate love of order came to the fore as he tried to categorize everything so that it would be clear and easily remembered by the reader. Knowing that the task was more than one man could accomplish in a single lifetime, he hoped only that he could at least have "constructed the machine itself and the fabric, though I may not have employed or moved it."[18] He was to point the way, to be a watch candle, a bell ringer, a lantern in the night.

Two books whose "author was God" were at the base of his philosophy—the Bible and the book of nature. The first revealed the will of God for the humble walk of man, and the second revealed the power of God as given in the world of form. If man could learn to read nature rightly, he could come to know and use the power of God. Only thus would come relief from mankind's pitiable state and a return to the blessing forfeited by Adam in "the fall."* Without the character of God, "man is a busy, mischievous, wretched thing, no better than a kind of vermin."[19] This was basically Francis Bacon's philosophy, that science and the service of mankind were the two prongs of the doctrine of creation.

Plainly and simply, Bacon was aiming for the enlightenment of all men. If his methods seem obvious to modern scholars, they

---

* This was a radical departure from the orthodoxy of the day. A wrong understanding of the biblical story of man's fall (through eating of the fruit of the tree of knowledge of good and evil) had led to a sense that it was the search for knowledge in itself that ultimately caused man's expulsion from paradise. Bacon proposed a new idea—that *true* knowledge, of God and his creation, could be the means for man's return to a golden age.

can gain perspective by realizing that he was scaling the summit of a mountain and surveying the landscape where no trails had been blazed. He had no textbooks, no scientific treatises, no university studies to which he could turn for aid in charting such a new course. He was "coming to the obscurest of all subjects without guide or light."[20]

There is little in Advancement that men cannot relate to today once they get used to the sometimes archaic words and the frequent references to classical sources which are now out of vogue in any but the most scholarly circles. An edition of Bacon's works stripped of these things would be a most useful guide for students, especially for their clear understanding of the matter, and also for the average citizen of our own time.

Eiseley gives us a glimpse of the dilemma facing Bacon as he sought to lay out his plan for the advancement of mankind:

> We must enter into the intellectual life of Bacon's period if we are fully to grasp the enormity of the task that confronted him, or his challenge to his epoch. I have said that science does not come easily to men; they must be made to envision its possibilities.... The magnitude of his educational vision can be perceived only when we realize that well toward the close of the nineteenth century the greatest universities in England were still primarily devoted to the classical education of gentlemen. This fact is both a measure of Bacon's perception and a revelation of the glacial slowness with which ancient institutions are modified.[21]

Bacon was well aware of the "glacial slowness" with which his work would be accepted, which is clearly seen in his cipher.

> I have undertaken great labour in behalf of men for the further advancing of knowledge, awaiting a time when it shall be in every language as in our own, but that this may be kept to other ages.... If God doth grant me a long life so

to complete these varied labours, it shall be well for the world, since I am seeking not my own honour, but the honour and advancement, the dignity and enduring good of all mankind.[22]

So it was the new king who was honored by the hopeful dedication of this astonishing book. He might have been flattered and impressed to have his name connected with such deep learning and philosophy, but this we don't know. Years later, when Francis dedicated another major book to him, *Novum Organum,* his real opinion seems to have been more clearly revealed. Presented with a gift copy, James wrote a note of thanks, promising "to read it through with care and attention, though I should steal some hours from my sleep; having otherwise as little spare time to read it as you had to write it."[23] Perhaps he did attempt to read it, but he probably didn't finish it—he was heard later to comment that Francis Bacon's latest book "is like the peace of God for it passeth understanding."[24]

Chapter Fifteen

A Slippery Climb

In the discharge of thy place
set before thee the best examples.

Looking over Bacon's letter to Robert Cecil in 1603 requesting to be knighted, an interesting item catches one's eye. Francis confesses that he is ready "to marry with some ... advancement." Then he adds, "I have found out an alderman's daughter, an handsome maiden, to my liking."[1]

It had been twenty-four years since the teenage Francis returned from France determined to banish his lovely French princess from his memory. He had succeeded only in banishing her portrait "to the walls of memory ... where it doth hang in pure, undimmed beauty of those early days, while her most lovely presence doth possess this entire mansion of heart and brain."[2] It had been less than ten years since his plans to marry Lord Burghley's granddaughter, Lady Hatton, had come to naught. He had never been very successful in his encounters with romance. But the years have a way of mellowing heartaches, and time cools even the most intense passions of the heart. He was now forty-two years old; if he was ever to marry, this was the time.

One doubts that his ardor for the alderman's daughter was the first consideration. It seems likely that he had other pressing motives, including a desire to prove to James and Cecil that he was fully sincere about giving up all ambitions to the throne. Choosing the daughter of a commoner should be proof enough to convince James of Francis's sincerity in abandoning all claims to his heritage, since such a marriage partner would not be acceptable for royalty. The message would be clear; it was worth a try. And then, too, he may have hoped to alleviate a certain loneliness in his life.

Just why Alice Barnham was the fortunate one to be chosen as Lady Bacon is a question. She was the daughter of a former member of Parliament who had died when she was young. An inheritance from her father gave her property worth £6,000 pounds and an income of £300 per annum. Elizabeth Hatton's vast wealth would have been a great boon to Francis, and he might well have considered that he had a certain right to share in it, since it had principally been derived from his mother's Lord Chancellor.[3] Young Alice's inheritance, however, was not great enough to have been the motivating factor in their marriage. But he was determined to convince James of his renunciation of the temporal crown. An immortal crown that rust shall do no ill nor evil men deny would be enough for him.[4] Marriage to Alice would set a seal to his promise.

He would have first met Alice at the home of her stepfather, the jovial Sir John "Lusty" Packington, whom Bacon visited occasionally, probably to discuss their mutual interest in gardens and landscaping. Sir Francis was intrigued with Alice, no doubt, by "the morn and liquid dew of youth"[5] still fresh on her face. And she apparently had "a quick tongue," as noted by du Maurier, which may suggest "a certain intelligence that would ripen with years."[6] Francis's love of jesting with Anthony (and

Francis Bacon in his parliamentary robes
This portrait, by an unknown artist, is a copy of an earlier Jacobean one.

flirting with Elizabeth Hatton) suggests that Alice's quickness
would be for him a treasured quality.

Francis enjoyed the young, not only because of the alertness
of their minds but also for their comparative lack of prejudice
and inflexibility. In his essay "Of Youth and Age," he quotes the
biblical verse "Your young men shall see visions, and your old
men shall dream dreams,"[7] and he interprets it to mean that
"young men are admitted nearer to God than old, because vision
is a clearer revelation than a dream. And certainly, the more a
man drinketh of the world, the more it intoxicateth."[8] Although

he appreciates the wisdom and stability that comes with the years, it is youth in whom he places his hope.

Jean Overton Fuller admits to being somewhat mystified by Bacon's choice of a bride. After all, with the marriage her formal schooling would be over, and yet she was not of the same background and experience as her philosopher-poet-author husband. "One feels she was not endowed with intellectual gifts or one would have heard of them,"[9] writes Fuller.

She was not a great beauty judging from her portraits, although Catherine Drinker Bowen's description from a painting of Alice in her thirties may well be accurate:

> It shows a handsome oval face with strong high-bridged nose, bold eyes heavy-lidded, a firm mouth and dark hair smooth above the forehead. Alice is richly dressed and wears her clothes with style; the face and carriage are those of a woman who could hold her own, even against a Francis Bacon. One small hint we have, from a writer who remarked that Alice Bacon's wit "lay forward, viz. in her tongue."[10]

Fuller points to an interesting parallel from *Othello*, a play written in 1604, at about the time of Bacon's courtship of Alice. In this play Othello, the Moor, was a friend of Senator Brabantio, Desdemona's father. While the young woman listened to conversations between the two men, she became intrigued by the older Othello as he talked of his exciting life experiences, and her imagination was so stirred that she became more than half the wooer. While Othello might have questioned whether his person of "tann'd antiquity"[11] would appeal to this attractive young maiden, Desdemona convinced him otherwise. Perhaps Alice was likewise charmed by the brilliant mind of this older man who conferred with her father. It is an interesting point and deserves more investigation.

Desdemona, her father and Othello, from *Othello*
Historians have long puzzled over the marriage of Alice Barnham and Francis Bacon. He was forty-five at the time of their marriage and she was only fourteen. While marriage at such a young age was not uncommon in that era, it does raise questions. Some commentators see a parallel between Alice and Desdemona, who was smitten with the glamorous Othello, a friend of her father, and eloped with him.

Whatever the attraction may have been, on May 10, 1606, Francis Bacon and Alice Barnham were married. The next day the letter writer Dudley Carleton wrote to Chamberlain describing the ceremony:

> Sir Francis Bacon was married yesterday to his young wench in Maribone [Marylebone] Chapel. He was clad from top to toe in purple, and hath made himself and his wife such store of fine raiments of cloth of silver and gold that it draws deep into her portion.[12]

Lusty Packington gave a dinner for the wedding party at his lodging "over against the Savoy." It appears that Cecil, now Lord Salisbury, used the occasion to insult Francis one more time. Although he was invited to the wedding, he turned down the invitation and sent his secretary and two other knights in his stead. This must have been a disappointment to Lady Packington, who, no doubt, was elated to have her daughter traveling in such lofty circles. Unfortunately, this new mother-in-law of Francis's would prove a trial for him, and it would take all his tact and diplomacy to keep their relationship on an even keel.

Francis's choice of purple for his wedding attire is one of the more intriguing aspects of the affair. A law had been passed a century and a half earlier by the Yorkist Edward IV making it illegal for a commoner to wear purple. Classes and professions were carefully color graded in medieval England. Russet, yellow, gray, green and sky blue were for the lower classes (peasants, servants, and so on). The upper classes loved their lush, sophisticated colors and gave them appropriate names—Marigold, Maiden Hair, Gingerline, Carnation. Purple, however, was reserved for royalty and nobility. Bacon's contemporary French biographer, the elusive Pierre Amboise, wrote that Bacon was "born amidst the purples"[13]—perhaps a veiled hint to his royal beginnings.

Francis knew that the laws regarding the color of clothing had been repealed two years earlier in a dispute between Parliament and the king. At last he could wear the royal purple without fear of loss or harm. Was there more to his choice of a glorious purple wedding garment? We'll never know, but his purple outfit would be an unmistakable sign of his royal heritage (for those in on the secret) and his wedding to a commoner would signal his renunciation of that heritage. Perhaps it was a message he hoped James wouldn't miss.

Alfred Dodd believes that for their wedding day, Bacon wrote a sonnet to his bride comparing her to "April's first-born flowers and all things rare." Sonnet 21 ends with these lines:

> And then believe me, my love is as fair
> As any mother's child, though not so bright

As those gold candles fixed in heaven's air:
  Let them say more that like of hearsay well;
  I will not praise that purpose not to sell.

Francis had not hesitated to compare his first love, Marguerite, to the heavenly bodies. Speaking through Romeo, he said, "Juliet is the sun," with eyes like "two of the fairest stars in all the heaven."[14] With Alice he is more restrained—she is "as fair as any mother's child" but not to be compared to the stars, the "candles fixed in heaven's air."

The following lines from sonnet 22, show further proof of Bacon's affection, not passion, for his new wife:

My glass shall not persuade me I am old,
  So long as youth and thou are of one date ...
  How can I then be elder than thou art?...
  I, not for myself, but for thee will,
  Bearing thy heart, which I will keep so chary
  As tender nurse her babe from faring ill.

This marriage was no "grand passion"; it was the tender promise of a mature husband to cherish the young bride in his care. Catherine Bowen writes: "The surprising thing about Bacon's marriage was that it went along so smoothly through the years. There were no children, but for two decades no breath of scandal touched the pair."[15] The marriage was, by the standards of the time, a suitable one.

This may have been so, but we know that for a time Bacon's mother-in-law was stirring up trouble for the newlyweds. Lady Packington's meddling was such that Bacon sent her a letter to the effect that if she continued to cause dissention in his household, she would no longer be welcome there.[16]

If Bacon had hoped to enter a new cycle of activity and service to the state after his marriage, and we know that he did, he was once more to be disappointed. The position of solicitor general became open in December 1605; he applied for it and was once more turned down. "What a discomfortable thing is it for me," he wrote to Lord Ellesmere, "to have that little reputation which by my industry I gather to be scattered and taken away by continual disgraces, every new man coming above me."[17] No man ever deserved more and received less. "It is impossible not to lay this at Robert Cecil's door," wrote Mrs. Bowen,[18] whose orthodox viewpoint does not explain the why and wherefore of Cecil's bitter enmity toward Bacon.

But a year and a half later, the post of solicitor general was finally granted to Bacon. And a year after that, in 1608, he became clerk of the Star Chamber (a post granted by Elizabeth but only recently vacated). Though the positions were given after so many years of delay and futility, he does not seem to have been overjoyed with his reward:

> I have found now twice upon amendment of my fortune, disposition to melancholy and distaste.... For upon my Solicitor's place I grew indisposed and inclined to superstition. Now upon Mill's place [the Clerkship in Star Chamber] I find a relapse unto my old symptom as I was wont to have it many years ago, as after sleeps: strife at meats, strangeness, clouds, etc.... Strangeness in beholding, darksomeness, offer to groan and sigh.[19]

After years of struggle, Francis's reaction was one of profound melancholy. Was this post to be the height of the career for one who was born to be a king? It would turn out to be only the first of his promotions under James, but for a number of years Francis was merely solicitor general.

One huge achievement of these years was the publishing of a

new translation of the Bible. Three translations were in popular use at the time and the Puritans had asked James for a new one that would be accurate and free of partisan interpretation. In James's first year on the throne he gave the go-ahead to arrange what is surely the best-known and most influential book in the English language—the King James Version of the Bible. Francis would become involved, as we shall see.

In 1604 James announced that he had "appointed certain learned men to the number of four and fifty for the translation of our Bible." The list, which finally dwindled to "seven and forty," included Anglican churchmen, Puritans and laymen—"the best biblical scholars and linguists of their day."[20] These were organized into six groups—two at Westminster, two at Oxford and two at Cambridge.

Strict rules were laid out for them, and it was arranged that the work of each translator would be compared with the work of every other translator. When any one book was completed it was sent to all the other groups for review and suggestions—an ingenious plan of organization. When the group work was finished, two members of each group were chosen to act as a review committee. This interim version next went to the Bishops of Winchester and Gloucester and then in 1609 it was sent to James for review. This entire procedure is duly recorded and documented. Only when the translation leaves the hands of the clergymen does the mystery begin.

The Cambridge History of English and American Literature says that this new version

> profited by all the controversy regarding previous trans-
> lations. Practically every word that could be challenged had
> been challenged.... The whole ground had been fought over
> so long that great intimacy with the Bible had resulted....
> Much of it [the King James Version] was literally learned by

heart by great numbers of the English people. Thus, it grew to be a national possession ... a national classic.... What Homer was to the Greeks, and the Koran to the Arabs,... the Bible has become to the English. Huxley writes: "... It is written in the noblest and purest English, and abounds in exquisite beauties of pure literary form.".... Macauley regarded the Bible as "a book which, if everything else in our language should perish, would alone suffice to show the whole extent of its beauty and power."[21]

Imagine the results of forty-seven men in different locations trying to come up with a unified version of anything, and one cannot help but realize that somebody had to be the organizer. None of the men who were chosen for the translation had any claim to literacy genius, and yet the result is the loveliest of all prose translations. Professor Quiller-Couch of Cambridge, sensing the truth, wrote:

> That a large committee of forty-seven, not one of them outside of this performance known for any superlative talent, should have gone steadily through the mass of holy writ, seldom interfering, seldom missing to improve; that a committee of forty-seven should have captured (or even should have retained and improved) a rhythm so personal, so constant that our Bible has the voice of one author speaking through its many mouths: that is a wonder before which I can only stand humble and aghast.[22]

In 1609 the translators presented their final version to James, and in 1610 James returned it to them completed. What had occurred in the interim?

Pondering the situation, biographer William Smedley says

> James was incapable of writing anything to which the term beautiful could be applied.... When the last stage came there was only one writer of the period who was capable of

turning the phrases with that matchless style which is the great charm of the Shakespeare plays. Whoever that stylist was, it was to him that James handed over the manuscripts which he received from the translators.... He produced a result which, on its literary merits, is without an equal.[23]

The original manuscripts from the translation process no longer exist, but in the Records Office of the British Museum there are documents that indicate Francis Bacon was involved in many proceedings related to this new translation, even the editing.[24] Do they confirm he was the final editor? That is unclear at this point. But many believe that only Francis had the genius to pull off such a monumental task with such literary grace and beauty. It was a far-reaching accomplishment for all involved. An estimated billion copies of the King James Bible (or Authorized Version) have been published in the English language alone.

In the year 1612 Francis's prospects for advancement began to change. Robert Cecil had finally departed from this earth and gone to be judged at the courts of heaven. After years of enduring the venom of his little "cousin," Francis was at last free from his treachery. It had been more than thirty years since he had made the mistake of beating up "the spy, the informer to the Queen" in that boyhood scrap that had such continuing repercussions—thirty years of being spied on, tattled on, scorned and humiliated.

> Those two men [Robert Cecil and his father, Lord Burghley] ... their subtle acts apparent. They were my worst, aye, my only foes.... [With their] overt insolence, acts so wicked, such violent deeds, I had a just [cause for] fear.... Upon every occasion they were mindful of my whereabouts.[25]

Now they were both gone. Was it too late for Francis? Bowen writes that "Robert Cecil died one of the richest men in England

and perhaps the most hated. No man is loved whose business it is to stand in the middle and play both sides."[26] Francis was not alone in his dislike of Cecil. On the London streets, ballads circulated about Cecil, including this one:

> Here lies, thrown for the worms to eat,
> Little bossive Robin that was so great:
> Owning a mind for dismal ends,
> As traps for foes and tricks for friends.[27]

With Robert gone, Francis's hope for better things immediately began to bear fruit. Once again Francis wrote a letter to James:

> I have served your Majesty above a prenticehood, full seven years and more, as your solicitor, which is, I think, one of the painfulest places in your kingdom.... God hath brought mine own years to fifty-two, which I think is older than ever any solicitor continued unpreferred.[28]

In his cipher he wrote: "Old men have been laid in the tomb and children have become men, yet this matter is still in the cradle, nor can I have great hope to see the maturity of this long-cherished dream."[29] Now James appointed him attorney general, a post that had previously been held by his jealous rival Edward Coke. It was October 1613 and the post was vacated when Coke was "promoted" from his judgeship to a higher position, and the attorney general promoted to Coke's spot. Coke was furious; he knew he had been "bumped upstairs," given a more prestigious position but one with less influence on the king. Although Coke had several times before won out over Francis—in acquiring the position of attorney general under Elizabeth, in winning Lady Hatton's hand—he was still jealous of the younger and superior man.

James was delighted when he finally understood the sincerity of Bacon's attitude. Judges should "be lions," Bacon wrote, "but yet lions under the throne, being circumspect that they do not check or oppose any points of sovereignty."[30] This was just what this inept king from Scotland wanted—someone who would assume the burden of authority but never question his own royal authority. It was the premise on which Francis had based his life.

Pleased beyond measure with Bacon's adroit services, James eventually gave him a choice. Would he prefer to become a member of the Privy Council immediately or lord chancellor of England in the event of the death of the incumbent chancellor? Francis chose the former and was sworn in as a privy councillor in June of 1616. The following year, James appointed him to be lord keeper, the post that his father had held many years earlier. And then the next year, in January of 1618, James appointed him to the office of lord chancellor.

Francis was also "promoted" to the peerage in 1618. By the grace of James, he was created Baron Verulam, or, as he signed himself, Francis Verulam, Chanc. [Chancellor]. For the first time in his life, Francis Tudor was free from the pseudonym he had always used, Francis Bacon. At last he was entitled to sit in the House of Lords. A few years later, he was given an even greater title—Viscount St. Alban, the highest title that this particular Prince of Wales would ever attain. For a son of Nicholas Bacon, it was a great honor; for a son of Elizabeth Tudor, it was only the first rung of the ladder—earl, marquess, duke and prince all taking precedence. Nevertheless, it must have been gratifying for this uncommon man to at last move out of the ranks of commoner.

A magnificent ritual in honor of Francis's new status as viscount was held at Theobalds, the king's favorite residence. It was now the new year of 1621. James showed particular favor to Bacon by investing him with the robes and coronet of a viscount, a departure from the usual custom of merely delivering papers of patent to the newly promoted peer.

We learn that once again Francis chose the royal color of purple for his robes. Perhaps it was an opportunity to wear his wedding clothes once more. Knowing Francis's taste for elegance, however, one suspects that the clothes for himself and Alice, the new viscountess, were the latest thing in style. Francis had never ceased to remember his royal heritage. The new Viscount St. Alban (for that is the title which he had chosen for himself) wrote a long letter to James in gratitude for his recent favor. He used an enigmatic phrase, "And so I may without superstition be buried in St. Alban's habit or vestment."[31]

The phrase suggests a private little conundrum which he expected James to appreciate. It seems to have been a gentle reminder to His Majesty that there was more between them than meets the eye. Saint Alban, as we've seen, was the first Christian martyr of England and a local hero in Francis's home environment of Hertfordshire. It appears that Francis felt he had much in common with Alban, both of them having sacrificed their true identity for the good of others.*

Baron Verulam, Viscount St. Alban—these were the names Francis was now allowed to use. "What's in a name?" he had written many years earlier, "A rose by any other word would smell as sweet."[32] Nevertheless, it had to be a satisfaction to choose his own titles, so justly deserved and so long delayed.

In that same month of January 1621, the lord chancellor of England gave a banquet of his own at York House, currently his home once again as the residence of England's top legal official. He and Lady Alice had moved there on the demise of his old friend Chancellor Ellesmere. About sixty years had now passed since Bacon was born in "York House or York Place"[33]; the occasion for the entertainment was his sixtieth birthday. At this

*See page 37 for the story of Saint Alban.

celebration, his close friend Ben Jonson wrote a somewhat enigmatical ode to him:

> Hail, happy Genius of this ancient pile!
> How comes it all things so about thee smile?
> The fire, the wine, the men! and in the midst,
> Thou stand'st as if some mystery thou didst...
> Son to the grave, wise Keeper of the Seal,
> Fame, and foundation of the English weal.
> What then his father was, that since is he,
> Now with a title more to the degree;
> England's high Chancellor: the destin'd heir
> In his soft cradle to his father's chair;
> Whose even thread the Fates spin round, and full,
> Out of their choicest, and their whitest wool....[34]

Here we see Jonson going along with Francis's commitment to drop all claims to his royal birth and to again reassure James that he meant only to lay claim to his Bacons' heritage.

The banquet would have been a festive one, we can be sure, with the usual warmth of Bacon's hospitality, the lavishness of his table, the brilliance of his dinner table conversation, and his courtesy to his guests at all levels. He was a host without compare. Wrote John Aubrey:

> At every meal, according to the season of the year, he had his table strewn with sweet herbs and flowers, which he said did refresh his spirits and memory. When his Lordship was at his country-house at Gorhambury, St. Albans [it] seemed as if the Court were there, so nobly did he live. His servants had liveries with his crest (a boar); his watermen were more than employed by gentlemen than any other, even the King's.[35]

His gifts and bounties to all who served him were unprecedented. There was always music playing softly in the background. "His Lordship would many times have music in the next room when he meditated. I have now forgot what Mr. Bushel said," admits Aubrey, "whether his Lordship enjoyed his Muse best at night or in the morning"[36]—perhaps both.

The lord chancellor had a saying to describe his attitude toward worldly possessions and high living: "The world was made for man,... not man for the world."[37] He believed that all the bountiful gifts of the Creator were to be used for the benefit of man and for the relief of his estate and that man's fortune was in his own hands.

Alfred Dodd, himself a Freemason, believes that the pictures and figures with which Bacon adorned his home were secret symbols of the "Craft," pregnant with meaning to the initiated. "By Masonic tradition," he writes, "St. Albans and Gorhambury are regarded as the birthplace and cradle of Freemasonry in England."[38] A discussion of the probable connection of Francis Bacon with the secret societies of England and Europe, one he carried on simultaneously with his public service to England, is due at another time.*

These times were the pinnacle of Bacon's career—a well-earned reward after so many years of untiring yet unheralded service. One wonders if his sense of prophecy would have revealed to him the not-too-distant collapse of all of his dreams. Did he foresee that his charming Verulam House, a mile from Gorhambury manor, and the lovely grounds would be sold for £400 in less than fifty years and torn down by two carpenters for the materials they contained?

---

* Virginia Fellows was unable to complete this further study of Francis Bacon and his work. For those who would like to explore this topic further, Alfred Dodd's biography, *Francis Bacon's Personal Life-Story,* has a great deal of information.

Chapter Sixteen

A Final Sacrifice

The welfare of the people is the supreme law.

It was on March 7, 1617, that Francis Bacon carried the Great Seal of Britain for the first time, contained, as tradition dictated, in the embroidered pouch of the lord chancellor. Lady Alice Bacon was content, for her special position was only one step from the top (as the wife of a lord chancellor), and even Lord Francis was at last seeing himself as a success.

Francis now had a very large income (although not as much as he was spending), and he was now living in the beloved York House of his childhood. He was respected everywhere, even by those who most resented his success. Every imaginable difficulty had been met and honorably conquered, and Lord St. Alban and his lady were graciously returning the smiles that Fortuna was at last beaming upon them, secure in the knowledge that they were, to a large degree, deserved. The view from the top was magnificent after so many years in the vale. It must have seemed good to have a moment to bask in the sun. But the moment was all too short.

Just four years later, this man who had tried in every way to make all things right, this grandson of kings, Francis Tudor, was imprisoned in the Tower of London—the same old Tower where his grandmother and brother had lost their lives, where his father and mother had first been bold enough to love, where the young princess who was to be his mother had scratched with her ring on the window glass: "Nothing by me, ever proven can be." She had protected herself by her silence. Francis's silence was for the protection of someone else, someone whose reputation he valued more than his own.

The story of the "fall" of England's lord high chancellor is sad to read and sadder to tell.

Things had not gone well in Britain that winter of 1621. The weather had been atrocious. The river highway, the Thames, had been frozen over, halting trade and traffic, and the city was clogged with refuse and filth. Because of the inept policies of the government, soaring prices burdened everyone with debts they could not pay. It seemed that every citizen, high and low, was complaining that they had never had it so bad. Some believed that the very existence of the Commonwealth was in peril.

And yet, how much did the king care? Very little, it seemed. As long as money could be eked out for his continued extravagances at court, the endless complaints seemed to affect James not at all. As long as nothing interfered with the privileges allowed to his favorite, "Steenie"* (George Villiers, later duke of Buckingham), not much else mattered. Everyone was nervous about just how far it would go. James's first son, the promising Prince Henry, had a tragically early death, and his younger brother, Charles, was now Prince of Wales. Through friendship and

---

* The king used to refer to Villiers affectionately as "Steenie," an allusion to St. Stephen, who is described in Acts 6:15 as having the "face of an angel."

George Villiers, duke of Buckingham
by Peter Paul Rubens, 1625

flattery, Buckingham had the young prince pretty well in his power. Some even believed that the prince was the slave of the duke, not vice versa.

Historian J. R. Green writes: "The immorality of James's Court was hardly more despicable than the imbecility of his government.... After the death of [Robert] Cecil, all real control over affairs was withdrawn ... from the Council and entrusted to the worthless favorite [Buckingham]."[1]

Buckingham was wearing the nation's most prestigious honor around his neck, the gilded chain of the ancient Order of the Garter. The favor of the king gave him the confidence and airs of a privileged member of the royal family. The lowborn Villiers clan was now raised to the highest level and their demands were insatiable. If one had a project to achieve, then one need only to please the king by pleasing Buckingham, and this meant pleasing Buckingham's demanding old mother too.

The lack of respect for the king at last began to be so pronounced that even James took notice. Fracases and ill-tempered quarrels between formerly peaceful citizens burst out everywhere —symbols of the lawlessness that is a result of poor leadership. James fretted, but he refused to change his ways; perhaps he could not. As he saw his influence slipping, his only recourse was to demand more obedience to the royal prerogatives that he claimed as his right. He was king—that was enough. But it became clear that the intellectual and philosophical qualities he had claimed to possess upon his accession were nothing but a coat of veneer on a complex personality that was now falling apart under the influence of infatuations.

Bacon had quietly hoped that James would be an ally in his plan for the enlightenment of the nation, but it had not worked out that way. He was, no doubt, flattered by the idea, but his interests lay far more in drinking and hunting and in his favorites, first Somerset and then Buckingham. He certainly had been a disappointment in his failure to support the spiritual (and perhaps Rosicrucian) activities of his daughter and her husband, the Winter Queen and King of Bohemia.

As the king's subjects became increasingly disillusioned with their Scottish ruler, things became dangerous. They began calling him the Prince of Humbugs. One biographer attempted to compare him with Elizabeth: "With all Elizabeth's defects, she was royal to the core, steadfast in purpose, fearless and wise." As for James, "There was never a less kingly king."[2] His much vaunted learning and intelligence was, according to some, a kind of crooked wisdom, a kind of cunning and craftiness substituted for the royal qualities of wisdom and grace.

Green's *History of the English People* gives a most un-flattering picture of James. The reader will be spared its entirety, but it ends with: "The Court of Elizabeth had been as immoral as that of her successor, but its immorality had been shrouded by a veil of grace and chivalry. But no such veil hid the degrading grossness of the court of James. The King was suspected of vices compared with which drunkenness was almost a virtue."[3]

In spite of this degrading atmosphere, in neither cipher nor letter did Bacon criticize his king. By gentle and humble means, he had won his trust and respect. The last lines of sonnet 58 show the patience and forbearance he had taken with Elizabeth. It must have been equally hard with James.

> I am to wait, though waiting so be hell,
> Not blame your pleasure, be it ill or well.

His private diary, recorded in cipher, refrains from rebuking the king except for one comment on James's jealousy of his lord chancellor. (James knew that his own claim ranked second to that of Elizabeth's kin.)

> The danger is past long ere now, and nought but the jealousy of the King is to be feared, and that more in dread of effect on the hearts of the people, than any fear of the presentation of my claim, knowing as he doth, that all witnesses are dead and the required documents destroyed.[4]

It was not for him, a prince who had never been crowned, to complain about a legally crowned king. There was, however, a deep sense of meriting compensation that had come with the years of dedication:

> Yet in this work of my hands, I am heir-apparent to a much loftier seat, a scepter of power that must extend to posterity. Nor time nor death can take my second kingdom from me.[5]

The problem that climaxed in Bacon's disgrace had begun long before with the royal tradition of granting monopolies and "patents" to certain favored British subjects. Patents were the rights granted to specific persons to collect a percentage of revenue from various businesses and manufacturers.

Far from abolishing the custom of awarding such favors, James granted more of them to the privileged few, leaving the lower classes increasingly short of the means to earn their own support. The granting of these revenues was an inexpensive way for the Crown to repay favors and an effective way for King James to heap benefits on Buckingham and his family. The Villiers were into every jam pot, it was said.

Lord Francis wrote to Buckingham urging him to influence the king to cease the practice of monopolies. This, he pointed out, would gain credit for him as the generous act of a caring monarch. "Put off the envy of these things (which I think in themselves bear no great fruit), and rather take the thanks for ceasing them, than the note for maintaining them."[6]

It was good advice, but the king was not about to heed it. James was desperately short of money. There was no alternative other than to call for a Parliament and have extra subsidies* levied. Bacon knew that it was the ancient and royal way of providing the king with treasure, but he also knew that it could be disastrous. He ended his advice, as he always did: "But howsoever, let me know your mind, and your Lordship shall find I will go your way."[7] "Not my will but thine be done" was always his attitude toward the Crown, as we shall see.

It had been seven years since the last Parliament was called, and James did not wish to call one now. It meant giving the two houses opportunity to comment on state affairs, a circumstance

---

* subsidy: a sum of money formally granted by Parliament to the king and raised by special taxation.

he was hoping to avoid. But the need for money was pressing. If he was to support his beleaguered daughter, Queen Elizabeth of Bohemia, and her husband, Frederick, and if he and Steenie were to continue their lifestyle, he would have to persuade Parliament that he deserved additional income. It was not a project he looked forward to.

The mood around London was one of belligerence on the opening day of Parliament—discontent among the people, friction between the Lords and the Commons, and a general urge to see heads roll. James was not too blind to see the danger he was in, but he was crafty enough to know how to handle the situation. He would have to paint himself in glowing colors and find some scapegoats to take the blame.

James was prepared to play his role when he had himself carried into the chambers of Parliament (his arthritis had made him almost a cripple). Dodd writes that he made a "long rambling speech in which he stated their relative duties: he was to distribute justice and mercy and they, without meddling with his royal prerogative, were by petition to acquaint him with their distresses and to supply his pecuniary wants."[8] It was a gracious speech that impressed hearts and minds, as intended.

The Commons passed his money bills and soon took up the contentious issue of monopolies and patents. Everyone knew that the king had granted the patents but only on the advice of the "referees." So if there was blame to be cast, it was not on the king but on the advisers. The king should only be blamed, perhaps, for taking bad advice. Everyone also knew that the king's chief advisor was the lord chancellor—ergo, the lord chancellor was the one guilty of the misuse of monopolies.

The mood in the Commons had shifted. Where they had been critical of the king, they were now somewhat taken by his unaccustomed humility and the great love he obviously felt for

Sir Edward Coke
engraving from "Gallery of Portraits" (1833)
Edward Coke and Francis Bacon clashed on a number of occasions. At Francis's urging, the king removed Coke from his post in 1616 and "promoted" him to a less influential position. Coke had his revenge in 1621, redirecting the anger of the Commons over corruption in the royal court into a personal attack on Bacon. R. W. Church described him as "one of the most truculent and unscrupulous of English lawyers. He was a potent element in Bacon's ruin."

his people. But they wanted somebody's blood. The higher the person, the more satisfying would be the charge.

The field was open for Bacon's enemies. For Edward Coke, still bitter in his rivalry with Bacon, it was payback time. He was the leader of the reformers in the House of Commons and the ringleader of a group of secret conspirators, all who felt snubbed or mistreated in some way by Bacon or sought their own advancement at Bacon's expense. They would do their part to bring down this justest of judges under the guise of upholding the state. All this is confirmed by Dodd in his careful analysis of Dixon, Spedding and other early biographers.[9]

Two men were found who were willing to swear that they had given bribes to the lord chancellor while he was hearing their cases—one of £100 and the other of £400. The fact that these gifts had not changed the chancellor's decisions against the suitors was not mentioned. Neither was the fact that one of the accusers was an angry clerk who had been dismissed by Lord St. Alban for misconduct.

In those days, there was a difference between bribes and gifts, and the giving of gifts to government officials was not considered bribery. All costs of the courts of law were paid by fees of the litigants and no official (be it attorney general, the lord admiral or the secretary of state) was paid more than a nominal sum by the government. Everything else came from fees or "gifts" by those concerned. It was hoped, undoubtedly, that the bigger the gift, the more favorable would be the decision, but that was not an indispensable condition.

It was obviously a poor system for handling costs, but it had been done for centuries. It was the custom, and it could not be changed in an instant by those seeking reform. The members of the bench and bar in England had inherited the tradition and they were supported in this way. They did not receive grants from the government, only from litigants who gave generous fees in gratitude for the service received.

It was an impractical system and one that needed reform, as Bacon was well aware. The only real crime would be if a judge changed a decision in return for a fee. Of this neither Attorney General Bacon nor Lord Chancellor Bacon had ever been guilty. In fact, as Bacon said—and his servants backed him up on it—he did not even receive the gifts himself (with only one exception). They were made to his household steward. Bacon was seldom aware of the size of the gifts and it is known that he paid little attention to the finances of his office.

Money had never been important to Francis except that it was a nuisance that was essential for carrying out his projects. As we know from his essay "Of the True Greatness of Kingdoms and Estates," he considered it a monarch's duty to demonstrate opulence and generosity as an example of his country's good fortune.[10] Money is like "muck," he wrote; the more it was spread, the more things grew.[11] This judge was far more interested in carrying out the official duties of his office justly and honorably than in fussing over money.

The general public, understanding little of the near miraculous accomplishments of the king's new judge, had been incensed by the unjust granting of these patents that made prices high and rewarded the rich and burdened the poor. They were now willing to be persuaded that the fee system must be changed—not with orderly procedure but, as is usual with mass frenzy, by attacking whoever was at hand. A friend of Bacon's had tried to warn him of the mood that was beginning to grow dangerous. "Look around you," he advised. Lord Francis answered, "I fear not! I look above,"[12] and calmly went on with his business.

When Bacon found that charges were brought against him, he was concerned, but he knew the motives of his own heart and mind. He would investigate the charges and mount a vigorous defense. But he also knew where to look for the source of the trouble. "I woo nobody," he said to Buckingham. "I do but listen and I have doubt only of Sir Edward Coke, who I wish had some round *caveat* given him from the King; for your Lordship hath no great power with him, but I think a word from the King mates him."[13]

The seed of Bacon's downfall was planted the very moment James decided to put the Great Seal into Bacon's hand without so much as a "by your leave" from his precious Steenie. Although Lord Francis had managed to gain a certain amount of respect from Buckingham, he never did have much luck with Steenie's mother, Lady Compton.

From what we are told of her, the term "lady" was grossly inappropriate. Although she seems to have had a certain measure of vivacious physical attractiveness, she was shrewish and crafty. She was a commoner, a kitchen maid by one account, who had married well, improving her station. And she did bear three unusually good-looking sons, one of whom had the good fortune to catch the king's roving eye. Outliving several husbands, she found herself a widow with one asset, a son who was close to the king. She ruled her family as despotically as any queen ever had, and it was said by some that her influence over the king in national affairs was greater than that of James's own wife, Queen Anne.

Dixon gives a detailed report of how Buckingham and Lady Compton had tried to manipulate the old chancellor, Ellesmere, out of his office, not wishing to wait until he died. She saw a chance to sell her influence for the office for £30,000. She managed to dig up all kinds of false reports of scandal against the honorable old man, and it was said that he finally died of a broken heart due to the charges of Lady Compton.[14] Bacon's promotion to the chancellorship rested in her hands, or so she thought.

For once, however, James had ideas of his own. Without consulting Buckingham, Lady Compton or a single member of the Villiers clan, he had put the Great Seal into the hands of his own cousin, Francis Bacon. To make matters worse in Lady Compton's eyes, James had not asked for a single penny from

Bacon in return for the favor.

When Bacon was first named to his high office, he had set about immediately to make some changes that he had felt were needed. One was to speed up the process of justice. He had long deplored the endless dragging on of lawsuits that enriched the lawyers but impoverished the litigants. There were cases in which a decision had been delayed for years. He would look at each case seriously, but he promised:

> I will pronounce my decree within [a] few days after the hearing....Justice ought not to be delayed.... Because justice is a sacred thing, and the end for which I am called to this place, and therefore is my way to heaven. I shall, by the grace of God,... add the afternoon ... and some fortnight of the vacation to the terms, for clearing of the causes of the Court. Only the depth of the three long vacations I would reserve for the studies of arts and sciences to which I am most inclined.[15]

It was a bold promise but one which he made good. Thousands of chancery cases had been handed to him with the gift of the seal, some of ten or twenty years standing. By early summer he could proudly say:

> This day I have made even with the business of the kingdom for common justice. Not one cause unheard. The lawyers drawn dry of all the motions they were to make. Not one petition unheard. And this I think could not be said in our time before.[16]

Not one single judgment of Francis Bacon's was ever overturned. He was a blessing to the oppressed subjects of the Crown. To those who were losing fees because of his prompt decisions, he was "gall and wormwood."

According to Dodd, it was people like Lady Compton, Coke,

a man named Williams and others who set about to destroy Lord
Chancellor Bacon as deliberately as they had attacked Lord
Chancellor Ellesmere. John Williams, a cleric, was the dean of
Westminster at the time. He was a handsome, charming man,
only slightly older than Lady Compton's sons. He was "courting"
the lady, seeking her favor in obtaining Bacon's office should
Bacon be disgraced and removed. There was even talk that he
might become more than the lady's dear friend.

An added complication in the plot against Bacon seems to
have been that Buckingham wanted the handsome old York
House for his private residence, but that was now Bacon's house
as the home of the chancellor. It had been Sir Nicholas's home,
the home of Bacon's childhood, and he was in no way to be
persuaded to give it to a member of the Villiers clan without a
direct order from the king. James didn't dare to force the issue on
behalf of Steenie, but it was an extra thorn in his side.

Coke and the others had succeeded in turning things to their
advantage. What had begun in the Commons as seeking redress
for burdensome patents and monopolies had now evolved into a
campaign against Bacon. Now with bribery charges against the
lord chancellor, the House of Lords took over the matter.

When Lord Francis heard the accusations against him, he
was profoundly shocked, so much so that he became seriously ill
and took to his bed. He called his secretary to his bedside and
had him draw up a last will, leaving his "soul to God above," his
body "to be buried obscurely" and his name "to the next ages
and to foreign lands." But however discouraged he may have
been, the end was not yet to come; one final chapter of the drama
was yet to be outplayed.

There were, as to be expected, those who would accuse Bacon
of feigning illness in order to avoid facing the charges against

him. He wrote a letter to the House of Lords assuring them that this was not so. He hoped that they would think of him without prejudice until he had the opportunity to defend himself, to cross-examine the witnesses against him, and to call in his own witnesses to testify on his behalf.[17] Furthermore, he asked if they would they please examine the thousands of cases he had completed to see if they could find any fault with them. Once everything was brought out into the open, he had no doubt that he would be completely cleared. "I have clean hands and a clean heart.... My mind is in a calm," he had assured them.[18] "I have nothing to fear but fear."[19] Lord Bacon preceded by three hundred years the famous remark made by F.D.R.[20]

Of course an open discussion was exactly what the enemies of Lord Francis did not want. Everyone knew that he could clear himself if he took the stand in his own defense, and his accusers knew it better than anyone else. They could no more stand up under his penetrating cross-examination than murky shadows can withstand the light of day. The corruption of King James's court might be exposed if the honorable lord chancellor decided to reveal all he knew—the squandering of the treasury on personal gratification, the selling of public offices, the favoritism and nepotism that was running rampant. The mood of the people was for reform; someone would have to pay. James and Buckingham were growing nervous. Few, including themselves, would survive such a day in court unscathed.

By the end of April, the lord chancellor was charged with twenty-eight counts of bribery and corruption, all the accusers claiming that they had given gifts of money to him in return for favors received. Now it was his turn to stand up in court and refute the charges. But, incredibly and unexpectedly, he did not do so. What could have gone wrong?

In a letter to King James on April 21, Bacon offered to surrender the seal. He would not refute the charges. This was paramount to admitting that he was guilty as charged. Both the Lords and the House of Commons were stunned—this was the biggest bombshell of all. The greatest lawyer of the time refusing the right to defend himself? It could mean only one thing—the great Lord Francis was guilty of corruption. In a letter to the lords, he wrote: "I do plainly and ingenuously confess that I am guilty of corruption,... do renounce all defense, and put myself upon the grace and mercy of your Lordships."[21] The letter was written from Bacon's sickbed; it was thought that he would not live more than a few days longer.

Lord Chief Justice, James Ley, another of Bacon's enemies, handed out the judgment:

(1) a fine of £40,000;

(2) imprisonment in the Tower during the king's pleasure;

(3) barred from ever holding office again;

(4) banishment from Parliament and never to come within the verge of the court.

This last condition meant that Francis St. Alban was banished from an area of twelve miles around the royal court, that is, he was never to enter London again. It was a severe sentence, far beyond the normal judgment of such a matter as bribery.[22] The greater the man, the harder the fall.

He was not sent immediately to the Tower—not until Southampton (who had never forgiven Francis for his part in the Essex trial) complained to the House of Lords that he was not yet in the Tower. Buckingham explained that the king had delayed his incarceration because of Bacon's illness. Both he and James knew that Bacon did not deserve the punishment, but those who wanted revenge insisted he be sent up immediately. In spite of Buckingham's obvious efforts to prevent it, Bacon was sent to the same dread Tower where so many of his kin had been imprisoned.

We know that Lord St. Alban signed a paper confessing himself guilty of all charges against him. We know that he abandoned his own defense. But why?

It is clear from other writings that he never regarded himself to be guilty of any crime. The only crime he allowed himself was that of carelessness or neglect, of trying to carry out duties which were not his natural bent. We know that he himself was opposed to the very crimes of which he was charged. What happened at the last minute to cause "the justest Chancellor ... since Sir Nicholas Bacon's time"[23] to admit to crimes for which he did not believe himself to be guilty ?

Alfred Dodd and Hepworth Dixon are among those who have found evidence explaining the whole puzzling situation. When James had first succeeded to the Crown, Bacon had written to him in terms of sacrifice, sacrificing himself "to your Majesty's service." He was about to be sacrificed again.

When things had begun to look serious for Francis, Buckingham apparently paid a visit. Dodd believes that he was seeking information about Francis's intended defense.[24] We don't know what transpired between the two, but there is extant an indignant letter written by Lord Francis to Buckingham the next day:

> Your Lordship spoke of Purgatory. I am now in it, but my mind is in a calm; for my fortune is not my felicity.... But Job himself, or whoever was the justest judge, by such hunting for matters against him as hath been used against me, may for a time seem foul, specially in a time when greatness is the mark and accusation is the game.[25]

Buckingham must have replied to Bacon in person, for a few days later he received another letter from the lord chancellor saying, in indignation, the same thing:

> I perceive ... that some wretched detractor hath told you

that it were strange I should be in debt, for that I could not but have received an hundred thousand pounds [in] gifts since I had the Seal. [It] is an abominable falsehood!... I praise God for it, I never took a penny for any benefice or ecclesiastical living, I never took a penny for releasing anything I stopped at the seal, I never took a penny for commissions or things of that nature, I never shared with any servant for any second or inferior profit.[26]

Bacon was not guilty, and in this letter he was defending himself hotly. He was confident of his ability to clear himself. The lord chancellor had a plan and every hope of clearing his name. An audience with James, however, changed that. James not only requested but absolutely *commanded* him to abstain from defending himself for fear of exposing Buckingham.[27] He was little comforted by Francis's comment: "Those that will strike at your Chancellor, it is much to be feared will strike at your Crown. I wish that as I am the first, I may be the last of sacrifices."[28]

Dodd believes that Buckingham was responsible for Bacon being sent to the Tower.[29] We have the letter he sent to Buckingham indignantly demanding his release—not requesting it, but *demanding* it. Buckingham would have taken the letter to James.

Good my Lord,

Procure the warrant for my discharge this day. Death, I thank God, is so far from being unwelcome to me, as I have called for it (as Christian resolution would permit) any time in these two months. But to die ... in this disgraceful place is even the worst that could be; and when I am dead, he is gone that was always in one tenor, a true and perfect servant to his master, and one that was never author of any immoderate, no, nor unsafe, no (I will say it) nor unfortunate counsel; and one that no temptation could ever make other than a trusty, and honest, and thrice loving friend to your Lordship.

Your Lordship's true and loving friend, living and dying,

Fr. St. Alban[30]

This letter could not be more explicit concerning Francis's trust in his own innocence and his indignation that James has not yet released him from the judgments. One does not command kings (or a king's favorite), yet that is what Francis is doing—and James, amazingly, did what he was commanded to do. In three days time Lord St. Alban was out of prison and in the lavish house of the comptroller of the Prince of Wales. His fine was remitted by the Crown.

The title of chancellor was not taken from him; that was a title for life even though he was relieved from duty. The king was often heard thereafter to bemoan the absence of his old chancellor's advice. "O, had I my old Chancellor here, I would speedily have an end to the affair," he said more than once. His Majesty longed for his best counselor when the problems of kingship seemed unsolvable.

Nevertheless, Francis was still barred from court. He was not to appear within an area of twelve miles around it, and this included the better part of London. There was nothing he could do but to move to his country home at Gorhambury. When he rode out to the country, a retinue of many friends and well-wishers rode with him, showing their faith in his innocence. When Prince Charles observed this procession, he is said to have remarked: "This man scorns to go out like snuff."[31] It was true. John Chamberlain, in his nonstop correspondence with Carleton, had written:

It seems he doth either dissemble or not feel the ignominy that hangs over him, but carries himself as was his wont.[32]

And three months later:

He is gone this day, as I hear, to his own house at Gorham-bury, having (as should seem) no manner of feeling of his fall, but continuing as vain and idle in all his humours as when he was at highest.[33]

Bacon knew it would take time for the truth to prevail:

I keep the future ever in my plan, looking for my reward, not to my times or countrymen, but to a people very far off, and an age not like our own.[34]

In spite of this hope that in future ages his reputation and his "fall" would be cleared, even now, almost four hundred years later, there are writers who seem not to have grasped the truth of it or even the essence of his mission.

Chapter Seventeen

New Worlds

I have taken all knowledge to be my province.

Now freed from his duties and banished to Gorhambury, for the first time in years Bacon could spend his hours doing what he liked most—writing and publishing. A project was already under full sway, and by efficiently using his time and delegating to coworkers he could accomplish much. Although he had enemies aplenty, he also had devoted friends and colleagues who were only too happy to help with his grand scheme—Ben Jonson, his literary assistant; Thomas Meautys, one of his devoted secretaries; Sir John Constable, his brother-in-law (who had married Alice's sister); Thomas Bushell, a gentleman usher in Bacon's household; Bishop Lancelot Andrewes; Tobie Matthew, who retained Bacon's friendship in spite of having turned Catholic; and the most unconventional earl of Arundel. These and many others were now members of his inner and secret circle.

Among the projects that now filled his mind, Bacon's plans for an ideal commonwealth received top priority. He was not forgetting his vision of the "land far away and many years in the

Ben Jonson, Francis's literary assistant (left), and Thomas Howard, earl of Arundel (right)

future"; he wrote a description of this place and, typically, created an adventure story to make sure people would read about it. The designs for a more perfect nation had been in the back of his mind for as long as he could remember, and if they could not be brought to fruition in England, the only thing to do was to try the new land across the ocean.

The New Atlantis, Bacon's adventure story about an ideal society in a new land, was based on Plato's fable (if fable it was) of the ancient submerged continent. Plato, as well as Aristotle, knew that the world was round, not flat, and many scholars believe that he had a new land across the vast ocean in mind. Marco Polo, Roger Bacon, and many others knew the earth was in the shape of a globe. "Tierra! Tierra!" (Land! Land!)—the cry of Columbus's lookout when he spotted solid ground at last—still echoed in England seventy years later when Francis was born.

Some were concerned that the various enterprises to explore the New World were based on greed and despotism. It took the English, they said, to build colonies. This was a springboard for Bacon to use in launching his design for the Utopia that he envisioned across the sea. He had been planning it ever since Sir Francis Drake's return from his memorable voyage around the world. It is likely that Drake was, if not at that time, then certainly later, a member of Bacon's Masonic group. The winds of democracy were beginning to blow.

Three years after Drake's return, Sir Humphrey Gilbert sailed to Newfoundland and claimed the land for the British Crown. Francis and his associates formed the Newfoundland Colonization Company, and in 1610 they sent John Guy with a charter from the king that mentioned fishing, timber, sheep raising and other commercial ventures. Guy founded a settlement with forty-one colonists at Cupids in Conception Bay. Even today, although biographers seldom mention it, Sir Francis Bacon is honored in Newfoundland as a founder of the oldest British colony in Canada, and in 1910 a commemorative stamp was issued in his honor.

Certainly the ideal of democracy was not new in the world, but in the seventeenth century it was challenging the entrenched special privileges and injustices of oligarchical (and monarchial) systems which had held sway for far too long. It is not difficult to understand how legends of a golden land had fired the imagination of the young pragmatic idealist Francis Bacon, and now that he was involuntarily retired, he had time to continue the work he had begun years earlier on plans for settling the New World. In *The New Atlantis* he outlined his vision for an ideal commonwealth, a golden age that could be born in this new land.

The New Atlantis was not published until after Bacon's death, and his chaplain Rawley says that it was never finished. Even so, it has been called one of the most remarkable tales ever written and a model for writers who aim for a fine English style. Abraham Cowley wrote that Bacon, like Moses, led men from the wilderness of ignorance and

> Did on the very border stand
> O the bless'd promised land;

Newfoundland stamp honoring Francis Bacon
This stamp is one of a series issued by Newfoundland in 1910 to
commemorate the three hundredth anniversary of the establishment of
the first permanent settlement. The caption under Bacon's portrait
proclaims him as "the guiding spirit in colonization scheme."
Newfoundland became a province of Canada in 1949.

> And from the mountain top of his exalted wit,
> Saw it himself, and showed us it.[1]

Bacon had the dream, he had the vision, and he was involved
in more than one venture in the new land. We find that today few
know how vital a part Francis Bacon played not only in Newfoundland but in the founding of Jamestown. A careful search of
the archives of history reveals that Bacon drew up the papers for
the king's signature granting the charter for the Virginia
Company of London. The charter, notes author Peter Dawkins,
contained the beginnings of a new system of governance for the
colony—constitutionalism.[2] Bacon, along with the earls of
Pembroke, Montgomery and Southampton, was on the Virginia
Company's council and "had become directly involved with [its]
schemes to colonise North America."[3] At the time, "Virginia"
was the name given to a vast span of North America's coast,
extending even to parts of Canada.

The years of Bacon's retirement were tremendously productive, a torrent of books pouring from the press. One of the most important was his monumental work (published under his own name) *De Augmentis Scientiarum*. This was a translation into Latin of his *Advancement of Learning*, with many additions, including a description of his Bi-literal Cipher. Some scholars consider the book to be one of the most unusual documents the world has seen.

In addition, the curious treatise called *History of Winds* and another called *History of Life and Death* appeared during this period. The latter is an intriguing collection of observations on the durability of not only objects but also of people and animals—the lasting qualities of all created things. Why do certain forms last as long as they do? Why don't they last longer? What characteristics determine their longevity or the lack of it?

Another remarkable scientific work was *Sylva Sylvarum*, or *A Natural History in Ten Centuries*, a collection of observations, experiments, teachings and discussions on natural phenomena. It was arranged into ten chapters with one hundred items in each. Several smaller works also appeared at this time, including a history, a biography, and additional scientific treatises.

The major work of this period, the one the world will never forget, was the great collection of the dramatic poetry of "William Shakespeare" known as the First Folio—*Mr. William Shakespeare's Comedies, Histories, & Tragedies Published according to the True Original Copies*. The volume contained thirty-six plays, exactly half of which had never been published before. Of the previously unprinted plays, many were entered in the Stationers' Register on November 8, 1623, just in time for publication.

Will Shaksper had been dead seven years and scarcely anyone had noticed. Why did a monument to Will "Shakespeare"

Frontispiece from Bacon's *Sylva Sylvarum*
This work was published by Rawley in 1627, the year after Bacon's death. In this and other volumes cataloguing observations of scientific and natural phenomena, Bacon sought to lay the foundation for a new science, one that would allow man to understand the workings of God's creation and reclaim his dominion over them. His work laid a philosophical foundation for the scientific and industrial revolutions of the following centuries.

suddenly appear in Holy Trinity Church in Stratford? The bust was done by the sculptor Gheerart Janssen, whose shop was near the Globe Theatre in London, which has caused speculation that it was commissioned, not by the remaining "Shakspers" of Stratford, but by someone from the city. (Country villagers seldom, if ever, made it into London.)

There has been a bit of controversy about the lack of expression and personal characteristics of the face. The bust shows a face with a peculiarly bland, masklike appearance, graced by no expression or distinguishing features. Some have called it the face of "Anonymous." But the Shaksper family and friends, if they

The Shakespeare memorial in Stratford
This memorial to Shakespeare in Holy Trinity Church, Stratford, raises a number of questions. The face, like that of the famous Droeshout portrait of Shakespeare, has a curiously bland appearance. His paper is resting on a pillow (rather than a desk), a means to present something for display but not a practical arrangement for writing.

had commissioned the monument, would surely have approved of the likeness.[4]

It wasn't until fifty years after the event that any explanation of Shaksper's death was released. John Ward, a vicar of Stratford, reported that Ben Jonson, Bacon's secretary and collaborator, had been one of those who gathered at a tavern in Stratford, perhaps to celebrate Will's upcoming fifty-second birthday. "Shakespeare, Drayton, and Ben Jonson had a merry meeting, and it seems drank too hard, for Shakespeare died of a fever there contracted." A fever? The vicar also noted a reminder to himself to "peruse Shakespeare's plays, and be versed in them, that I may not be ignorant in that matter."[5]

Suspiciously, there had not been a single eulogy lamenting or even remembering the death of the Stratford actor. However Will

Shaksper may have died, he had been gone seven full years by the time the First Folio was published with its collection of plays. Many of the earlier plays had been added to, subtracted from or changed in some way.

The dedication in the Folio to William Herbert, earl of Pembroke, and his brother, Philip, earl of Montgomery, is flowery and flattering to excess. One suspects it to be almost satirical, especially when we realize the closeness between Bacon and the Herberts. They were nephews of Francis's cousin Philip Sidney and certainly knew whose book was being dedicated to them.

In the dedication it was claimed that two men who had been fellow actors in Shakespeare's company were the ones who had collected the thirty-six plays published in the Folio. They call them "trifles," just as Bacon most likely spoke of plays as "toys" or "trifles." These men, who gained literary fame because of their connection with the works of "Shakespeare" as coeditors, are John Heminge and Henry Condell. Both were members of the King's Men, for whom Shaksper also acted, and both had been shareholders in the Globe playhouse and the Blackfriars theater. Condell was not an original shareholder but acquired some shares later on. He retired from the stage in 1616 before the Folio was published, which raises suspicion that he was paid well for the use of his name by Bacon, Pembroke, Jonson and company—so well that he could afford the retirement.

Part of the Folio's "Epistle Dedicatorie" was apparently patterned on an ancient text, the dedication of Pliny the Elder's *Natural History* to Emperor Vespasian.[6] In it Pliny even speaks of his works as "my toys and fooleries."[7] How had the work of this classical Greek author found its way to the dedication of the First Folio? Many point to Ben Jonson, Bacon's assistant, who was a scholar and author in his own right. They conclude that he was the real editor, that he wrote the dedication and also supervised the folio's publication.[8]

We know too that Francis was always in search of cover text for his ciphers, and it is believed he suggested to Anthony that one could "pad out" the contents of books by borrowing prefaces and dedications from older works. Bacon was always padding out his works to make more cover text for his cipher. In the First Folio, *The Merry Wives of Windsor* has twelve hundred more lines than it had in 1602,[9] *Titus Andronicus* has a whole new scene, and *Henry V* is double the length of the 1600 edition.[10] Much padding had been done.

Who could have written these additions if the author had been dead for seven years? And where had the manuscripts been all this time? Scholars generally agree that the Shaksper family never held the manuscripts in their possession, and we know they were not mentioned in Shaksper's will. How does one account for the new plays? The mystery can never be solved by orthodox thinking.

In the Folio's opening letter to the reader, the editors deceptively assert that the plays published therein were written by the stage actor and collected by two of his fellow players for posterity. The editors are made to say that these plays were printed from the true and original manuscript, that they were "absolute in their numbers as he conceived them," and that they "scarce received from him a blot in his papers." And yet scholars often insist that these plays were made up from prompt books and that Shakespeare took little interest in what happened to his manuscripts. Someone has to be wrong.

The exact nature of the relationship between Ben Jonson and "Shakespeare" has been a source of endless conjecture. The confusion exists, obviously, in not knowing which "Shakespeare" old Ben is speaking of in a particular writing. Is it his employer and friend, Francis Bacon, whom he said he loved and honored "on this side of idolatry"? Or is it the actor Will Shaksper, whom

Ben ridiculed in *The Alchemist?* Attached to the Folio is a eulogy, an ode, written by Jonson. It begins:

> To the memory of my beloved,
> The Author
> MR. WILLIAM SHAKESPEARE:
> AND
> what he hath left us.

> *To draw no envy* (Shakespeare) *on thy name,*
> *Am I thus ample to thy Book, and Fame.*

In the ode, the name Shakespeare is unnecessarily written in a different style and enclosed in parentheses. Why? No one has an explanation except the Baconian detectives who see it as one of many deliberate and carefully executed clues to the mystery.

The ode contains lavish praises to the poet—he is the "Soul of the Age," "the wonder of our Stage," "thou Star of Poets." Stratfordians* accept these extravagant phrases as proof that Jonson was echoing the popular attitude toward "the Bard" at the time. Outside these deliberately manufactured eulogies in the Folio, however, there had been little or no praise for the supposed playwright—not a word about him when he died, no eulogies from his contemporaries in London or in Stratford. Jonson's ode also says

> *Thou art a monument, without a tomb,*
> *And art alive still, while thy Book doth live.*

Enigmatic? Not to one who knows the cipher story, particularly since there was a very visible physical monument back in the Stratford Holy Trinity Church. Will Shaksper was not without a tomb—it was Francis Bacon who had no tomb.

---

* Stratfordian: one who believes that William Shakespeare, the man from Stratford-on-Avon, was the true author of the works bearing his name.

Christopher Marlowe (1564–1593)
Marlowe's play *Doctor Faustus* was first published in 1604. A revised and greatly expanded version was published in 1616, twenty-three years after his death. The new material matched Marlowe's style exactly. Scholars have proposed a number of theories about this "post-mortem" activity, including that Marlowe faked his own death and went into hiding in 1593. But why would he publish new material under his own name if he was trying to hide? The cipher story reveals that it was Francis Bacon who was the author of the stage plays published under the name of Marlowe.

One cannot help but wonder why Shakespearean scholars are so ready to believe whatever is printed on a title page, as if they didn't know the exigencies of Elizabethan publishing. There seems also to be an odd kind of myopia in cases in which a work first appeared anonymously and only later had a name attached to it (like so many of the "Shakespeare" plays).

Names such as Laneham, Puttenham, Spenser, Greene, Marlowe, Shakespeare and Burton have been accepted without question, and yet a brief review of the quotation from *The Arte of English Poesie,* published in 1589, should be a reminder that all is not always what it seems: "I know very many notable Gentlemen in the Court that have written commendably, and suppressed it again, or else suffered it to be published without their own names to it."[11]

We can puzzle over this as much as we choose, but we have direct information in cipher of just what role this pair of actors, Heminge and Condell, played in the First Folio. In the Bi-literal Cipher that Mrs. Gallup found in the *Novum Organum* printed in 1620, we find Lord Francis discussing the dilemma of how to publish the plays which he had "put forth" in the name of Shakespeare now that his mask was dead:

> In our plays, just spoken of as being in the name of a man not living, there is still more of this secret history. By following our good friend's advice [Ben Jonson?], we have not lost that mask though our Shakespeare no longer liveth, since two others, fellows of our play actor,—who would, we doubt not, publish those plays,—would disguise our work as well. This will not, however, be done until a most auspicious time.
>
> Much work must be accomplished in a short time if many new plays should be added which doth now seem desirable, inasmuch as it suiteth us far better than prose or a lighter verse, while it giveth more satisfaction to our readers.[12]

At this point, the cipher explains, thirteen new plays have been written—five histories, five historical tragedies, and three comedies. And yet, Francis explains, some are not completely finished: "Coming lately into new honors and new duties we have, as may be supposed, written much less than formerly. All interior work, nevertheless, is completed, and made ready for incorporation into these diverse works."[13]

First he composes the secret interior, or enciphered, play; then the outer play, which is designed as the cover text and is created to use various identical lines in an entirely different content according to the principles of the Word Cipher. The titles of the interior plays ready for enciphering are given:

> *The Life of Elizabeth*
> *Anne Bullen* [Anne Boleyn]
> *Mary Queen of Scots*
> *The Life of Essex*
> *The White Rose of Britain*
> *The Life and Death of Edward III*
> *The Life of King Henry VII*
> *The Earl of Essex* [Bacon's late brother, Robert]
> *Earl of Leicester* [Bacon's true father]
> *The Life of Marlowe*
> *The Mouse Trap*
> *The Seven Wise Men of the West*
> *Solomon the Second*[14]

This is an intriguing list, and only two of them were deciphered by Dr. Owen—*The Tragedy of Mary Queen of Scots* and *The Tragical History of the Earl of Essex*.[15] The remainder, as far as we know, are still hiding under the cover-text pages glued to the Owen cipher wheel, waiting to be discovered by bright young eyes and alert minds.

One of the most intriguing features of the Folio is the portrait attached to it, that most familiar of literary faces known as the Droeshout portrait of Shakespeare. There are only two portraits of Shakespeare ever considered as possible authentic likenesses. One is the "anonymous" memorial bust in Holy Trinity Church. The other the equally "anonymous" engraving by Martin Droeshout in the Folio. Droeshout was only a boy of fifteen when Shaksper died in Stratford, and there is no evidence that they ever met. Why does the address "To the Reader" (by Jonson) claim that he tried to "outdo" nature when he probably had never seen the man he was depicting?

> This figure, that thou here seest put,
> It was for gentle Shakespeare cut;
> Wherein the graver had a strife
> With Nature, to out-do the life.
> O, could he but have drawn his wit
> As well in brass, as he hath hit
> His face, the print would then surpass
> All that was ever writ in brass.
> But since he cannot, Reader, look
> Not on his picture but his Book.

Friends of Bacon must be struck right off by the similarity of this verse to the sentence Hilliard wrote around the edge of his portrait of eighteen-year-old Francis: "O that I could have drawn a picture worthy of his mind."

Samuel Schoenbaum, a great Shakespearean scholar who, although orthodox, deserves credit for trying to be fair, describes the engraving in his *Shakespeare's Lives*:

> Even before being coarsened by touching up, the Droeshout engraving shows defects that are all too gross and that can be ascribed only to the artist's ineptitude. The same stiffness, the same hard line would appear in his later portraits of distinguished men.... In the Shakespeare engraving a huge head, placed against a starched ruff, surmounts an absurdly small tunic with over-sized shoulder-wings.... The mouth is too far to the right, the left eye lower and larger than the right, the hair on the two sides fails to balance.[16]

Schoenbaum speaks of the "vapid engraving" as a "Rorschach blot on which the biographer projects the Shakespearean image of his own conceit," the forehead being a "horrible hydrocephalus development," and so on.[17]

The Droeshout engraving of Shakespeare from the First Folio

The one biographer (orthodox, naturally) who seems to see the engraving as a work of art which truly depicts the character of the great poet-dramatist is A. L. Rowse:

> We all know quite well what Shakespeare looked like from the one authentic portrait of him, the engraved frontispiece [the title page] to the First Folio. The whole impression is dominated by that magnificent bald cranium, like another dome of St. Paul's—plenty of room there for the most lively (and living), the most universal brain among the Elizabethans. It is absolutely convincing. Then there are the arched eyebrows, the large fine eyes that we can see would

> GOOD FREND FOR IESVS SAKE FORBEARE,
> TO DIGC THE DVST ENCLOASED HEARE:
> BLESE BE Y MAN y SPARES HES STONES,
> AND CVRST BE HE Y MOVES MY BONES.

Inscription on Shakespeare's tomb
Is this the best that the Immortal Bard could do for his own epitaph? Or is someone having a jest with us?

easily be capable of a wide range of expression, full of intelligence. The nose is large and rather sensual, yet with sensibility indicated in the flare of the nostril—and we know that he had an acute sense of smell.[18]

Fortunately, most of the mainstreamers, even the most dedicated, do not agree with Rowse that this staring, lifeless mask could actually look like the real flesh-and-blood poet who wrote so many lines that the world will never forget. "It is the face of anonymous."

Author John Michell has pointed out that in a second printing of the Folio (in 1640 by a "John Benson") the address "To the Reader" has been edited. Where it previously said "This figure" it now said "This Shadowe." Michell concludes: "It looks as though someone is having a game with us."[19]

The entire First Folio—in spite of its innumerable seeming mistakes, misspellings, mispaginations and enigmatical meanings —is proven by the cipher to have been a production printed with amazing skill and care. Each letter, each number, each comma is in exactly the place that the author (who carefully supervised either in person or through his secretary, Ben Jonson) intended it to be. This amazing First Folio, which the orthodox consider to be a bungled, sloppy job of publication by two of Shaksper's fellow actors, is considered by Baconians to be a brilliantly executed example of craftsmanlike printing under the most

Gorhambury today
Francis Bacon's last years were spent at this country estate, the birthplace
of some of the key works of the English Renaissance.

difficult of circumstances. Every misprint, every seeming error
carries a fully calculated purpose and meaning.

It is small wonder that critics have puzzled over this volume
for so long. It was written to be puzzled over—written by a
brilliant man who knew exactly what he was doing and how best
to do it.

Chapter Eighteen

Into the Shadows

Old men go to death, and death comes to young men.

"Death is no such terrible enemy," wrote Francis Bacon in his essay "Of Death." "But, above all, believe it, the sweetest canticle is *Nunc dimittis,* when a man hath obtained worthy ends and expectations. Death hath this also, that it openeth the gate to good fame, and extinguisheth envy."[1]

The *Nunc Dimittis* is from the gospel of Luke. It begins, "Lord, now lettest thou thy servant depart in peace."[2] Permission to leave this life behind was Lord Francis's greatest longing now. Many years earlier when he wrote this essay, he observed that a man could die of boredom—"only upon a weariness to do the same thing so oft over and over."[3] Was this something to be faced in these last years? Who would he have been speaking of other than himself? It was only his writing that now kept his spirit alive.

Although he was mortally weary, he did not allow himself to fret over the sudden, bitter collapse of his affairs. Long ago he had taught himself to dwell wholly in the present. The past was only for learning. That excellent training stood him in good stead now: We must not dwell long on cares and worries. We must be creatures of today, not tomorrow, for tomorrow will have its turn and become today. But for the future, how could we bear the burden of the day?

Lord Francis's zeal for service did not slacken, but he was living in a human body and it was growing weary. By the end of January of 1626, he had passed his sixty-fifth birthday and was beginning to feel the strain of age and the stress of disgrace. He had tried to allay the pains by herbs and "physics" of various kinds, but they had not helped much. For some time it had been said of him that he looked older than his years. Decades of burdens, disappointments, frequent illnesses and sleepless nights had etched lines of fatigue on his noble face. Not even his wholesome state of mind and soul had been able to erase the telltale signs.

England was changing before his eyes, some of the change for the better perhaps but much of it disappointingly worse. Not many of his own generation were still living, that creative mix of Elizabethans—confident, self-assured British yeomen, shop-keepers, courtiers—who were all equally convinced that their little offshore islands had been particularly favored from above. Had not God arranged the storm that had driven back the Armada? The wholesome optimism of the Elizabethans was slipping into the nostalgia of memory now. Even James was gone, having died of "tertian ague" in March of 1625. And though he had sat on the throne which Francis had thought would one day be his, at least he had been a link to the Tudor clan. The Crown Prince Charles was not the king his brother Henry would have been. Lord Francis knew that, for he had spent hours tutoring them both.

Things would be different with Charles at the helm. Everybody agreed that it was now Buckingham who ruled. The young king was a mere puppet in his hands, weak and lacking in judgment. Bacon must have foreseen the inevitable end of his reign—the near collapse of monarchy brought about by the corruption and self-serving of the Stuart kings.

As soon as Charles succeeded his father, Bacon again petitioned for the remission of his sentence, which would have allowed him to return to office. Others had received full pardons, and he knew that James would have finally granted it to him. But Charles was stalling. "I hope I deserve not to be the only outcast"[4]—sad words from one of the most faithful servants of the kingdom. But the pardon did not come. Why not? Did Buckingham feel safer with Bacon out of the way? Was Charles jealous of him? Afraid of him? Suspicious of him? We don't know, and apparently Lord Francis didn't know either. Whatever the reason, he felt that his days of service to his country were drawing to a close.

Lady Alice made a trip to London to plead with Buckingham on her husband's behalf. She might have spared herself the trip, for it had not helped. She had enjoyed the preferment of the wife of the lord chancellor, precedence over all but the royal ladies at court, and she seems to have relinquished the privilege with poor grace.

From the biography of Alice Bacon by A. Chambers Bunten, one learns that little Alice Barnham had grown into a proud and dignified woman, not very pretty but having a certain pride of place which may have made her attractive in a somewhat haughty way. She dressed elegantly and drove about London in the finest of coaches. She was one of the leading ladies of Queen Anne's court. Her husband would not have objected; it was always his belief, as we know, that one's surroundings should reflect one's rank and standing—noblesse oblige. But Alice lacked the inner grace of her husband and she was humiliated by his fall.

Had she ever really loved him? It seems doubtful. He may have seemed like a tedious old man to her, if not at the time of their marriage, then later. He was closer to her father's age than to her own. The sonnets suggest that Lord Francis was well aware of her feeling toward him:

> My glass shall not persuade me I am old,
> So long as youth and thou are of one date,
> But when in thee Time's furrows I behold,
> Then look I death my days should expiate.
>
> *Sonnet 22*

> Love's not Time's fool, though rosy lips and cheeks
> Within his bending sickle's compass come;
> Love alters not with his brief hours and weeks,
> But bears it out even to the edge of doom.
>
> *Sonnet 116*

Whoever may have had a change of heart, it would not have been Francis. His love altered not when it "alteration finds."

> Tell me thou lov'st elsewhere; but in my sight,
> Dear heart, forbear to glance thine eye aside.
>
> *Sonnet 139*

> In loving thee thou know'st I am forsworn,
> But thou art twice forsworn, to me love swearing;
> In act thy bed-vow broke and new faith torn
> In vowing new hate after new love bearing.
>
> *Sonnet 152*

For some time, Lord Francis and his lady seem to have lived apart. In 1625 Francis had his will rewritten. The reason for this is not clear.

The first will had been drawn up in 1621 during the desperate illness at the time of his trial. "I bequeath my soul to God

Alice Barnham, wife of Francis Bacon

above.... My body to be buried obscurely. My name to the next ages and to foreign nations," he wrote. Lawyer that he was, he left instructions for the disposal of his estate with detailed provisions for Alice—funds for the "competent abilities to maintain the estate of a viscountess."

Four years later, there was a definite change. A terse and enigmatic codicil to the will revoked the earlier provisions for Alice completely: "Whatsoever I have given, granted, confirmed or appointed to my wife, in the former part of this my will, I do now, for just and great causes, utterly revoke and make void, and leave her to her right only."[5]

British law required certain benefits to a widow. Beyond this, Francis left nothing at all to Alice. What were the "just and great" causes? Was it that Lord Francis discovered some unwifely indiscretions on the part of his younger spouse?

Just eleven days after Sir Francis's death, Alice married the gentleman usher of their household, one Sir John Underhill. Lest we be guilty of judging Alice by circumstantial evidence, a look at sonnet 138 gives a further hint:

When my love swears that she is made of truth,
I do believe her though I know she lies,
That she may think me some untutored youth,
Unlearnèd in the world's false subtleties.
Thus vainly thinking that she thinks me young,
Although she knows my days are past the best,
Simply I credit her false-speaking tongue;
On both sides thus is simple truth suppressed.
But wherefore says she not she is unjust?
And wherefore say not I that I am old?
O, love's best habit is in seeming trust,
And age in love loves not to have years told.
   Therefore I lie with her, and she with me,
   And in our faults by lies we flattered be.

And in sonnet 139 there is this:

O, call not me to justify the wrong
That thy unkindness lays upon my heart;
Wound me not with thine eye but with thy tongue;
Use power with power and slay me not by art.
Tell me thou lov'st elsewhere; but in my sight,
Dear heart, forbear to glance thine eye aside;
What need'st thou wound with cunning when thy might
Is more than my o'erpressed defense can bide?
Let me excuse thee; ah, my love well knows
Her pretty looks have been mine enemies,
And therefore from my face she turns my foes,
That they elsewhere might dart their injuries.
   Yet do not so; but since I am near slain,
   Kill me outright with looks and rid my pain.

It was now the following year after Francis had rewritten his will. The weather at the beginning of April in 1626 was anything but springlike. The air was damp and chilly, and there was still snow upon the ground. Nevertheless, Viscount St. Alban, accompanied by a Scotch physician by the name of Dr. Witherborne, left London for a carriage drive toward the better air of Highgate, on the verge of the city. Suddenly, reports Aubrey in his *Brief Lives* (not written until many years later), "it came to my Lord's thoughts, why flesh might not be preserved in snow, as in salt." Impetuously, Bacon is supposed to have told his driver to halt in front of a farmer's cottage, where he climbed down, knocked on the door and asked to buy a chicken. When the housewife had killed and dressed the bird, Bacon proceeded to pack it with snow, an experiment with refrigeration. During the process, he became suddenly gripped by a chill and was too ill to return home. He ordered his driver to take him to the house of his friend Lord Arundel at nearby Highgate.[6]

Arundel was away serving time in the Tower for having allowed his son to secretly marry a girl of royal blood, and Bacon would have known that he was not at home. Arundel's faithful steward welcomed the unexpected guest and hastily prepared a bed for him. Unfortunately, the bed had not been slept in for a year and it was damp. The combination of chill and the damp bed was fatal—Lord Francis developed a fever "whereby the defluxion of rheum" caused his death. It was Easter morning, April 9, 1626. We hear no more of Dr. Witherborne.

From this bed Francis had dictated a letter to his absent host: "I was likely to have had the fortune of Caius Plinius the elder, who lost his life by trying an experiment about the burning of the Mount Vesuvius." He went on to explain that he intended an experiment or two "touching the conservation and induration [strengthening] of bodies."[7] But Bacon had already talked about the effects of cold on preserving the body in his *Sylva Sylvarum*. Why was he trying another experiment on a chilly spring drive with a physician accompanying him?

Aubrey's is one of the few reports we have of the death of Francis Bacon. Rawley's report agrees that Bacon died of an excess of "rheum." Another report talks of his death from "a long languishing illness."[8] Still another has Bacon dying in a different house.[9] How could there be such confusion?

Lord Francis St. Alban was both famous and infamous. Ever since his impeachment, there where those who revered him, as Ben Jonson did, "this side of idolatry," and there were those who detested him. Either way, he was not a man to be ignored—and yet his death went almost unrecorded and the records we do have are inconsistent. What about his funeral service? Who walked in the procession? Of all these things we know very little. There appears to be "something rotten in the state of Denmark," to use a phrase from *Hamlet*.

In his will, Francis Bacon had requested burial at St. Michael's, near St. Albans. He gave as his reason, "there was my mother buried,... and it is the only Christian church within the walls of old Verulam."[10] It was the church founded on the memory of the heroic Saint Alban. Francis requested that he be buried in the same church as Lady Anne Bacon, the one woman in his life who had never abandoned him. Such was his choice of a final resting place.

But is he buried at St. Michael's? No one has been able to locate his coffin. In the early part of the twentieth century, the then earl of Verulam told the prestigious Baconian Mrs. Henry Pott that he had checked the burials in the crypt when his father was buried. There was no casket for Sir Francis Bacon.[11]

It has been thought in the past that he may have been buried under the statue erected to him by his devoted servant Sir Thomas

Meautys (at Meauty's expense) in the chancel at St. Michael's. Oddly enough, the original wording of the monument had been obliterated—intentionally or by accident?[12] Jean Overton Fuller points out that the inscription reads "here sits" rather than the usual "here lies," that recent excavation shows no tomb there, and that the present Verulam family insists that he was never buried there.[13] The relevant page from the burial register is likewise missing. She finds it impossible to locate any reference to his funeral.[14]

Arundel House, where Bacon is said to have breathed his last breath, stood on Highgate Hill just outside London. Once owned by the Catholic Queen Mary's comptroller, it was thought to have been used during Elizabeth's reign as a hiding place for Catholic recusants.[15] It was from here that Lady Arabella Stuart escaped when she was suspected of having designs on the Stuart Crown.

An architect by the name of Owen was known to install "anything and everything in the way of sliding panels, double floors, trap doors, and innocent-looking cupboards, the backs of which, by removing pegs, swung back into recesses, slanting tunnels, handy ropes dropping fugitives down into cellars and subterranean passages a mile or more in length."[16] He was, in other words, an escape specialist. A writer in *Baconiana* believes that this man was commissioned to provide Arundel House with some or all of these devices. One of his favorite tricks was to build a long, narrow place of concealment at the back of the enormous curtained bedsteads[17] favored at the time. Perhaps the damp bed into which Bacon was put to overcome his chill had such a hiding place. It may have had one of those subterranean passages leading to Sir Julius Caesar's house, not far away. Sir Julius was a nephew by marriage.

Some accounts place Bacon in his last moments with Sir Julius, either dying in his arms at Arundel House or in Sir Julius's home.[18] The oddly named Sir Julius Caesar was married to a granddaughter of Sir Nicholas Bacon, and Lord Francis, her "uncle," had given her away at the wedding. Aubrey again said that the lord chancellor, "in his necessity," had received £100 from Sir Julius.[19] Most intriguing of all, it was reported that Caesar "possessed the secret of longevity," whatever that may have meant.[20] All this suggests that together they may have been delving into some of the secret laws of spiritual freedom that had always intrigued Lord Francis.

What are we to make of this confusion concerning the disappearance of so famous a man?[21]

It was a major tenet of the Rosicrucians that instead of being buried in tombs with identification on the headstones, they would be "buried obscurely" so that their good deeds might be recorded in heaven rather than on earth. Bacon had expressed the desire in his first will that his "body be buried obscurely" and his name be "left to future ages." Some would go further than this.

Rosicrucians speak of a "philosophic death," a dying to the world rather than a physical death. The individual who so "died" would retire to a contemplative life in a secret location or carry on his work incognito. A number of investigators believe that Francis Bacon did just that. He feigned death and left his beloved England in disguise to continue life in a land across the Channel that was more friendly to him than his own.

In 1671, a prefix to Rawley's *Resuscitatio,* written by Charles Molloy, says that Bacon,

> with a head filled up to the brim, as well with sorrow as with wisdom, and covered and adorned with gray hair, made a holy and humble retreat into the cool shades of rest, where he remained triumphant above fate and fortune, till heaven was pleased to summon him to a more triumphant rest.[22]

It is particularly interesting to learn that a Thomas Meautys was planning to travel abroad at the exact time of Bacon's supposed death. Was this the Thomas Meautys who was Bacon's personal secretary? Or was it the secretary's second cousin of the same name? At this point we are left without answers since researchers disagree on the man's identity. But if Bacon was to succeed in a scheme to leave England secretly, he would of course have needed the aid of a few devoted friends and allies.[23]

Two centuries after these events, Dr. Owen (who discovered the Word Cipher) and Dr. Prescott (an ardent Baconian) found a cipher passage giving an account of Bacon's disappearance. It was in the 1638 edition of *The Countess of Pembroke's Arcadia*.

The frontispiece of this edition was clearly marked with an emblem picture. In it a boar, Bacon's crest, is suspended between a bear, the crest of the Dudley family (representing Robert Dudley, Lord Leicester, his real father) and a lion, the crest of Elizabeth (his mother). An intriguing detail is that the boar has the quills of a porcupine, which is the animal that signifies Sir Philip Sidney, *Arcadia's* author. Is the boar-porcupine creature telling us that Francis (or his cipher) is taking cover in Sidney's book? Or even that Bacon is masquerading as Philip Sidney?[24]

One can imagine the excitement of the two doctors when they deciphered the code and realized that they had found an account of Lord Bacon's escape from England in 1626. Unfortunately, we do not have a copy of Prescott's work, and we have only Mrs. Prescott's report that it was found. Here is her account of the decipherment:

> Fearing for my life lest King Charles should kill me, I feigned death, being put to sleep with opium. I was sewn in a sheet and taken to St. Michael's Church where I was found seventeen long hours later by Sir Thomas Meautys who brought me back to life by the injection of nightshade into my rectum. I escaped from England dressed as the

serving maid of Lady Delaware.[25]

This Lady Delaware would have been the daughter of Sir Francis Knollys (a relative of Francis's) and wife to Thomas West, Baron de la Warr, who was a close friend of Bacon's and a fellow member of the Virginia Company. Some believe that Bacon attended his own funeral, perhaps disguised as a serving woman, before exiting this stage of his life.

Mrs. Prescott, remembering Bacon's statement that he left a book in every known language, believed that he also "spoke" through emblem books and that pictures were a universal language. She relates how Dr. Owen obtained a Spanish emblem book from a bookshop in London and was rewarded by finding in it two amazing pictures. One shows a table on which there lie four dice giving an anagram for F. Bac. or, arranged a different way, the numbers 1623 (the date of the First Folio). The other emblem shows a figure dressed in the garb of a serving woman, but the face, amazing though it may be, looks much like Francis Bacon—beard and all.[26] The words "Soy hic and hac and hoc" are printed under it. "Soy" in Spanish means "I am." The "hic, hac, hoc" is taken from a little joke on Latin grammar in *The Merry Wives of Windsor:*

> *William:* Articles are borrowed of the pronoun, and be
>   thus declined: "Singulariter, nominativo, hic, haec,
>   hoc."
> *Evans:* "Nominativo, hig, hag, hog." Pray you, mark:
>   "genitivo, hujus." Well, what is your accusative case?
> *William:* "Accusativo, hinc."
> *Evans:* I pray you, have your remembrance, child:
>   "accusativo, hung, hang, hog."
> *Mistress Quickly:* "Hang-hog" is Latin for bacon, I
>   warrant you.
>
> *act IV, sc. 1*

This would have been hilarious wordplay to the audiences of Bacon's time, who would remember their struggles with Latin declensions from their school days. One can easily understand why Dr. Owen was elated with his find.

This cipher from *Arcadia* is the last discovered of Bacon's ciphers. From here on, all that we have concerning Lord Francis is conjectural or is the result of detective work. There are many hints to an active and rewarding life spent incognito. Was he one of the mysterious writers whose mystic works and treatises on occultism and spiritual alchemy continually flowed from the presses of Holland, Germany and Europe? Did he go to the Winter King and Queen of Bohemia, whose aims were so close to his? Did he spend time in Paris? The city was the love of his youth, and his lifelong love of mystical activities would have drawn him there many times. Did he take a trip to America? Mrs. Prescott is among those who are sure that he did. [27]

There is certainly more, *Plus Ultra*,* to be revealed about Lord Francis. Mystery surrounded his death, just as it had surrounded his birth.

---

* *Plus Ultra* is a Latin motto meaning "More Beyond."

Memorial to Francis Bacon in St. Michael's church, St. Albans
"Thus leaning on my elbow I begin..."

About Those Ciphers

by the Editors of Summit University Press

In the sixteenth and seventeenth centuries, the highest of high tech was cipher writing. As in today's world, governments had to be able to receive reports and send instructions to their agents in foreign lands safely and without the risk of interception. Some of the greatest minds of the time devoted themselves to devising codes that would accomplish the task. Among them was Francis Bacon.

Francis wrote briefly about ciphers in his 1605 *Advancement of Learning*:

> For ciphers, they are commonly in letters or alphabets, but may be in words. The kinds of ciphers (besides the simple ciphers, with changes, and intermixtures of nulls and non-significants) are many, according to the nature or rule of the infolding, wheel-ciphers, key-ciphers, doubles, &c. But the virtues of them, whereby they are to be preferred, are three; that they be not laborious to write and read; that they be impossible to decipher; and, in some cases, that they be without suspicion.[1]

Francis had been using the Bi-literal Cipher for over twenty-five years at the time *Advancement* was published. In the late 1800s Elizabeth Gallup found the earliest examples of this cipher in *The Shepherd's Calendar,* a book of poems published anonymously in 1579 and attributed to Edmund Spenser after his death. In all those twenty-five years of Francis embedding coded messages in various published works, no one had discovered the cipher. Clearly it met one of Francis's criteria, that the document containing the coded writing should be without suspicion of the existence of the hidden message.

It would not have been safe for the secrets hidden in the ciphers to be revealed in 1605, when *The Advancement of Learning* was published. But eighteen years later, in 1623, circumstances had changed. The cipher had still not been discovered, but many of the people involved in the secret history had died and Francis's succession to the throne was no longer an issue. It seems that he felt safe in giving some further clues.

In 1623 two events took place. Francis translated *The Advancement of Learning* into Latin so that it could be read by people all over Europe, and he took the opportunity to significantly expand it—"a translation, but enlarged almost to a new work."[2] In this new version, *De Augmentis Scientiarum,* he gave complete instructions for the operation of the Bi-literal Cipher. It was in 1623 that the plays of Shakespeare were published in the First Folio, providing additional material to be decoded.

Mrs. Gallup Discovers and Decodes the Bi-literal Cipher

In the introduction to the book of her discoveries, Elizabeth Gallup describes how she found the Bi-literal Cipher in the works of Francis Bacon:

> This Bi-literal Cipher is found in the Italic letters that
> appear in such unusual and unexplained prodigality in the

original editions of Bacon's works. Students of these old editions have been impressed with the extraordinary number of words and passages, often non-important, printed in italics, where no known rule of construction would require their use. There has been no reasonable explanation of this until now it is found that they were so used for the purposes of this Cipher. These letters are seen to be in two forms—two fonts of type—with marked differences. In the Capitals these are easily discerned, but the distinguishing features in the small letters, from age of the books, blots and poor printing, have been more difficult to classify, and close examination and study have been required to separate and sketch out the variations, and educate the eye to distinguish them....

I became convinced that the very full explanation found in *De Augmentis,* of the bi-literal method of cipher writing, was something more than a mere treatise on the subject. I applied the rules given to the peculiarly Italicized words and "letters in two forms," as they appear in the photographic Fac-simile of the original 1623, Folio edition, of the Shakespeare plays.... Original editions of Bacon's known works were then procured, as well as those of other authors named in these, and claimed by Bacon as his own....

From the disclosures found in all these, it is evident that Bacon expected this Bi-literal Cipher would be the first to be discovered, and that it would lead to the discovery of his principal, or Word-Cipher, which it fully explains, and to which is intrusted the larger subjects he desired to have preserved. This order has been reversed, in fact, and the earlier discovery of the Word-Cipher, by Dr. Owen, becomes a more remarkable achievement, being entirely evolved without the aids which Bacon had prepared in this [the Bi-literal Cipher], for its elucidation.[3]

Bacon Reveals the Cipher Workings

The following is a description of the Bi-literal Cipher from an English translation of *De Augmentis*, with the illustrations from the original Latin edition. After an introduction to ciphers similar to the one in the *Advancement*, the text continues:[4]

We will annex another invention, which, in truth, we devised in our youth, when we were at Paris*: and is a thing that yet seemeth to us not worthy to be lost. It containeth the highest degree of cipher, which is to signify *omnia per omnia*,[†] yet so as the writing infolding, may bear a quintuple proportion to the writing infolded; no other condition or restriction whatsoever is required. It shall be performed thus: First let all the letters of the alphabet, by transposition, be resolved into two letters only; for the transposition of two letters by five placings will be sufficient for 32.[‡] Differences, much more for 24. which is the number of the alphabet. The example of such an alphabet is on this wise.

---

* Francis was in Paris from 1576 to 1579 (see chapter 6) when he accompanied Sir Amyas Paulet, the newly appointed ambassador, to France. One of the members of the accompanying party was Thomas Phelippes, the English master of intelligence ciphers. Phelippes had been a student at Trinity College in the years that Francis was there, and the two remained close during the following years. It is also likely that in Paris Francis met Blaise de Vigenere, the pioneering French cryptographer. Vigenere was associated with the *Pleiade*, the French literary society. He published his textbook on ciphers, *Traicte de Chiffres*, in 1585.

[†] Latin, lit. "everything by means of everything": a reference to the fact that any cipher message may be hidden within any outer message.

[‡] Five positions, each of which has two possible options, gives a total of $2^5 = 32$ different possibilities, which is sufficient for the letters of the alphabet. (At that time, the alphabet had 24 letters, the modern *i* and *j* using the same letter, and *u* and *v* using the same letter.) This coding system is similar in principle to binary coding that is used in modern computing systems, which generally use eight positions (eight bits), giving $2^8 = 256$ different possibilities. The most common encoding system is known as ASCII. The 256 different codes are sufficient for upper and lower case letters of the alphabet, numbers, punctuation, accented characters and other symbols. Some protocols for communication between computers have used seven bits, enough for 128 different characters. Languages such as Japanese and Chinese are encoded using sixteen-bit codes, which give $2^{16} = 65,536$ possible characters.

$$\mathcal{A}_{aaaaa}.\quad \mathcal{B}_{aaaab}.\quad \mathcal{C}_{aaaba}.\quad \mathcal{D}_{aaabb}.\quad \mathcal{E}_{aabaa}.\quad \mathcal{F}_{aabab}.$$

$$\mathcal{G}_{aabba}.\quad \mathcal{H}_{aabbb}.\quad \mathcal{I}_{abaaa}.\quad \mathcal{K}_{abaab}.\quad \mathcal{L}_{ababa}.\quad \mathcal{M}_{ababb}.$$

$$\mathcal{N}_{abbaa}.\quad \mathcal{O}_{abbab}.\quad \mathcal{P}_{abbba}.\quad \mathcal{Q}_{abbbb}.\quad \mathcal{R}_{baaaa}.\quad \mathcal{S}_{baaab}.$$

$$\mathcal{T}_{baaba}.\quad \mathcal{V}_{baabb}.\quad \mathcal{W}_{babaa}.\quad \mathcal{X}_{babab}.\quad \mathcal{Y}_{babba}.\quad \mathcal{Z}_{babbb}$$

An example of a bi-literary alphabet
Each letter of the alphabet is signified by a five-letter group made up of a unique combination of the letters *a* and *b*. The dots separate the different 5-letter groups.

Neither is it a small matter these cypher-characters have, and may perform: For by this art a way is opened, whereby a man may express and signify the intentions of his mind, at any distance of place, by objects which may be presented to the eye, and accommodated to the ear: provided those objects be capable of a twofold difference only; as by bells, by trumpets, by lights and torches, by the report of muskets, and any instruments of like nature.* But to pursue our enterprise, when you address your self to write, resolve your inward-infolded letter into this Bi-literary alphabet. Say the interior letter be

Fuge.

Example of Solution.

$$\mathcal{F}_{abab}.\quad \mathcal{V}_{baabb}.\quad \mathcal{G}_{aabba}.\quad \mathcal{E}_{aabaa}.$$

Together with this, you must have ready at hand a *Biformed Alphabet,* which may represent all the letters of the common alphabet,

---

* This binary encoding system, invented by Francis Bacon, is the principle that was used by Samuel Morse in his code for telegraphy. Morse code is usually described as using dots and dashes. These could be transmitted as long and short sounds (using radio waves), electrical signals (telegraph), flashes of light (still used by navies for ship-to-ship communication) and other similar methods.

as well capital letters as the smaller characters, in a double form, as may fit every mans occasion.

An example of a bi-formed alphabet.

An example of a bi-formed alphabet
Each letter of the alphabet may be written or printed in one of two styles, shown here as "a" and "b." The differences are very obvious in the capitals and some of the lowercase letters. In a few cases, the variants are more difficult to distinguish, such as the lowercase *a* and *m*. In order to make the principle more obvious, the differences between the two alphabets are exaggerated in this example. A practical application would have two alphabets that were more closely matched in order not to arouse the suspicions of a casual reader.

Now to the interior letter, which is biliterate, you shall fit a biformed exterior letter, which shall answer the other, letter for letter, and afterwards set it down. Let the exterior example be,

Manere te volo, donec venero.

An example of accommodation.

a a b a b . b a a b b . a a b b a . a a . b a u

Manere te volo donec venero

Short sample of the Bi-literal Cipher

The lower line shows the exterior text which is used to conceal the interior, coded message. Each letter of the exterior text is compared with the two letter forms in the chart of the bi-formed alphabet. For example, the M in this text matches the "a" style M in the bi-formed alphabet. Therefore "a" is written above that letter. The next letter in the exterior text matches the "a" style (more rounded) a in the bi-formed alphabet, so "a" is written above it, and so on for each letter of the exterior text. The "a"s and "b"s are then divided into groups of five. (These divisions are indicated by the dots between the groups in the above example.) Each group of five decodes to a single letter using the bi-literary alphabet. For example, the first group of five is "aabab," which corresponds to F.

We have annexed likewise a more ample example of the cipher of writing *omnia per omnia*: an interior letter, which to express, we have made choice of a Spartan letter sent once in a Scytale or round cyphered staff.

All is lost. Mindarus is killed. The soldiers want food. We can neither get hence nor stay longer here.

*Perdita Res. Mindarus cecidit Milites esu-
riunt. Neque hinc nos extricare, neque
hic diutius manere possumus.*

An exterior letter, taken out of the first epistle of Cicero, wherein a Spartan letter is involved [encoded].

*Ego omni officio, ac potius pietate erga te;
caeteris satisfacio omnibus: Mihi ipse nun-
quàm satisfacio Tanta est enim magni-
tudo tuorum erga me meritorum, vt quoni-
am tu, nisi perfectâre, de me non conquiês-
ti; ego, quia non idem in tuâ causâ efficio,
vitam mihi esse acerbam putem. In causâ haec sunt. Ammonius Regis Legatus
apertè pecuniâ nos oppugnat. Res agitur,
per eosdem creditores per quos, cùm tu ade-
ras, agebatur. Regis causâ si qui sunt,
qui velint, qui parati sunt omnes ad Pompe-
ium rem deferri volunt. Senatus Reli-
gionis calumniam, non religione, sed ma-
leuolentiâ, et illius Regiae Largitionis
inuidia comprobat &c.*

Example of coded message using Bi-literal Cipher
The opening *E* is "a" style, the following *g* is "b" style, the two following
o's are "b" style, and the following *m* is "a" style. The first five letters thus
decode to "abbba," the sequence for *P*, the first character of the Spartan
letter shown on the previous page. The remaining text may be decoded in
the same way to give the complete text of the Spartan letter on the
previous page: *Perditae res. Mindarus cecidit,* etc.

Bacon Reveals the Word Cipher

As Gallup deciphered the messages hidden in the Bi-literal Cipher, she found instructions for other codes that the works also contained. (It seems that Francis openly published the instructions for only the Bi-literal Cipher. For once this was discovered, it would provide the key to unlock all the others.) Gallup deciphered the following text from Bacon's *Novum Organum:*

> We have sometime found our other inventions of some worth, in our work, and we have spent occasional idle minutes making such masks serve instead of the two ciphers so much used [the Bi-Literal Cipher and the Word Cipher], for of so many good methods of speaking to the readers of our works, we must quite naturally have a preference, and we own that the Word-Cipher seemeth to us superior to all others we have invented. We have, however, devised six [ciphers] which we have used in a few of our books. These are the Bi-literal; Word; Capital Letter; Time, or as more oft called Clock; Symbol; and Anagrammatic....
>
> Next the great cipher spoken of so frequently [the Word Cipher]—termed the most important invention, since 'tis of far greater scope—shall here be again explained. More rules and instructions are necessary than were needed in any of the others, but in the first work, only such as will be readily seen need be sought. These now follow:
>
> Keys are used to point out the portions to be used in this work. These keys are words employed in a natural and common way, but are marked by capitals, the parentheses, or by frequent and unnecessary iteration; yet all these [key words] are given in the other ciphers, also making the decipherer's part less difficult.*

---

* In his deciphered passages, Bacon gives examples of key words, including Friendship, Fortune, Honour, Strife, Fortitude, Truth and Art. See Gallup's *Bi-literal Cypher*. These examples are taken from part II, pages 170–71.

Next sort carefully all the matter thus obtained and place it in boxes and drawers for timely use. There will, with a little observation, be discerned words which are repeatedly used in the same connection. These must be noted specially since they form our series of combining or joining words, which like the marks the builder putteth on the prepared blocks of stone showing the place of each in the finished building, point out with unmistakable distinctness its relation to all other parts....

As while writing these interior works, these keys and joining words did deter the advancement [i.e., made their writing more difficult], it shall work a contrary effect on this part of the design, and the part of our ready decipherer is made easy for his hand; but his sight shall accordingly need to be as the sight of the keen-eyed eagle, if he would hunt this out, losing nothing.[5]

The text then continues with further explanation of the operation of the cipher, giving the example of the words used to distinguish the story of Bacon's love for Marguerite. These words that act like a flag or marker include

... such familiar and common terms as the mind and every faculty or power, memory, reason, and so forth, also the heart with its affections—as we term the emotions or passions slightly understood—the spirit and soul. These accompanying a key-word show that this portion belongs to the part of my history I have mentioned in this way....

Of my devices nothing excels that of the employment of words in common use to direct our decipherer. Tables should contain all such, because no man's memory can long retain such a number of words.[6]

The text then gives further instructions for the use of the Word Cipher and explains that the instructions have been given in a number of different outer works so that if one set is not found, this will not impede the process of deciphering.

How does the Word Cipher work in practice? Dr. Owen provides an explanation of his work at the beginning of the second volume of *Sir Francis Bacon's Cipher Story*. A number of other accounts have also been written by those who studied Owen's decipherings and learned to work the cipher themselves. The following account, written by P. J. Sherman, was published in *Baconiana,* volume IV, number 14, 1896. It is printed here in its entirety because of the insight it provides into the operation of the cipher and the assistance it would give to anyone seeking to personally experiment with it. The reader will note some material overlaps portions discussed by Gallup.

DR. OWEN'S CIPHER

The following are extracts from a long article lately published in the Detroit *Tribune*, and written by an eye-witness and experimenter upon Dr. Owen's Cipher System. Since the particulars here reprinted coincide with other reports contributed by several independent witnesses, and since the description is considered to be the most lucid and satisfactory which has yet appeared, we consider it only just to draw attention to it. An article on the subject specially written for this Magazine by another eye-witness and decipherer has, unfortunately, been delayed, and cannot reach us in time for publication in April. We hope to insert it in the June number [of *Baconiana*]:—

THE MYSTERY OF THE BACON CIPHER.—
DR. O. W. OWEN'S DISCOVERY INVESTIGATED.

"And now that the entrance to the secret has been found out,
     The world will wonder how it could miss it so long."— BACON

What is a cipher?

It is an internal story, told by external words, letters, marks or hieroglyphics.

"Sir Francis Bacon's Cipher Story, as Discovered by Dr. Orville W. Owen," is deciphered by words, and is one of the most remarkable literary productions of the world. So astounding, indeed, is it that it is not strange that those who have had neither desire nor opportunity to investigate the matter thoughtfully, should have condemned it offhand. Yet, secret modes of communication have been in use from earliest times, Ciphers are used by governments for sending secret dispatches, and in times of war especially, have proven of incalculable value. It is, in fact, if the reader will stop and consider, the most natural and yet the safest manner in which these histories could have been concealed, and thus transmitted to coming generations.

The Bacon cipher, as discovered by Dr. Owen, consists, I find, of a series of (1) guide words. Around these guide words are clustered (2) key words, and these key words again have (3) concordant words, both single and double. The (4) sentences containing the guides, key words, and concordants are (5) collected together, by (6) system, when it is found that the new story unrolls itself with hardly a hitch. Nothing needs to be added or taken therefrom. It is all necessary to the complete narrative.

However, the most satisfying knowledge is that obtained by working out the results one's self, and, having conquered the cipher and made actual applications of it, I will endeavour to relate how it is done, in as concise and comprehensive a manner as possible. But first let us look a little into what this discovery signifies.

What the Cipher Reveals.

The cipher reveals the fact that all the works of William Shakespeare, Robert Greene, George Peel, Christopher Marlowe's stage plays, the "Fairy Queen," "Shepherd's Calendar"; and all the works of Edmund Spenser; the "Anatomy of Melancholy" of Burton; Bacon's "History of Henry VII," the "Natural History," the "Interpretation of Nature," the "Great Instauration," the "Advancement of Learning," the "De Augmentis," "Essays," and all his other works were actually written by Sir Francis Bacon only, he using the other names as masks to conceal his own identity.

*   *   *   *   *   *

How to Work the Cipher.

The first time I talked with Dr. Owen concerning the cipher he gave me a few rapid instructions regarding the "wheel," and then placed in my hands the first published volume which was worked out by the cipher, telling me to read carefully the "Letter to the Decipherer," after which I might come to the office and make application of the directions therein given, which suggestion I acted upon as before stated. Upon page 3 [of the first volume of *Sir Francis Bacon's Cipher Story*] I found the following:—

> "Take your knife and cut all our books asunder,
> And set the leaves on a great firm wheel
> Which rolls and rolls, and turning the
> Fickle rolling wheel, throw your eyes
> Upon FORTUNE, that goddess blind, that stands upon
> A spherical stone, that turning and incessant rolls
> In restless variation.
> Mark her the prime mover:
> She is our first guide."

This advice has been literally acted upon. An immense wheel has been constructed, consisting of two reels, on which is rolled a great stretch of cloth, 1,000 feet long and over two feet wide. The arrangement is so simple that by turning the reel in one direction for a time the entire 1,000 feet of canvas come under the eye, and by reversing the motion all passes back again in the other direction. Upon this stretch of cloth are pasted the printed pages of all the works of all the supposed authors above mentioned. A more simple or convenient arrangement for examining a great number of pages in a short time could not be devised.

THE KEY WORDS.

The "Letter to the Decipherer" now goes on to add to "the first great guide"—Fortune—four others, Nature, Honour, Reputation, and Pan, the god of nature. The next act of Dr. Owen after pasting all the works upon the wheel was to carefully scan them, every word, and with coloured pencils to mark these guide words every time they occurred, which of itself was no small task, the first four words being repeated 10,641 times by actual count.

Let it now be borne in mind that these five words are not keys to the hidden stories, but guides whereby to find the key words. And around every guide clusters these keys. They are repeated over and over, so plainly and definitely that the earnest seeker cannot fail to find them. The next thing done is to pencil around every sentence containing the guide word being used, thus enclosing the keys as well, and these sentences are now read from the wheel to an operator, who typewrites them upon sheets of paper. At the head of every page thus written is placed the key word, or words, of the sentences, thus avoiding all confusion when the papers come to be sorted.

I find to be absolutely true the instructions given in the "Letter to the Decipherer" on page 8 of the first volume:—

> "And, sir, though far and wide the secret thread
> Of these rules seem scattered,
> This distribution ceases if you
> To one place carry all the words of your cue.
> Then may you see the great flood
> Or confluence of materials carries along with it
> The key of every story for the instruction
> Of the decipherer."

The sorting of the papers means placing in piles by themselves all pages containing the same key words, thus bringing to one place all the words of the cue, or all that relates to the story to be deciphered from these especial sentences or paragraphs:—

> "And sifting it as faithful secretaries and clerks
> In the courts of kings, set to work with diligence and
> Judgment, and sort into different boxes, connaturals,
> Concerning matter of state, and when he has
> Attentively sorted it, from the beginning to the end,
> And united and collected the dispersed and distributed
> Matter, which is mingled up and down in combination,
> It will be easy to make a translation of it."

CONCORDANT WORDS.

Dr. Owen worked and delved for nearly eight years before he discovered how to decipher the hidden stories. But for me, under his instructions, the task was a comparatively easy one. It is also a fascinating, though complicated one, for I soon found that not by key words alone could the stories be deciphered, but that about the keys again cluster concordant words, designed to help the searcher on his way, and leading him on and on into almost illimitable mazes of connecting sentences, which, though collected from perhaps scores of places in half-a-dozen different works, "Scattered wider than the sky or earth," still, by this rule, bringing out hidden histories and astounding revelations.

I will give an example of these concordant words. Let us suppose that the key words are "love" and "king." We must not look for "love" and "king" only, by which to be guided, but for all synonymous words. For "love's" synonyms we find "devotion," "adore," "adoration," etc. For "king" we follow such words relating to royalty as "majesty," "highness," "kingdom," "court," etc. As long as sentences containing a repetition of these words are found the student may safely continue to walk along the outlined path, gathering the story as he goes. If, however, a paragraph contains the keys, and yet refuses to "make sense," turn it how you may—in fact, seems superfluous—it should be put aside for the time being, and by-and-bye a gap will be found into which it fits with astonishing exactness.

WHEN THERE ARE COMPLICATIONS.

Occasionally there comes a disconnection in the story. Something is missing; it does not read smoothly. In taking the matter from the wheel a passage has been overlooked, or in sorting the papers one has been placed in the wrong box.

Now comes a hunt. A whole day has been given to the finding of a single line or paragraph. But it is there somewhere, and simply must be found. Then is the time when, as Dr. Owen expresses it, "my hair stands up on end," and the brain fairly reels with the immensity of complications which might arise from one small oversight.

Sometimes passages intrude themselves which do not contain the key being used, and which actually have no bearing on the story in progress. Simply leave these over, reserving them for future use. They belong to some other story, and will fall into place in good time. Nothing will be lost. Again a sentence reads in a vague or unnatural manner. In this case the decipherer is plainly instructed to transpose it, when the true meaning is revealed at once:—

"Therefore let your own discretion be your tutor,
And suit the action to the word, and the word to the action,
With this especial observance that you match
Conjugates, parallels and relatives by placing
Instances which are related, one to another,
By themselves; and all concordances

> Which have a correspondence and analogy
> With each other should be commingled with the connaturals."

The above is from *Hamlet, Novum Organum, Aphorisms*, and *Advancement of Learning*. For the first time it is brought together in the "Letter to the Decipherer," on page 8. This is a good example of the way the sentences are scattered. On page 21 are also found these lines:—

> "Some of the story
> Has more feet than the verses would bear,
> And you must exercise your own judgment;
> And give it smoothness when it lamely halts."

Proper Names

Reference is made to compound words, and the question is asked: "What mean you, sir, by compound words?" And the answer is given:—

> "No one can be so dull as to believe
> That we would set the whole name of any man
> Open among the subject matter.
> That certainly would be childish in the highest degree.
> On the contrary, though, the names are set
> So frequent, you must understand the device,
> (And our device, I think, will outstrip all praise)
> Before you can discover how we overcome the difficulty
> We use the simple and safe plan of consort.
> The similarity of word with word
> Contributes to save the whole from discovery.
> However, we will show you how, for the speedy
> And perfect attaining of names, to fit the words.
> And if you know how one is obtained,
> You know how all are coupled.
> So please take our on-hers, and we'll strive
> To let you under-stand the method that you must employ
> In unravelling and unlocking the double words."

I quote an example of a name hidden on page 142 of the 1623 edition of Shakespeare. It is a part of *Love's Labour Lost*, where the company of counterfeit actors play before the queen. Read the passage of wit between them and the spectators, see how one of the auditors compounded the name of one of the actors:—

"'Therefore, as he is an asse, let him go;
And so adieu, sweet Jude. Nay, why dost thou stay?'
'For the latter end of his name.'
'For the asse to the Jude; give it him, Jud-as away.' "

PARALLEL SENTENCES.

Here may be given an illustration of parallel sentences taken from seemingly widely different sources, yet mingling like the fragrance of the very flowers described:—

"O'er-embellished with knaps and flowers of all kinds
Cut in pure gold, pomegarnets, lavender, mint, savory,
Marjoram, marigold, gillivors, maidenheads, carnations,
Lilies (the flower-d-luce being one), columbines, pinks,
Honeysuckles, roses, sweet satirium, poppies, wild thyme,
Bean flowers, daisies, anemones, tulips, hyacinth-orientals,
Perrywinkles, bullices and virgin branches of the almond, etc."

This description of flowers and trees covers nearly all of page 39 of the "Letter to the Decipherer." Anyone who will look upon page 292, act IV, scene 4, *Winter's Tale*, and the "Essay on Gardens," by Bacon, will at once see where all the flowers mentioned were taken from. In other words, the parallels, concordances and similar matter.

FINDING THE COMMENCEMENT OF A HIDDEN STORY.

"How does the decipherer know where a story begins?"

This is as plain as anything can be. Having collected the material for the story, by means of the guides and keys, I find that somewhere among the passages the eye is startled with words like these: "Begin here," "We will commence here," "We will now commence," etc. Could anything be more definite? A good example of this is found in Shakespeare's *Life and Death of King John*, act I, scene 1:—

"My Dear Sir:
"Thus leaning on my elbow I begin the letter," etc.

The question of knowing what the next story will be, when one is completed, seems an important one, but I find that Bacon has inserted the title of the one to follow, very plainly, at or near the close of each story. At the close of the "Letter to the Decipherer," he tells in plain

English, "The next letter is the author's 'Epistle Dedicatory.' " At the close of the "Epistle" I find:—

> "The next letter that followeth is the 'Description
> Of the Queen, the General Curse, and the Story of Our Life,'
> Which, the instant you begin, will bring forth secret
> And original narratives woven into a continuous history."

PICKING OUT THE KEYS.

Following this naturally comes the question, "How find the keys for stories?" These, too, are at the close of each story, being one or more words of significance, strong enough to attract attention. As soon as the passages containing the key or keys are collected, and the student begins work, it is almost startling to discover the numerous keys that cluster around the one or two that lead, and concordant words sometimes almost countless.

       *   *   *   *   *   *

"We have enclosed our name without regard to safety, in the different texts," says Bacon in his letter to the decipherer, "in such capital letters that, as the prophet saith, 'He that runneth by may read.' And if you have digested a sufficient number of our books no doubt the first point you found was our name." This astonishing statement is literally true. Any one who will search the 1623 edition of Shakespeare, and the other works mentioned, will find Bacon's name appearing frequently, and in capital letters, as in Shakespeare's *Henry IV*, "I have a gammon of BACON," or in Peele's "Old Wife's Tale," "My grandmother was a gammon of BACON." And yet Bacon often warns the decipherer concerning the danger attendant upon its discovery. He says:—

> "For my good lord, in this secret way
> We enfold a dangerous chronicle, and by starts
> Unclasp a secret book to your quick conceiving,
> And read you matter deep and dangerous."
> "Swear never to publish that we conceal under the names
> Of others our own, till we are dead."

Notwithstanding the intricacy of the cipher, Bacon alludes to the ease with which it may be worked if the rules are strictly followed. "You will not fail, if to the work you give time enough," he says, "for it is translated so easy it is almost mechanical." This is my experience, for the key-words to the hidden stories are

"Interspersed in sufficient quantities to allow
The correspondence to be revealed so clearly
That any purblind eye may find them out.
They are so clear, so shining, so naked, and so evident,
That they will, in the full course of their glory,
Glimmer through a blind man's eye."

Bacon does not assert that every man can plunge into the labyrinth and find his way safely out again unscathed. He even tells the would-be decipherer:—

"Yet you may not be
Capable of detecting the ciphers. Many a man
Promises to himself more than he can perform,
And it is impossible to discover the subtlety of the work
Unless he that works loves it."

As to Chance.

"Does every story continue through all of the words used?" was the question I asked. The answer was, "Yes, and no." That is, if the facts of the story or history were not complete until the whole number of books had been written, portions of it were concealed in all. But the narration of some events came to an end prior to the publication of Bacon's later works. Consequently it would be useless to search for more after all had been given. For example, if a person is dead his history is ended, and the world cannot consistently expect any more from him.

Upon page 28 the decipherer says to Bacon concerning the deciphered stories:—

"But may they not say it is chance that doth this?"

The answer is:—

"We thought of that; and if any man conceive
That it is done without system or common
Center, let him proceed to form a history,
And neglect the guides. He cannot go through with it
To its completion, for if a man runs the wrong way,

> The more active and swift he is, the further will
> He go astray; for the lame man that takes the right road
> Outstrips the runner that takes the wrong."

And so the cipher stories are worked out:—

> "As many arrows loosed several ways come to one mark;
> As many winding ways meet in one town;
> As many fresh streams meet in one salt sea;
> As many straight lines close in a dial's center,
> Then so may a thousand ciphers, once afoot,
> And in one purpose be all well borne."

*   *   *   *   *   *

The ridiculous idea that the cipher stories are emanations from Dr. Owen's own brain is not abroad in the land as much as it was a year ago. Too many conclusive proofs abound, one of the most convincing being the fact that the fifth volume of the Cipher series, containing the continuation of "Sir Francis Bacon's Life at the Court of France," has been deciphered entirely by Dr. Owen's assistants, he having had nothing whatever to do with it, and yet it continues as smoothly as could be desired.

To me the continued patience and perseverance of Dr. Owen in this work is almost as wonderful as the discovery of the cipher.

"This work need not stop if I should stop," said the doctor. "If I should die to-night, my assistants could go right on with the decipherings. If one of them should die, or for any other reason leave the work, I should have some one else learn it. Thus it would continue right on."

The learning and applying of the Baconian cipher has thoroughly convinced me of its genuineness. The rules governing it are positive, though flexible. The stories told are connected and concise, for the period in which they were written, and cannot be twisted into other than the designed conclusion. While no two decipherers might tell the story in exactly the same way, still there would be no conflict of facts. It is a true cipher.

P. J. SHERMAN.

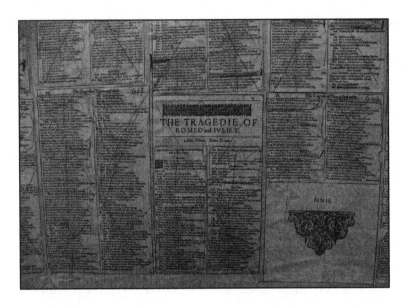

Pages from the cipher wheel
These pages show notations in colored pencil made by Owen and his assistants as they worked on the cipher. (These pages include marks in red, yellow, purple, blue, magenta and black.) As passages and whole pages were examined for cipher text, they appear to have been marked to indicate progress and avoid duplication of effort.

Further Testimony on the Word Cipher

It is perhaps not surprising that Orville Owen's announcement of the word cipher was controversial. Its revelations literally rewrote the history of the Elizabethan era. Furthermore, Dr. Owen gave no detailed description of his methods in the first volume of his work. Many critics called him a fraud. A very few sought to weigh the evidence for themselves. One who did was a Mr. J. B. Millett of Boston, who visited Dr. Owen's workshop in Detroit in February of 1893.

The following is excerpted from the account of his experiments with the cipher:

To test the accuracy of the method, the key-word relating to the "Story of the Spanish Armada" (afterwards published by Dr. Owen*) was given to the writer [Mr. Millett], who was shown how to proceed. With pencil in hand he copied about one hundred lines from various parts of the wheel, following the key-words, and then put these disconnected sentences and parts of sentences together in such a way as to make an intelligible statement without adding a word. Having finished, he was about to read aloud the result, when Dr. Owen stopped him, and taking from a drawer a type-written manuscript (the existence of which the writer did not know), read it also aloud. The two copies corresponded almost exactly, and the differences proved to be slight errors in copying on the part of the writer. Other shorter tests were made, and the writer soon after left, reserving his opinion "until he had time to think it over," and had found opportunity to investigate independently as to whether some new law of rhetoric were not involved. The thing was, at all events, extremely puzzling; and, if a fraud, there were at least six persons living up to an ingenious and elaborate lie and committed to this attitude for some time to come....

Vol. 1 made it plain that one of two things was true: either Dr. Owen invented the matter contained in that book, and then proceeded to hunt for scattered sentences all through the Folio, Bacon's acknowledged works, Spenser, Peele, Green, and Marlowe, laboriously fitting these sentences together so as to make continuous sense (which sense must also conform to the plot of the book he was inventing), or else he had invented a method which enabled him in some mechanical way to find these sentences and put them together....

Notwithstanding the fact that Dr. Owen's results are in some degrees astounding and unconformable with history, there still remains no other escape from the above conclusions....

On the writer's third visit to Detroit (December, 1895), he was at once admitted to the workshop, and spent considerable hours there before Dr. Owen made his appearance. During that time he was permitted to see anything that he asked to see, all questions that he asked were answered freely, and explanations made. He satisfied himself from the testimony of the clerks, and the members of the publishing

* Millett's visit was after the first volume of Owen's work had been published in 1893. The cipher play *The Story of the Spanish Armada* commenced in volume II and concluded in volume III, which were both published the following year.

firm, as well as from the testimony of individuals in Detroit personally known to him (and familiar with Dr. Owen's movements) that for many months Dr. Owen had nothing whatever to do with the deciphering, which was going on in his office, but that this work was actually done by two and sometimes three of his assistants, one of whom had been with him from the beginning, and two others who had been taught later. From all this it follows that Dr. Owen's method is capable of being readily explained to others, and it does not require that they should be familiar, as Dr. Owen is, with Shakespeare's plays or Bacon's acknowledged works.

A part of the work upon which Dr. Owen's assistants were engaged at the time of the writer's last visit was the deciphering of the translation of the Iliad from the "wheel." The writer has always been, from his university days, familiar with Homer, both in the original and translation, and it required but a few moments to find out that Dr. Owen's assistants were none of them in the least conversant with the Iliad. Upon examining a large pile containing about 2,000 sheets of large foolscap covered with extracts made from various works above mentioned, the writer became satisfied, much to his surprise, that these notes contained many passages from the Iliad, some obscure and not to be recognized by any one unfamiliar with the Iliad from beginning to end, unless that person had some guide like a key-word to go by....

It will be remembered that the "Omnia per Omnia" cipher invented by Francis Bacon [the Bi-literal Cipher] was made up entirely of the use of two letters—"a" and "b." It was a very laborious task to write a long letter by this method, because five letters were used to indicate one letter of the alphabet.* Dr. Owen's cipher, depending entirely upon key-words, or concordants and key-words growing out of them, is such a method, as can be readily conceived, Francis Bacon would naturally have invented as a sequel to the "Omnia per Omnia." It grows out of it.

The practicability of this method has been very thoroughly illustrated by the work of several amateurs in Detroit, who, in response to a prize offered by a Detroit newspaper, wrote a series of five stories in which was concealed a sixth, and this sixth story was to be found by the

---

* Another disadvantage of the Bi-literal Cipher is that when the type is reset using a single font in later printings, the cipher text is lost. With the Word Cipher, although the deciphering is made more difficult (since the seemingly random capitalization or italicizing that has been used to highlight key words may be "corrected" by later editors), the cipher text itself will not be lost.

use of Dr. Owen's method. It was required of a successful competitor to write out the sixth story without any assistance, and a number were able to do so, thus demonstrating that without altering the sense, without changing the construction, or without hampering himself in any way apparent to the reader, the author of these five stories was able to conceal in them a sixth, readily deciphered after the method was known, but entirely different in construction and meaning. In this particular case the sixth, or hidden story, was a poem of some length.[7]

Ignatius Donnelly's Cipher

The third cipher that this book has drawn from is the one discovered by Ignatius Donnelly and described in his two volumes of *The Great Cryptogram* (1888). Francis Bacon left no instructions regarding this cipher (or at least none have been found so far), and we have only Donnelly's explanations of its operation.

He explains that it is a cipher of words and that the words are selected from the text according to certain complex arithmetic principles. Donnelly gives an example of the principle in the following paragraph, which is an outer text containing a cipher message:

> For there can be no doubt whatever, that if it be examined closely, there is reason to believe that a cunningly adjusted and concealed cipher story, and one not of alphabetical signs, but of words, may be found hidden, not only in books, but letters of those ages, of which the very intricate key is lost. It may be revealed by some laborious student in the future, but for the present age all the great stories told therein, in cryptogram, are hopelessly buried.

The hidden message within this text is revealed by extracting every fifth word.

> No; it is a cipher of words, not letters, which is revealed in The Great Cryptogram.

Donnelly's method is similar in that it extracts words from the text according to numerical calculations to reveal a hidden message. However, his arithmetical formulas are much more complex than simply taking every fifth word. He describes a complex process of deriving them from "root-numbers," which are then modified by other numbers to give a numeric sequence by which words may be picked out from the text.

Other researchers have not been able to duplicate Donnelly's work, perhaps because of the complexity of the system or because Donnelly did not fully explain it. For now, it remains one of the many mysteries surrounding Francis Bacon and his works.

Beyond the Cipher Story

There are other ciphers that people claim to have discovered in the works of Shakespeare and his contemporaries. Some are derived from the initial letters of lines or phrases, some are interpretations of symbols in frontispieces and title pages, and some are substitution ciphers or anagrams. These ciphers, however, do not reveal a narrative but simply glyphs, hints at the hidden story of Francis Bacon.

All the other ciphers are not without their critics. Some seem unwilling to accept a story that differs from the orthodox view of history. Some think that those who pursue these ciphers are finding what they want to find, that the First Folio has become a kind of inkblot test into which people will read what they already believe to be there.

One thing seems clear, however—whatever shortcomings or errors there may have been in their methods, those who devoted years of their lives to the quest to uncover the ciphers were sincere in their desire to find the untold story of Francis Bacon. And isn't it the story that is really paramount?

He was free from malice....

He was no revenger of injuries; which if he had minded, he had both opportunity and place high enough to have done it....

He was no defamer of any man to his prince....

I have been induced to think that if there were a beam of knowledge derived from God upon any man in these modern times, it were upon him.

William Rawley
Preface to *Sylva Sylvarum*

INDEX OF PRINCIPAL PLAYERS

King Henry VIII   Henry Tudor. Father of Elizabeth.

King Edward VI   Edward Tudor. Son and successor to Henry VIII. Half-brother of Elizabeth.

Queen Mary   Mary Tudor. Daughter of Henry VIII and Catherine of Aragon. Half-sister of Elizabeth. Successor to Edward VI. Popularly known as "Bloody Mary."

Queen Elizabeth I   Elizabeth Tudor. Daughter of Henry VIII and Anne Boleyn. Successor to Queen Mary. The "Virgin Queen." Gloriana. Mother of Francis and Essex.

Lord Leicester   Robert Dudley. Queen Elizabeth's "Robin." Former husband of Amy Robsart. Lover and secret husband of the Queen. Father of Francis and Essex.

Francis Bacon   Prince Francis Tudor. Secret son of Queen Elizabeth and Leicester. Attorney General, Lord Chancellor. Baron Verulam, Viscount St Alban.

Nicholas Bacon   Lord Keeper of the Seal. Father to Anthony. Foster father to Francis.

Anne Bacon	Daughter of Sir Anthony Cooke. Wife of Sir Nicholas. Mother to Anthony. Foster mother to Francis.
Anthony Bacon	Birth son of Nicholas and Anne Bacon. Loyal friend and foster brother of Francis.
Lord Essex	Robert Devereux. Second son of Elizabeth and Leicester. Prince Robert Tudor. Real brother of Francis. Another "Robin."
Lord Burghley	William Cecil. Secretary of State to Queen Elizabeth. Husband of Mildred Cooke. Brother-in-law of Anne Bacon. Father of Robert Cecil.
Robert Cecil	Earl of Salisbury. Son of William and Mildred Cecil. Life-long enemy of Francis Bacon. "The Sly Fox."
King James I	James Stuart. James VI of Scotland. James I of England. Successor to Elizabeth. Son of Mary, Queen of Scots. Usurper of Francis's rightful throne.
Lord Buckingham	George Villiers. Duke of Buckingham. King James's favorite, "Steenie."
Edward Coke	Attorney General. Chief Justice of the Common Pleas. Chief Justice of the King's Bench. Rival and enemy of Francis Bacon.

CHRONOLOGY

1533	Sep 7	Birth of Elizabeth Tudor
1557		Elizabeth secretly marries Robert Dudley in the Tower of London
1558		Birth of Anthony Bacon
	Nov 17	Elizabeth succeeds to the throne
1560	Sep 8	Death of Amy Robsart, Dudley's wife
	Sep 12	Second marriage of Elizabeth and Dudley, in the house of the Lord Pembroke
1561	Jan 22	Birth of Francis Bacon
1564		Robert Dudley is created the Earl of Leicester
1566	Nov 10	Birth of Robert Devereux, Francis's younger brother
1572	Nov	Supernova appears in the constellation Cassiopeia
1573	April	Anthony and Francis enter Trinity College, Cambridge
1575	July 9–27	Entertainment of queen at Kenilworth, believed to be the inspiration for *A Midsummer Night's Dream*
1576	June 27	Anthony and Francis admitted to Gray's Inn
	Sep	Francis finds out about his royal birth

	Sep 25	Francis arrives in France with Sir Amyas Paulet, Elizabeth's ambassador to the French court
1579	Feb 20	Death of Sir Nicholas Bacon
	Mar 20	Francis arrives back in England
	Apr	Anthony and Francis take up residence at Gray's Inn
	Dec	Anthony leaves for France
1581	Jan 16	Francis sits in parliament for the first time
1582		Francis admitted as a barrister at Gray's Inn
1588		Defeat of the Spanish Armada
	Sep 4	Death of Lord Leicester
1592	Feb 4	Anthony returns from Europe
1594		First quarto editions of Shakespeare plays appear, anonymously
1596	June-July	Triumph of Essex at Cadiz
1597		First edition of *Essays* published
1598	Aug 4	Lord Burghley dies. Robert Cecil (his son) takes on his position as secretary of state
1599	March 27	Essex leaves to subdue rebellion in Ireland
		Globe Theatre built; first recorded performance: *Julius Caesar*, Sep 21
	Sep 28	Essex returns from Ireland, placed under house arrest by the queen
1601	Feb 8	Essex's failed coup
	Feb 25	Essex beheaded at Tower Green
	April 29	Death of Anthony Bacon
1603	March 24	Death of Elizabeth, James succeeds to the throne
	July 23	Francis knighted by James I
1604		New translation of the Bible commenced
1605		*Advancement of Learning* published

1606	April 10	James I grants a charter for the Virginia Company
	May 10	Francis marries Alice Barnham
1607	May 13	Jamestown settlement founded
	June 25	Francis appointed Solicitor General
1609		"Shakespeare" sonnets first published
1610	Aug	Death of Lady Anne Bacon
		First permanent colony established in Newfoundland
1611		King James Bible published, edited by Bacon
1612		Second edition of the *Essays* published
	May 24	Death of Robert Cecil, Lord Salisbury
	Nov 6	Death of Prince Henry
1613	Oct 26	Francis appointed Attorney General
1616	April 23	Death of William Shaksper
1617	March 7	Francis appointed Lord Keeper
1618	Jan 4	Appointed Lord Chancellor
	July 12	Made a peer. Receives the title Baron Verulam
1620	Oct 12	*Novum Organum* published
1621	Jan 27	Elevated in the peerage. Receives the title Viscount St. Alban
	March 14	Accused of accepting bribes
	April 22	Pleads guilty at the king's command
	May 3	Sentenced by House of Lords
	May 31– June 4	Imprisoned in the Tower
	June 23	Retires to Gorhambury
1623	Oct	*De Augmentis Scientiarum* published, including detailed instructions for the Bi-literal Cipher
	Nov	First Folio of "Shakespeare" plays published
1625		Third edition of the *Essays* published

	March 27	Death of James I. Charles I succeeds to the throne
1626	April 9	Reported death of Francis Bacon
1627		*New Atlantis* and *Sylva Sylvarum* published by William Rawley
1856		Delia Bacon proposes that Francis Bacon wrote works attributed to Shakespeare
1888		Ignatius Donnelly publishes *The Great Cryptogram*
1893–1895		Dr. Orville W. Owen publishes *Sir Francis Bacon's Cipher Story*
1899–1901		Elizabeth Wells Gallup publishes *The Biliteral Cypher of Sir Francis Bacon*

SELECT BIBLIOGRAPHY

Arensberg, Walter Conrad. *The Baconiana Keys*. Pittsburgh: Walter Conrad Arensberg, 1928.

Arthur, James. *A Royal Romance*. Madras, India: Vasanta Press, 1941.

Aubrey, John. *Brief Lives—edited from the Original Manuscripts by Oliver Lawson Dick*. Ann Arbor: University of Michigan Press, 1957.

Bacon, Francis. *Advancement of Learning—Novum Organum*. New York: Colonial Press, 1900.

———. *Essays and New Atlantis*. New York: Walter J. Black, 1942.

———. *The Essays*, ed. by John Pitcher. London: Penguin Books, 1985.

———. *Novum Organum*. Translated and edited by Peter Urbach and John Gibson. Chicago: Open Court Publishing, 1994.

Baconiana. Published periodically by the Francis Bacon Society, London, England.

Barsi-Greene, Margaret, comp. *I, Prince Tudor, Wrote Shakespeare*. Boston: Branden Press, 1973.

Baxter, James Phinney. *The Greatest of Literary Problems*. New York, 1956.

Bayley, Harold. *The Tragedy of Sir Francis Bacon*. New York:

Haskell House Publishers, 1970.

Begley, Gerald E. *Shakespeare: A Biographical Handbook*. New Haven: Yale University Press, 1961.

Bokenham, T. D. *Brief History of the Bacon-Shakespeare Controversy: With Some Cipher Evidence*. London: Francis Bacon Research Trust, 1982.

Bowen, Catherine Drinker. *Francis Bacon: The Temper of a Man*. Boston: Little, Brown & Company, 1963.

Brown, Ivor. *Shakespeare*. New York: Country Life Press, 1963.

Bunten, A. Chambers, *Life of Alice Barnham, Wife of Sir Francis Bacon*. London: Oliphants, 1928.
www.cybermesa.com.

Cambridge History of English Literature. Cambridge University Press, 1986.

Camden, William. *The History of the Most Renowned and Victorious Princess Elizabeth*. Chicago University Press, 1957.

Challinor, A. M., comp. "Francis Bacon: Philosopher, Statesman, Poet: An Index to Baconiana and Its Predecessors, 1886–1999." London: The Francis Bacon Society, 2001.

Chamberlin, E. R. *Marguerite of Navarre*. New York: Dial Press, 1974.

Chambers, Sir Edmund K. *A Study of Facts and Problems*. London: Clarendon Press, 1930.

Church, R. W. *Bacon*. New York: AMS Press, 1968.

Churchill, R. C. *Shakespeare and His Betters*. London: M. Reinhardt, 1958.

Chute, Marchette. *Shakespeare of London*. New York: E. P. Dutton, 1949.

Clark, Natalie Rice. *Hamlet on the Dial Stage*. Paris: H. Campion, 1931.

Crowther, J. G. *Francis Bacon: The First Statesman of Science*. London: The Cresset Press, 1960.

Dawkins, Peter. *The Shakespeare Enigma*. London: Polair Publishing, 2004.

Dixon, William Hepworth. *Personal History of Lord Bacon: From Unpublished Papers.* London: J. Murray, 1861.

Dodd, Alfred. *Francis Bacon's Personal Life-Story.* London, New York: Rider & Company, 1949.

———. *The Martyrdom of Francis Bacon.* London: Rider & Company, 1945.

———. *The Secret History of Francis Bacon (Our Shakespeare)—The Son of Queen Elizabeth.* London: C. W. Daniel Company, 1941.

Donnelly, Ignatius. *The Great Cryptogram: Francis Bacon's Cipher in the So-Called Shakespeare Plays.* London: S. Low, Marston, Searle & Rivington, 1888; St. Clair Shores, Mich.: Scholarly Press, 1972.

Du Maurier, Daphne. *Golden Lads: Sir Francis Bacon, Anthony Bacon and Their Friends.* Garden City, N. Y.: Doubleday & Company, 1975.

———. *The Winding Stair: Francis Bacon, His Rise and Fall. Garden City.* Garden City, N. Y.: Doubleday & Company, 1976.

Durning-Lawrence, Sir Edwin. *Bacon is Shake-speare.* London: Gay & Hancock, 1910.

Eiseley, Loren. *The Man Who Saw through Time.* New York: Charles Scribner's Sons, 1973.

Erickson, Carolly. *The First Elizabeth.* New York: St. Martin's Press, 1997.

Evans, A. J. *Shakespeare's Magic Circle.* London: A. Barker, 1956.

Fuller, Jean Overton. *Francis Bacon, a Biography.* London: East-West Publications, 1981.

Gallup, Elizabeth Wells. *The Bi-literal Cypher of Sir Francis Bacon.* London: Gay & Bird, 1901; reprint, Detroit: Howard Publishing Company, 1901.

————. *The Lost Manuscripts, Where They Were Hidden.* N.p. 1910.

Gibson, H. N. *The Shakespeare Claimants.* New York: Barnes and Noble, 1962.

Giroux, Robert. *The Book Known as Q.* Baylor University Press, 1981.

Goodrich, Norma Lorre. *The Holy Grail.* New York: Harper Perennial, 1992.

Green, A. Wigfall. Sir *Francis Bacon, His Life and Works.* Denver: Alan Swallow, 1952.

Greenblat, Stephen. *Will in the World.* New York: W. W. Norton & Company, 2004.

Greenwood, Sir George. *Is There a Shakespeare Problem?* London: John Lane Press, 1916.

Gundry, W. G. C., ed. *Manes Verulamiani* (Anthology of Poems to the Memory of Francis Bacon 1626). London, 1950.

Hall, Manly Palmer. *Masonic, Hermetic, Qabbalistic, Rosicrucian and Symbolical Philosophy.* San Francisco: H. S. Crocker, 1928.

————. *The Secret Teachings of All Ages.* Manly P. Hall, 1928.

Halliday, A. E. *Shakespeare and His Critics.* London: Duckworth & Co., 1929.

Hart, Joseph C. *The Romance of Yachting.* New York: Harper, 1848.

Hickson, S. A. E. *The Prince of Poets and Most Illustrious of Philosophers.* London: Gay & Hancock, 1926.

Hoffman, Calvin. *The Man Who Was Shakespeare.* London, 1955.

Hotson, Leslie. *Mr. W. H.* London: Hart Davison, 1964.

Ince, Richard. *England's High Chancellor.* London: Frederick Muller, 1935.

Inge, William Ralph. *England.* New York: C. Scribner's Sons, 1926; McGraw-Hill Co., 1963.

Jardine, Lisa, and Alan Stewart. *Hostage to Fortune*. New York: Hill and Wang, 1998.

Jenkins, Elizabeth. *Elizabeth the Great*. New York: Coward-McCann, 1958.

Kahn, David. *The Code Breakers*. New York: Macmillan, 1967.

Lacey, Robert. *Robert, Earl of Essex*. New York: Atheneum, 1971.

Lawrence, Herbert. *The Life and Adventures of Common Sense*. New York: Garland Publishing, 1974.

Leary, Penn. *The Second Cryptographic Shakespeare*. Omaha, Neb.: Westchester House, 1990.

Lee, Sidney. *Shakespeare's Life and Works*. New York: Macmillan, 1906.

Levin, Harry. *The Question of Hamlet*. Oxford University Press, 1970.

Luke, Mary M. *A Crown for Elizabeth*. New York: Coward-McCann, 1970.

MacNeil, Robert, William Crans, and Robert McCrum. *The Story of English*. New York: Viking Penguin, 1993.

Marder, Louis. *His Exits and His Entrance*. Philadelphia: Lippincott Co., 1963.

Martin, Milward W. *Was Shakespeare Shakespeare?* New York: Cooper Square Publications, 1965.

Mattingley, Garrett. *The Armada*. Boston: Houghton Mifflin Co., 1959.

McManaway, James G. *The Authorship of Shakespeare*. Washington, D.C.: Folger Library Booklet, 1962.

Melsome, W. S. *The Bacon-Shakespeare Anatomy*. London: George Lapworth & Company, 1945.

Michell, John. *Who Wrote Shakespeare?* London: Thames and Hudson, 1996.

Ogbum, Charlton. *The Mysterious Shakespeare*. New York: Dodd, Mead & Co., 1984.

Owen, Orville W., M.D. *Sir Francis Bacon's Cipher Story,* Vols. I–II, III–IV, V. Detroit: Howard Publishing Co., 1894.

Pott, Mrs. Henry. *Bacon's Promus.* London: Longmans, Green & Co., 1883.

———. *Francis Bacon and His Secret Society.* San Francisco: John Howell, n.d.

Prescott, Kate H. *Reminiscences of a Baconian.* New York: The Haven Press, 1949.

Puttenham. *The Art of English Poesie.* London: Robert Triphon, 1811.

Rawley, William. *Life of the Right Honorable Francis Bacon.* Available online at http://home.att.net/~tleary/rawley.htm.

———. *Resuscitatio.* N.p., 1657.

Roe, J. E. *The Mortal Moon.* New York: Burr Publishers, 1891.

———. *Sir Francis Bacon's Own Story.* Rochester, N.Y.: The DuBois Press, 1918.

Rossi, Paolo. *From Magic to Science.* Routledge, 1968.

Rowse, A. L. *William Shakespeare, a Biography.* New York: Harper and Rowe, 1963.

Schoenbaum, Samuel. *Shakespeare's Lives.* New York: Oxford University Press, 1970.

Shakespeare, William. *The Complete Signet Classic Shakespeare.* New York: Harcourt Brace Jovanovich, 1972.

Smedley, W. T. *The Mystery of Francis Bacon.* London: n.p.

Smith, Lacey. *The Elizabethan World.* New York: Houghton Mifflin, 1967.

Sobran, Joseph. *Alias Shakespeare.* New York: The Free Press, 1997.

Spedding, James, ed. *The Letters and Life of Francis Bacon,* 7 vols. London: Cambridge University Press, 1861–74.

———. *The Works of Francis Bacon,* 7 vols. London: Cambridge University Press, 1857–61.

Spurgeon, Caroline. *Shakespearean Imagery.* Cambridge University Press. 1935.

Stopes, Charlotte. *The Bacon-Shakespeare Question Answered.*
N.p., 1889.

Strachey, Lytton. *Elizabeth and Essex: A Tragic History.* New
York: Harcourt Brace & Co., 1928.

Strickland, Agnes. *The Life of Queen Elizabeth.* London: Hutchinson & Co., 1905.

Strong, Roy. *Portraits of Queen Elizabeth I.* Oxford: Clarendon
Press, 1963.

Sweet, George Elliott. *Shakespeare, the Mystery.* Calif.: Stanford
University Press, 1956.

Theobald, Bertram. *Enter Francis Bacon.* London: n.p., 1937.

Wadsworth, Frank. *The Poacher from Stratford.* Berkeley: University of California Press, 1958.

Waldman, Milton. *Elizabeth and Leicester.* Boston: Houghton
Mifflin, 1945.

Wigston, W. F. C. *The Columbus of Literature.* London: n.p.,
1892.

Woodward, Parker. *The Strange Case of Francis Tidir.* London:
Robert Banks & Son, 1901.

Yates, Frances A. *Astraea: The Imperial Theme in the Sixteenth
Century.* London: Pimlico, 1993.

———. *Majesty & Magic in Shakespeare's Last Plays.* Boulder,
Colo.: Shambala, 1978.

———. *The Occult Philosophy in the Elizabethan Age.* London:
Routledge Kegan Paul, 1979.

NOTES

The quotes at the beginning of each chapter are taken from Francis Bacon's *Essays* unless otherwise noted (*The Essays*, ed. John Pitcher [London: Penguin Books, 1985]).

Passages from Shakespeare's plays and sonnets are taken from *The Complete Signet Classic Shakespeare* (New York: Harcourt Brace Jovanovich, 1972).

In material quoted from older sources we have frequently modernized the spelling in order to assist the reader.

CHAPTER 1 · A TALE OF TWO STRANGERS

1. Delia Bacon (1811–1859) was an American author. Her book *The Philosophy of the Plays of Shakespeare Unfolded* (1857) was among the first to propound the idea that Francis Bacon wrote the works of Shakespeare, the so-called Baconian theory. Her book was published twenty-six years before those of Orville Owen.
2. Owen elaborates on how the Word Cipher poem "The Spanish Armada" was formed. He compares some excerpts from the Shakespeare plays with the passages in the cipher poem where those excerpts are used. It is a fascinating example of how the exact same phrases are used to form two different stories. See Owen's "Introduction" in *Sir Francis Bacon's Cipher Story*, book two (includes volumes III and IV) originally published by Howard Publishing Company of Detroit in 1894. For those who would like to read the entire poem on the Spanish Armada, it begins in book one (vol. II, pp. 263–400) and concludes in book two (vol. III, pp. 401–570).
3. "Elizabeth I's Response to a Parliamentary Delegation on Her Marriage," 1559.
4. George Goodale, quoted in Owen, *Sir Francis Bacon's Cipher Story*, vol. I (1893), p. 8 of the opening pages of the book.

5. Herbert Lawrence, *The Life and Adventures of Common Sense: An Historical Allegory* (1769; reprint, New York: Garland Publishing, 1974), pp. 146, 147.

6. S. Schoenbaum, *Shakespeare's Lives* (New York: Oxford University Press, 1970), pp. 544–47; and "The First Baconian," by Lord Sydenham of Combe, reprinted from the February 1933 issue of *Baconiana,* at http://www.sirbacon.org/firstbaconian.htm.

7. See Edwin Durning-Lawrence, *Bacon Is Shake-speare* (London: Gay and Hancock, 1910), p. 179.

8. Ibid., pp. 179–80.

9. Schoenbaum, *Shakespeare's Lives,* p. 571.

10. Mark Twain, *Is Shakespeare Dead? From My Autobiography,* chap. 8; text is available online through Project Gutenberg.

11. Ignatius Donnelly, *Atlantis: The Antediluvian World* (New York: Harper, 1882).

12. Owen, *Sir Francis Bacon's Cipher Story,* vols. I–II, p. 3.

13. See "Sir Francis Bacon's Letter to the Decipherer," in Owen, *Sir Francis Bacon's Cipher Story,* vols. I–II, pp. 1–44.

14. Ibid., pp. 28–29, 23.

15. See Kate H. Prescott, *Reminiscences of a Baconian* (Haven Press, 1949), pp. 27–29.

16. Ibid., pp. 30–31.

17. Peter Dawkins, *The Shakespeare Enigma* (London: Polair Publishing, 2004), p. 173.

18. P. B. Shelley, preface to *Prometheus Unbound,* quoted in "Imagery, Thought-Forms and Jargon," by M. P., *Baconiana,* Sept. 1969; available at http://www.sirbacon.org/jargonmp.htm.

CHAPTER 2 · A CHILDHOOD EDEN

1. Jean Overton Fuller, *Francis Bacon* (London: East-West Publications, 1981), p. 25.

2. Under the Julian calendar then in effect in England, the Sun entered Aquarius on January 10. On January 21, the Sun was at 11 degrees Aquarius.

3. For astrologer William Lily's information about Francis Bacon's astrological chart, see http://www.sirbacon.org/links/charts/htm. See also Fuller, *Francis Bacon,* p. 26, note 2.

4. See Fuller, *Francis Bacon,* p. 26, note 1; and Alfred Dodd, *Francis Bacon's Personal Life-Story* (London: Rider and Company, n.d.), p. 42.

5. Fuller, *Francis Bacon,* pp. 27–32.

6. Daphne du Maurier, *Golden Lads* (Garden City, N.Y.: Doubleday and Company, 1975), pp. 16–17.

7. S. A. E. Hickson, *The Prince of Poets and Most Illustrious of Philosophers* (London: Gay and Hancock, 1926), pp. 48–49.

8. Ibid., p. 60.

9. Shakespeare, *A Midsummer's Night's Dream,* act II, sc. 1, line 150.

10. Hickson, *Prince of Poets,* pp. 92–98.

11. Ibid., pp. 97–98. Alfred Dodd points out that "Laneham" is an anagram for "lean ham." This kind of word play was popular in Elizabethan times (and in Shakespeare's plays), and the use of this name provides another clue to Bacon's authorship of this piece (*Francis Bacon's Personal Life-Story,* p. 77).

12. William Rawley's life of Francis Bacon, *Resuscitatio,* published in 1657.

13. Dodd, *Francis Bacon's Personal Life-Story,* p. 64.

14. See Mrs. Henry Pott, *Francis Bacon and His Secret Society* (Kessinger Publishing's Rare Mystical Reprints), pp. 230–31.

15. See Catherine Drinker Bowen, *Francis Bacon: The Temper of a Man* (Boston: Atlantic Monthly Press, Little, Brown and Company, 1963), part I.

16. Du Maurier, *Golden Lads,* p. 18.

17. Margaret Barsi-Greene, comp., *I, Prince Tudor, Wrote Shakespeare* (Boston: Branden Press, 1973), p. 67. Barsi-Greene has compiled excerpts from Elizabeth Wells Gallup's *The Bi-literal Cypher of Sir Francis Bacon* (New York: AMS Press, 1901). The excerpts are organized by topic and have modernized spelling.

18. Roger Ascham, "Preface to the Reader," in *The Scholemaster, or plain and perfect way of teaching children...,* available at
http://www.classiclanguagearts.net/resources/the-schoolmaster.htm

19. See II Sam. 11.

20. Hickson, *Prince of Poets,* pp. xxiv–xxv.

21. Andrew Lyell, quoted in http://www.sirbacon.org/links/parentage.htm. For additional information on Elizabeth's relationship with Dudley, see Dodd, *Francis Bacon's Personal Life Story,* pp. 38–43.

22. See *Dictionary of National Biography,* vol. 16, published in 1888, p. 114 under the heading of "Dudley."

23. Barsi-Greene, *I, Prince Tudor,* p. 199.

24. Ibid.

25. "The Story of Robert Devereux, Earl of Essex," in *Baconiana,* vol. 13, no. 51 (July 1915), p. 114.

CHAPTER 3 · A LIFE-CHANGING REVELATION

1. Francis Bacon, "Of Envy," in *The Essays,* ed. John Pitcher (London: Penguin Books, 1985), p. 83.

2. Bacon, "Of Deformity," in *Essays,* p. 192.

3. See Barsi-Greene, *I, Prince Tudor,* pp. 82–84; or Owen, *Sir Francis Bacon's Cipher Story,* vols. I–II, pp. 137, 138, 142.

4. Loren Eiseley, *The Man Who Saw through Time* (New York: Charles Scribner's Sons, 1973), pp. 17, 20.

5. Francis Bacon, *Cogitata et Visa.* According to biographer William T. Smedley, this text, composed in 1607 and published in 1653, was a forerunner of *Novum Organum.* (See Smedley's *Mystery of Francis Bacon,* chapter 24.)

6. "The Medieval Bestiary: Animals in the Middle Ages" at http://bestiary.ca/beasts/beast78.htm.

7. Thus Bacon described his tutors in his 1605 manuscript *An Essay on Human Learning.*

8. Dodd, *Francis Bacon's Personal Life-Story,* p. 50.

9. Gallup, *Bi-literal Cypher,* part I, p. 85; Barsi-Greene, *I, Prince Tudor,* p. 70.

10. Owen, *Sir Francis Bacon's Cipher Story,* vols. I–II, p. 59.

11. Ibid., p. 90.

12. Ibid.

13. Ibid., pp. 91–94.

14. Agnes Strickland, *The Life of Queen Elizabeth* (London: Hutchinson and Co., 1905), p. 275.

15. Carolly Erickson, *The First Elizabeth* (New York: St. Martin's Griffin, 1997), p. 262.

16. Elizabeth Jenkins, *Elizabeth the Great* (New York: Coward-McCann, 1958), p. 208.

17. Owen, *Sir Francis Bacon's Cipher Story,* vols. I–II, pp. 94–98.

18. Gallup, *Bi-literal Cypher,* part II, p. 139; Barsi-Greene, *I, Prince Tudor,* pp. 71–72.

19. Owen, *Sir Francis Bacon's Cipher Story,* vols. I–II, pp. 98–99.

20. Ibid., pp. 99–100.

CHAPTER 4 · MORE REVELATIONS

1. Owen, *Sir Francis Bacon's Cipher Story,* vols. I–II, pp. 103, 105.

2. Ibid., pp. 106, 108.

3. Bacon, "Of Beauty," in *Essays,* p. 189.

4. Milton Waldman, *Elizabeth and Leicester* (Boston: Houghton Mifflin Company, 1945), p. 1.

5. Frances A. Yates, *Astraea: The Imperial Theme in the Sixteenth Century* (1975; reprint, London: Pimlico, 1993), p. xi.

6. Jenkins, *Elizabeth the Great,* p. 25.

7. Strickland, *Life of Queen Elizabeth,* p. 18.

8. Ibid., p. 50.

9. Waldman, *Elizabeth and Leicester,* pp. 46–47.

10. Mary M. Luke, *A Crown for Elizabeth* (New York: Coward-McCann, 1970), pp. 434–35.

11. Owen, *Sir Francis Bacon's Cipher Story,* vols. I–II, p. 200.

12. Ibid., p. 201.

13. Ibid., pp. 201–2.

14. Ibid., p. 224.

15. Ibid., p. 250.

16. Dodd, *Francis Bacon's Personal Life-Story,* pp. 41–42.

17. Owen, *Sir Francis Bacon's Cipher Story,* vols. I–II, p. 59.

18. Ibid.

CHAPTER 5 · BANISHED TO PARIS

1. Owen, *Sir Francis Bacon's Cipher Story*, vols. I–II, pp. 130–35.
2. Ibid., pp. 135–36.
3. Bacon, *Essays*, pp. 226–27.
4. Owen, *Sir Francis Bacon's Cipher Story*, vols. I–II, pp. 137–38.
5. Barsi-Greene, *I, Prince Tudor*, p. 74.
6. Owen, *Sir Francis Bacon's Cipher Story*, vols. I–II, p. 142.
7. Ibid., pp. 251–53.
8. Ibid., pp. 255, 256, 258.
9. Ibid., p. 260.
10. See Owen, *Sir Francis Bacon's Cipher Story*, vols. I–II, pp. 257–58.
11. Jenkins, *Elizabeth the Great*, p. 54.
12. Owen, *Sir Francis Bacon's Cipher Story*, vols. I–II, pp. 261–62.
13. See Parker Woodard, *Sir Francis Bacon*, p. 12, quoted in Alfred Dodd, *The Marriage of Elizabeth Tudor*. Portions of Dodd's book are available online at http://www.sirbacon.org. For Woodard's quote, see http://www.sirbacon.org/francisqueenleicester.htm.
14. See Owen, *Sir Francis Bacon's Cipher Story*, vols. I–II, p. 262, and vols. III–IV, p. 571.

CHAPTER 6 · JULIET AND HER ENGLISH ROMEO

1. Alfred Dodd, himself a Mason, provides much information on Bacon's work with Freemasonry and Rosicrucianism in his biography *Francis Bacon's Personal Life-Story* and in *Shakespeare: Creator of Freemasonry*.
2. Gallup, *Bi-literal Cypher*, part II, p. 337.
3. Ibid., pp. 79–80, 176. For the cipher accounts of Francis's love for Marguerite of Valois, see Barsi-Greene, *I, Prince Tudor*, pp. 89–98.
4. Dodd, *Francis Bacon's Personal Life-Story*, p. 91.
5. Owen, *Sir Francis Bacon's Cipher Story*, vols. III–IV, pp. 571–72.
6. Ibid., pp. 572–73.
7. Ibid., p. 573.
8. Ibid., pp. 574, 575.
9. Ibid., p. 575.
10. Fuller, *Francis Bacon*, p. 35.
11. Dodd, *Francis Bacon's Personal Life-Story*, p. 90.
12. See Owen, *Sir Francis Bacon's Cipher Story*, vols. III–IV, pp. 581–91.
13. Ibid., p. 587.
14. Ibid., vol. V, p. 949.
15. E. R. Chamberlin, *Marguerite of Navarre* (New York: Dial Press, 1974), p. 42.
16. In *Love's Labor's Lost*, the king and several lords decide that their court shall be a "little academe" committed to contemplation and learning and that they will uphold a monastic lifestyle, avoiding the company of women for three years. See act I.
17. Owen, *Sir Francis Bacon's Cipher Story*, vol. V, pp. 925, 926.

18. Ibid., pp. 928, 930, 931.
19. Barsi-Greene, *I, Prince Tudor*, p. 93.
20. Owen, *Sir Francis Bacon's Cipher Story*, vol. V, p. 948.
21. Ibid.
22. Shakespeare, *Troilus and Cressida*, act I, sc. 2, line 296.
23. Ibid., act IV, sc. 4, line 102.
24. Ibid., act V, sc. 2, line 104.

CHAPTER 7 · THE GLORY OF A KING

1. Bowen, *Francis Bacon*, pp. 39–40.
2. Fuller, *Sir Francis Bacon*, p. 44.
3. Bacon, *Essays*, p. 90.
4. See William Ralph Inge, *England* (New York: C. Scribner's Sons, 1926), p. 43.
5. Ibid., p. 57.
6. Owen, *Sir Francis Bacon's Cipher Story*, vols. I–II, p. 22.
7. Inge, *England*, pp. 57, 58.
8. Ibid., pp. 59–60.
9. Dodd, *Francis Bacon's Personal Life-Story*, p. 112.
10. Prov. 25: 2; Owen, *Sir Francis Bacon's Cipher Story*, vols. I–II, p. 32.
11. Ibid., pp. 33–35.
12. See Barsi-Greene, *I, Prince Tudor*, p. 90.
13. James Spedding, quoted in Harold Bayley, *The Tragedy of Sir Francis Bacon: An Appeal for Further Investigation and Research* (1902; reprint, New York: Haskell House Publishers, 1970), p. 31.

CHAPTER 8 · THE GOLDEN LADS

1. Gallup, *Bi-literal Cypher*, part II, pp. 108, 134, 172, 209–10; or Barsi-Greene, *I, Prince Tudor*, pp. 64–65, 176, 198.
2. Daphne du Maurier, *The Winding Stair* (Garden City, N.Y.: Doubleday and Company, 1976), p. 173.
3. Tobie Matthew, quoted in du Maurier, *Winding Stair*, p. 174, and John Michell, *Who Wrote Shakespeare?* (London: Thames and Hudson, 1996), p. 121.
4. Gallup, *Bi-literal Cypher*, part II, pp. 134–35.
5. Dodd, *Sir Francis Bacon's Personal Life-Story*, pp. 42–43, 83, 225.
6. William Camden, *Elizabeth*, p. 167, quoted in Dodd, *Sir Francis Bacon's Personal Life-Story*, p. 83.
7. Robert Lacey, *Robert, Earl of Essex* (New York: Atheneum, 1971), p. 18.
8. Ibid., p. 19.
9. Shakespeare, *The Two Gentlemen of Verona*, act II, sc. 3.
10. See Strickland, *Queen Elizabeth*, p. 72.
11. Hickson, *Prince of Poets*, p. 161.
12. Dodd, *Francis Bacon's Personal Life-Story*, pp. 132–36.

CHAPTER 9 · TWO BROTHERS

1. Lacey, *Robert, Earl of Essex*, p. 49.
2. The intent of the Spanish Armada was to overthrow protestant England and restore the Catholic faith. On board the fleet were ninety Spanish Inquisitors along with the needed equipment to set up the Inquisition in the conquered land. In a separate account, 180 priests are listed with the noncombat cargo of the fleet. See *Baconiana*, vol. 36, no. 144 (Nov. 1952), p. 114, and http://www.tudorplace.com.ar/Documents/defeat_of_the_armada.htm.
3. Letter from Lady Anne Bacon to Anthony Bacon, quoted in du Maurier, *Golden Lads*, pp. 73–74.
4. W. T. Smedley, *The Mystery of Francis Bacon*, pp. 109, 98, 101, quoted in Dodd, *Francis Bacon's Personal Life-Story*, pp. 133, 134. Dodd lists more than forty books published between 1579 and 1593 by Francis Bacon and his circle and released anonymously or under various pseudonyms (see *Life-Story*, pp. 136–38, 179–80).
5. According to the Bi-literal Cipher, Francis tells us that "to make choice of mouthpieces for our voice is far from being a light or pleasing, but quite necessary and important, mission; and it oft in truth swalloweth all we receive from our writings ere such cost be paid." In another section he says: "All men who write stage plays are held in contempt. For this reason none say, 'How strange,' when a play cometh, accompanied with gold, asking a name by which one putting it forward shall not be recognized, or thought to be cognizant of its existence." (Gallup, *Bi-literal Cypher,* part I, p. 89, part II, p. 77). In addition, we learn from Donnelly's cipher that the character Falstaff as played by Shakespeare was a huge success, drawing crowds to the plays and thereby increasing his share of the revenue. Even the German Minister said it was well worth it to see him as Falstaff (see p. 174 this volume). Shakespeare apparently owned a percentage of the Globe Theatre. See Ignatius Donnelly, *The Great Cryptogram: Francis Bacon's Cipher in the So-Called Shakespeare Plays* (London: Sampson, Low, Marston, Searle and Rivington, 1888), pp. 818–23; and *Baconiana,* vol. 36, n. 144 (Nov. 1952), p. 110.
6. Anne Bacon to Anthony Bacon, 17 April 1593, quoted in du Maurier, *Golden Lads*, pp. 80–81.
7. Lytton Strachey, *Elizabeth and Essex: A Tragic History* (New York: Harcourt Brace and Co., 1928), p. 4.
8. Gallup, *Bi-literal Cypher,* part II, pp. 209–10.
9. Ibid., p. 210.
10. Ibid., pp. 44, 45.
11. G. B. Harrison, quoted in Fuller, *Sir Francis Bacon*, pp. 58–59.
12. Lacey, *Robert, Earl of Essex*, p. 64.
13. Strachey, *Elizabeth and Essex*, p. 38.
14. Fuller, *Sir Francis Bacon*, p. 58.
15. Barsi-Greene, *I, Prince Tudor*, p. 200.
16. Ibid., p. 199.

17. Shakespeare, Sonnet 94.
18. T. Birch, *Memoirs of the Reign of Queen Elizabeth,* I, p. 152, quoted in Lacey, *Robert, Earl of Essex,* p. 113.
19. Ibid.
20. Anne Bacon, dialogue with Robert Cecil, 1595, quoted in du Maurier, *Golden Lads,* p. 104.
21. Robert Essex to Francis Bacon, 24 August 1593, quoted in Fuller, *Sir Francis Bacon,* p. 64.
22. Francis Bacon Robert Essex, 30 March 1594, quoted in Fuller, *Sir Francis Bacon,* p. 65.
23. Francis Bacon to Robert Cecil, quoted in Dodd, *Francis Bacon's Personal Life-Story,* p. 248.
24. Strachey, *Elizabeth and Essex,* p. 65.
25. Fuller, *Sir Francis Bacon,* p. 132.

Chapter 10 · Try, Try, Try Again

1. Shakespeare, Sonnet 90.
2. Gallup, *Bi-literal Cypher,* part II, p. 132.
3. Du Maurier, *Golden Lads,* p. 95.
4. John Chamberlain to Dudley Carleton, 22 November 1598, quoted in du Maurier, *Golden Lads,* p. 197.
5. See Owen, introduction to vol. II, in *Sir Francis Bacon's Cipher Story,* vols. I–II.
6. Du Maurier, *Golden Lads,* p. 97.
7. Anne Bacon to Anthony Bacon, 1594, quoted in du Maurier, *Golden Lads,* pp. 97–98.
8. Du Maurier, *Golden Lads,* p. 98.
9. Fuller, *Sir Francis Bacon,* p. 146.
10. Donnelly, *Great Cryptogram,* vol. II, pp. 814–17. See also Fuller, *Sir Francis Bacon,* p. 147.
11. Ben Jonson, *Every Man Out of His Humor,* ed. Helen Ostovich (Manchester University Press, 2001), p. 107.
12. Ibid., pp. 230–31.
13. See Barsi-Greene, *I, Prince Tudor,* p. 141.
14. Donnelly, *Great Cryptogram*, vol. II, pp. 812, 815–16.
15. Ibid., pp. 817–19, 820–22.
16. Greene, *Groatsworth of Wit.*
17. Donnelly, *Great Cryptogram,* vol. II, pp. 844–48.
18. Ibid., pp. 850–51.
19. Ibid., pp. 765–67.
20. Ibid., pp. 719–24.
21. Ibid., pp. 771–74.
22. Ibid., pp. 767–68.

CHAPTER 11 · TROUBLE FROM STRATFORD

1. See Donnelly's summary of the cipher account, *Great Cryptogram*, vol. II, pp. 873–76.
2. Ibid., p. 876.
3. Francis Bacon to Lord Puckering, 19 August 1595, quoted in A. Wigfall Green, *Sir Francis Bacon: His Life and Works* (Denver: Alan Swallow, 1952), p. 58.
4. Anne Bacon, quoted in Bowen, *Francis Bacon*, p. 73.
5. Dodd, *Francis Bacon's Personal Life-Story*, p. 251.
6. Strachey, *Elizabeth and Essex*, p. 61.
7. See "Celestial Visitation" in Barsi-Greene, *I, Prince Tudor*, p. 76. The complete celestial vision appears in chapter 7 of this volume, pp. 121–23.
8. Barsi-Greene, *I, Prince Tudor*, p. 199.
9. Erickson, *The First Elizabeth*, p. 387.
10. Strachey, *Elizabeth and Essex*, p. 100.
11. Ibid., p. 106.
12. French Ambassador De Maisse, quoted in Erickson, *The First Elizabeth*, p. 387.
13. Francis Bacon to Robert Essex, 4 October 1596, quoted in Dodd, *Francis Bacon's Personal Life-Story*, p. 261. This letter, excerpted in many biographies of Bacon, Essex and the queen, is found in its entirely in James Spedding, *The Works, Letters and Life of Francis Bacon* (London: Cambridge University Press, 1858–1874), vol. II, pp. 40–50.
14. Ibid., p. 262.
15. Dedication to the 1597 *Essays*, in Bacon, *Essays*, pp. 238, 239.
16. R. W. Church, *Bacon* (1889; reprint, New York: AMS Press, 1968), pp. 217–18.
17. Bacon, *Essays*, p. 219.
18. See Bacon's essay "Of Envy."
19. Robert Essex to John Harrington, quoted in Strachey, *Elizabeth and Essex*, p. 193.
20. Strachey, *Elizabeth and Essex*, pp. 197, 198.

CHAPTER 12 · ESSEX, BACON AND TRAGEDY

1. Lacey, *Robert, Earl of Essex*, p. 223.
2. Francis Bacon, quoted in du Maurier, *Golden Lads*, pp. 191–92.
3. Bacon relates in his Bi-literal Cipher the story of Essex and his rebellion that ended so tragically. See Gallup, *Bi-literal Cypher*, part II, especially pp. 29–32, 76, 209; or Barsi-Greene, *I, Prince Tudor*, pp. 198–213.
4. Lacey, *Robert, Earl of Essex*, p. 237.
5. Francis Bacon to Robert Essex, 20 July 1600, in Lisa Jardine and Alan Stewart, *Hostage to Fortune* (New York: Hill and Wang, 1999), p. 233.
6. See Gallup, *Bi-literal Cypher*, part II, p. 68; or Barsi-Greene, *I, Prince Tudor*, p. 206.

7. Bacon, *Apologia*, quoted in Dodd, *Francis Bacon's Personal Life-Story*, p. 276.
8. Gallup, *Bi-literal Cypher*, part II, p. 210; or Barsi-Greene, *I, Prince Tudor*, p. 198.
9. Daphne du Maurier points out that there were rumors about this time that Francis had used his influence with the queen to discredit the earl. Francis was quite disliked by the earl's supporters as evidenced from Francis's own letter: "My life hath been threatened, and my name libelled…. But these are the practices of those whose despairs are dangerous, and yet not so dangerous as their hopes" (*Golden Lads*, pp. 195–96).
10. Dodd, *Francis Bacon's Personal Life-Story*, p. 282.
11. Strachey, *Elizabeth and Essex*, pp. 236–37.
12. Gallup, *Bi-literal Cypher*, part II, p. 174.
13. Barsi-Greene, *I, Prince Tudor*, pp. 201, 202, 203–4.
14. Gallup, *Bi-literal Cypher*, part II, p. 20; or Barsi-Greene, *I, Prince Tudor*, p. 207.
15. For a summary of the views of different biographers on Bacon's presence at Essex's trial and the reasons for it, see Dodd, *Francis Bacon's Personal Life-Story*, pp. 291–92.
16. Francis tells us in cipher: "Truly, I did not welcome the task, for to me it grew to be less honorable, so to put forward my dear Lord, his misdeeds, at Queen Elizabeth's behest, though I did it but at her express commands and always as a Secretary to Her Majesty….

    "Yet this truth must at some time be known; had not I thus allowed myself to give some countenance to the arraignment, a subsequent trial, as well as the sentence, I must have lost the life that I held so priceless. Life to a scholar is but a pawn for mankind….

    "Remorse doth make my grief so bitter, for my very life did hang on that thread, and by the truth my brother was attaint [guilty], yet fain would I now choose an hundred shameful deaths than aid to send a brother into Eternity." Barsi-Greene, *I, Prince Tudor*, pp. 210, 208, 204. See also Gallup, *Bi-literal Cypher*, part II, pp. 43, 22, 104.
17. See Spedding, IX, p. 205, cited in Fuller, *Sir Francis Bacon*, p. 167.
18. Henri of Navarre, quoted in Lacey, *Robert, Earl of Essex*, p. 2.
19. Dodd, *Francis Bacon's Personal Life-Story*, p. 294.
20. Ibid.
21. Strachey, *Elizabeth and Essex*, p. 268.
22. Owen, *Sir Francis Bacon's Cipher Story*, vols. I–II, p. 63.
23. Barsi-Greene, *I, Prince Tudor*, p. 213.

CHAPTER 13 · TUDORS OUT

1. Jenkins, *Elizabeth the Great*, p. 323.
2. Gallup, *Bi-literal Cypher*, part II, p. 160; Barsi-Greene, *I, Prince Tudor*, p. 211.
3. Strickland, *Life of Queen Elizabeth*, pp. 344–45.

4. Gallup, *Bi-literal Cypher*, part II, pp. 33–34; Barsi-Greene, *I, Prince Tudor*, pp. 211–12.

5. Alfred Dodd, in *Francis Bacon's Personal Life-Story*, names several publications from the 1600s that included the story about the queen's ring. He presents the controversy about the story's authenticity, giving the opinions of early biographers who discredit the story as well as those inclined to accept it. See pp. 301–2.

6. For the description of these two rings, see "The Rings of Queens Elizabeth and Mary," at
   http://www.jjkent.com/articles/rings-queens-elizabeth-mary.htm.

7. See Owen, *Sir Francis Bacon's Cipher Story*, vols. I–II, p. 181.

8. Strickland, *Life of Queen Elizabeth*, pp. 362–63.

9. Ibid., p. 362.

10. See Owen, *Sir Francis Bacon's Cipher Story*, vols. I–II, pp. 97–98.

11. Piers Compton, *Queen Bess*, p. 194, quoted in Dodd, *Francis Bacon's Personal Life-Story*, p. 300.

12. Francis is referring to the biblical story of Jacob and Esau in which the younger son, Jacob, obtains the famished older son's birthright in exchange for a serving of pottage and bread (Gen. 25:31–34). Gallup. *Bi-literal Cypher*, part II, p. 133; or Barsi-Greene, *I, Prince Tudor*, p. 217.

13. Gallup, *Bi-literal Cypher*, part II, p. 215.

14. Barsi-Greene, *I, Prince Tudor*, p. 239.

15. John Chamberlain to Dudley Carleton, 27 May 1601, quoted in du Maurier, *Golden Lads*, p. 224.

16. See du Maurier, *Golden Lads*, p. 223.

CHAPTER 14 · STUARTS IN

1. Bowen, *Francis Bacon*, p. 100.

2. Francis Bacon to Tobie Matthew, April 1603, quoted in Bowen, *Francis Bacon*, p. 98.

3. Bacon, *Essays*, p. 98.

4. Although James became king of England in 1603, Scotland and England remained as separate states until 1707. At that time, with the passage of the Acts of Union, the two nations united to create a new state, the Kingdom of Great Britain.

5. Arthur Weldon, *Character of King James*, quoted in John MacLeod, *Dynasty: The Stuarts: 1560–1807* (New York: St. Martin's Press, 2001), p. 128.

6. Bacon, "Of Cunning," in *Essays*, p. 129.

7. Francis Bacon to John Davies, 28 March 1603, in Fuller, *Francis Bacon*, p. 182.

8. Church, *Bacon*, p. 63.

9. Francis made this statement about being tied to another's fist in the first draft of a letter he was composing to James, 29 May 29 1612. In his second draft he is more diplomatic and omits this phrase. There is no

evidence that the letter was ever sent. Quoted in Church, *Bacon,* p. 93.

10. Donnelly, *Great Cryptogram,* vol. I, p. 192.

11. In the Bi-literal Cipher, Francis tells us of the evil Cecil worked against him, first with the queen but continuing afterwards until the day Cecil died. "Through his wild influence on Elizabeth, he filled her mind with a suspicion of my desire to rule the whole world, beginning with England, and that my plan was like Absalom's, to steal the hearts of the Nation and move the people to desire a king…. In truth, Cecil worked me nought save evil to the day which took him out of the world." See Gallup, *Bi-literal Cypher,* part II, p. 335.

12. Francis Bacon, "Of the Interpretation of Nature: Proem," in Dodd, *Francis Bacon's Personal Life-Story,* pp. 392, 393.

13. Francis Bacon to James, March 1603. See du Maurier, *Winding Stair,* p. 11; Fuller, *Sir Francis Bacon,* p. 181.

14. Francis Bacon to Robert Cecil, 1603, quoted in Bowen, *Francis Bacon,* p. 100.

15. Gallup, *Bi-literal Cypher,* part II, p. 213; or Barsi-Green, *I, Prince Tudor,* p. 234.

16. Francis Bacon, *Novum Organum,* Aphorism X from *The Second Book of Aphorisms.*

17. Eiseley, *Man Who Saw through Time,* pp. 32, 33.

18. Francis Bacon, quoted in Eisley, *Man Who Saw through Time,* p. 34.

19. Bacon, "Of Goodness and Goodness of Nature," *Essays,* p. 96.

20. Eisley, *Man Who Saw through Time,* p. 33.

21. Ibid.

22. Gallup, *Bi-literal Cipher,* part II, pp. 26, 98; or Barsi-Greene, *I, Prince Tudor,* pp. 240, 242.

23. Jardine and Stewart, *Hostage to Fortune,* p. 438.

24. King James, quoted in A. Wigfall Green, *Sir Francis Bacon* (Denver: Alan Swallow, 1952), p. 232.

CHAPTER 15 · A SLIPPERY CLIMB

1. Francis Bacon to Robert Cecil, 3 July 1603, quoted in du Maurier, *Winding Stair,* p. 16.

2. Gallup, *Bi-literal Cypher,* part II, pp. 336–37; Barsi-Greene, *I, Prince Tudor,* p. 96.

3. Refers to Sir Christopher Hatton, the queen's lord chancellor, who died a bachelor. His nephew, Sir William Hatton (Elizabeth Hatton's husband), was his heir. When William died, he left the inheritance to his young wife, Elizabeth.

4. Gallup, *Bi-literal Cypher,* part II, p. 188; Barsi-Greene, *I, Prince Tudor,* pp. 234–35.

5. Shakespeare, *Hamlet,* act I, sc. 3, line 41.

6. Du Maurier, *Winding Stair,* p. 16.

7. Joel 2:28.

8. Bacon, *Essays,* p. 188.

9. Fuller, *Sir Francis Bacon*, p. 190.

10. Bowen, *Francis Bacon*, p. 116.

11. Shakespeare, Sonnet 62.

12. Dudley Carleton to John Chamberlain, 11 May 1606, quoted in Fuller, *Sir Francis Bacon*, p. 190.

13. Pierre Amboise, quoted in Fuller, *Sir Francis Bacon*, pp. 190, 194.

14. Shakespeare, *Romeo and Juliet*, act II, sc. 2, lines 3, 15.

15. Bowen, *Francis Bacon*, p. 115.

16. Ibid., p. 116.

17. Ibid., p. 117.

18. Ibid., p. 118.

19. Ibid., p. 119.

20. From *A Brief History of the King James Bible*, by Lawrence M. Vance, online at http://www.av1611.org/kjv/kjvhist.html.

21. From "The 'Authorized Version' and Its Influence," *The Cambridge History of English and American Literature*, vol. IV, at http://www.bartleby.com/214/0209.html.

22. J. Arthur, *A Royal Romance: Bacon-Shakespeare* (Madras: Theosophical Publishing House, 1941), p. 294.

23. William Smedley, *Mystery of Francis Bacon*, chap. XVII, at http://www.sirbacon.org/links/bible.html.

24. Tony Bushby, *The Bible Fraud* (Hong Kong: Pacific Blue Group, 2001), pp. 20–22. Chapter I, "What Was the Church Trying to Hide?" which contains these pages is also available as an online excerpt at http://www.sirbacon.org/links/bible.html.

25. Gallup, *Bi-literal Cypher*, part II, pp. 174, 175.

26. Bowen, *Francis Bacon*, p. 125.

27. Ibid., pp. 125–26.

28. Francis Bacon to James, 7 August 1613, quoted in Jardine and Stewart, *Hostage to Fortune*, p. 338.

29. Barsi-Greene, *I, Prince Tudor*, p. 234; Gallup, *Bi-literal Cypher*, part II, p. 213.

30. Bacon, "Of Judicature," in *Essays*, p. 225.

31. Francis Bacon to James, n.d., quoted in Jardine and Stewart, *Hostage to Fortune*, p. 443.

32. Shakespeare, *Romeo and Juliet*, act II, sc. 2, lines 43–44.

33. In his *Life of the Right Honorable Francis Bacon*, William Rawley, chaplain to Francis Bacon, wrote that Bacon was "born in York House, or York Place, in the Strand, on the two and twentieth day of January." The full text of Rawley's biography, dated 1657, is available online at http://home. att.net/~tleary/rawley.htm.

34. See Ben Jonson, "Lord Bacon's Birth-day," quoted in Bowen, *Francis Bacon*, p. 172.

35. John Aubrey, *Brief Lives* (University of Michigan Press, 1982), p. 9.

36. Ibid., p. 10.

37. Ibid.

38. Dodd, *Francis Bacon's Personal Life-Story*, p. 354.

CHAPTER 16 · A FINAL SACRIFICE

1. J. R. Green, quoted in Alfred Dodd, *The Martyrdom of Francis Bacon* (London: Rider, 1945), p. 57.
2. Dodd, *Martyrdom*, p. 56.
3. Ibid., pp. 56–57.
4. Gallup, *Bi-literal Cypher*, part II, p. 102; Barsi-Greene, *I, Prince Tudor*, p. 190.
5. Gallup, *Bi-literal Cypher*, part II, p. 190; Barsi-Greene, *I, Prince Tudor*, p. 190.
6. Francis Bacon to George Villiers, 29 November 1620, quoted in Jardine and Stewart, *Hostage to Fortune*, p. 447.
7. Ibid.
8. Dodd, *Martyrdom*, p. 73.
9. See Dodd, *Martyrdom*, especially chapters VI–X.
10. Bacon, *Essays*, pp. 147, 155.
11. Bacon, "Of Seditions and Troubles," in *Essays*, p. 105.
12. See Dodd, *Martyrdom*, p. 78.
13. Bowen, *Francis Bacon*, p. 182.
14. See Dixon, *Life*, p. 234, quoted in Dodd, *Martyrdom*, p. 69.
15. Francis Bacon in a speech on his first day presiding as Lord Keeper of the Great Seal, 7 May 1617. See Dodd, *Martyrdom*, p. 109; and du Maurier, *Winding Stair*, p. 99.
16. Francis Bacon, 8 June 1617, quoted in Church, *Bacon*, p. 109.
17. Francis Bacon to the Lords, 19 March 1621.
18. Francis Bacon to the Lords, 14 March, 1621, quoted in Bowen, *Francis Bacon*, p. 187.
19. Francis Bacon would later write that "nothing is terrible except fear itself." See *De Augmentis Scientiarum*, book II.
20. Franklin D. Roosevelt, in his first inaugural address, 4 March 1933, said, "The only thing we have to fear is fear itself."
21. Francis Bacon's letter of submission was read aloud in the House of Lords on 30 April 1621. See Dodd, *Martyrdom*, p. 101.
22. Biographer Lucy Aitkin, in *Memoirs of the Court of King James the First* (1822), says, "The sentence on the Lord Chancellor was more severe than any ever pronounced upon an impeachment: in all previous examples it had been the consequence of an Attainder [a dishonor]." See Dodd, *Martyrdom*, p. 144.
23. Francis Bacon, written while imprisoned in the Tower, quoted in Dodd, *Martyrdom*, p. 119.
24. See Dodd, *Martyrdom*, p. 86.
25. Francis Bacon to Buckingham, 14 March 1621, quoted in Dodd, *Martyrdom*, p. 86.
26. Bowen, *Francis Bacon*, p. 209
27. Alfred Dodd incorporates excerpts from a number of biographers as well as the evidence that James commanded Bacon to abandon his defense and plead guilty. See *Martyrdom of Francis Bacon*, chapter VIII, "The Confession of Guilt," particularly pages 94–102. It is a

compelling account. Many biographers and historians—Dixon, Spedding, Hacket, Montague and others—clearly understood what had occurred; they pieced together the evidence available to them at the time. Dodd has also discovered new material from the writings of "Shakespeare." In his foreword, which can be read online, he presents the controversy about Bacon's guilt and some of the evidence that appears in chapter VIII. See
http://www.sirbacon.org/links/martyrdom.htm.

28. Bowen, *Francis Bacon*, p. 183.
29. Dodd, *Martyrdom*, p. 124.
30. Ibid.
31. Church, *Bacon*, p. 137.
32. John Chamberlain to Dudley Carleton, 24 March 1621, quoted in Dodd, *Martyrdom*, p. 93.
33. Du Maurier, *Winding Stair*, p. 155.
34. Barsi-Greene, *I, Prince Tudor*, p. 243; Gallup, *Bi-literal Cypher*, part II, p. 208.

CHAPTER 17 · NEW WORLDS

Opening quote: Francis Bacon to Lord Burghley, c. 1592.

1. Abraham Cowley, excerpt from "To the Royal Society."
2. See "Francis Bacon's Life: A Brief Historical Sketch by Peter Dawkins," at http://www.fbrt.org.uk/pages/essays/essay-fb-life.html.
3. Ibid.
4. An interesting addition to the controversy—the depiction in the bust may correlate with the cipher story found by Ignatius Donnelly. In that deciphering, published in *The Great Cryptogram*, Donnelly found that the jolly, rotund character of Falstaff was based on the actor who played the part, Will Shaksper. Will passed on at age fifty-two. Perhaps the image of the bust with its round fleshy face reflects his appearance at that age more faithfully than believed. For more information, see page 173 this volume.
5. John Ward, quoted in Stephen Greenblatt, *Will in the World: How Shakespeare became Shakespeare* (New York: W. W. Norton, 2004), p. 387.
6. Penn Leary, *The Second Cryptographic Shakespeare* (Omaha, Nebr.: Westchester House Publishers, 1990), p. 90.
7. See Plinius Secundus, *The First Book of the Historie of Nature*, trans. Philemon Holland (1601), at http://penelope.uchicago.edu/holland/plinyepistle.html.
8. William T. Smedley, "The First Folio," in *Baconiana*, vol. XII, no. 46 (April 1914), p. 84; Michell, *Who Wrote Shakespeare?* pp. 78–79.
9. *Complete Signet Classic Shakespeare*, p. 967.
10. Scanned images of many of the Shakespeare quartos may be viewed on the web site of the British Library. See "Shakespeare quartos" at

http://www.bl.uk/treasures/shakespeare/quartos.html.

11. *The Arte of English Poesie* (1589), attributed to George Puttenham, book 1, chapter 8; available online at http://shakespeareauthorship.com/ptext1.html.

12. Gallup, *Bi-literal Cypher,* part II, p. 115.

13. Ibid., p. 117.

14. Ibid., pp. 117–18. See also Harold Bayley, *The Tragedy of Sir Francis Bacon* (New York: Haskell House, 1970), pp. 111–12.

15. *The Tragedy of Mary Queen of Scots* appears in volume IV of *Sir Francis Bacon's Cipher Story,* by Orville Owen. A synopsis of this play, summarizing its acts and scenes, is included in volume V's table of contents, which lists the contents of all six volumes, or books. (Unfortunately, volume VI, although prepared for publication, was never printed.)

    Owen gives us some background on *The Tragedy of Mary Queen of Scots.* The play, he says, "embraces Mary's attempts to gain the English crown, her trial, and the tragic end." It was published in 1894 and "has been pronounced a masterpiece." He explains that "portions of it were found in every play attributed to Shakespeare, and in the writings of Spenser, Peele, Greene, Marlow, Burton, and Francis Bacon.... It is believed to be the first of Bacon's writings of historical drama in Cipher, and it is chiefly drawn from the earlier works and plays, before they were re-written and enlarged in 1608–17–23." (See "Introduction" in volume V, following p. 1001.)

    The other cipher play, *The Tragical History of Our Late Brother, Earl of Essex,* was published by the Howard Publishing Company of Detroit, Michigan, circa 1895. A "Publisher's Note" following p. 1001 of vol. V of *Sir Francis Bacon's Cipher Story* says the play was published separately "being complete in itself, and of the most thrilling interest and historical value" that it "may be the earlier enjoyed as one of the marvels of literature, in advance of its appearance as a part of the later books of the series of Sir Francis Bacon's Cipher Writings." These later books were never published.

16. Schoenbaum, *Shakespeare's Lives,* pp. 10–11.

17. Ibid., pp. 13–14, 11.

18. A. L. Rowse, quoted in Schoenbaum, *Shakespeare's Lives,* p. 13.

19. John Michell, *Who Wrote Shakespeare?* (London: Thames and Hudson, 1996), p. 86.

CHAPTER 18 · INTO THE SHADOWS

Opening quote: *Sir Francis Bacon's Apophthegms,* no. 119.

1. Bacon, *Essays,* pp. 64, 65, 65–66.

2. Luke 2:26, 29.

3. Bacon, "Of Death," *Essays,* p. 65.

4. Francis Bacon, quoted in Church, *Bacon,* p. 169.

5. Francis Bacon, quoted in Bowen, *Francis Bacon,* p. 224.

6. Aubrey, *Brief Lives,* pp. 15–16.

7. Bowen, *Francis Bacon,* pp. 225–26. Biographers have theorized about Francis's experiment on the "conservation and induration" of bodies. Lisa Jardine and Alan Stewart, in their 1999 biography *Hostage to Fortune,* suggest that Bacon was using himself as a guinea pig in an experiment to prolong life and that he inhaled a remedial substance, possibly nitre or opiates, and died from an overdose (pp. 505–11). Parker Woodward also believes that Bacon was experimenting with opium or another substance to effect the "flight of the spirit" thus simulating a deathlike state from which he could later be revived after his "death" had been confirmed by those attending his bedside. He believes the experiment was a success and that the funeral was a mock one. (See Dodd, two-volume edition, *Francis Bacon's Personal Life-Story,* p. 541.)

8. James Howell to Dr. Thomas Pritchard, quoted in Jardine and Stewart, *Hostage to Fortune,* p. 504.

9. See Dodd, two-volume edition *Francis Bacon's Personal Life-Story,* p. 542.

10. Bacon's last will, 19 December 1625, in Jardine and Stewart, *Hostage to Fortune,* p. 518.

11. Prescott, *Reminiscences of a Baconian,* p. 84.

12. See Harold Bayley, *The Tragedy of Sir Francis Bacon* (New York: Haskell House Publishers, 1970), p. 142.

13. Fuller, *Sir Francis Bacon,* p. 345. Over the years additional information has come to light concerning the "burial" of Sir Francis. We have not independently investigated the following two accounts but present them as a sampling for the reader. An article by Roderick Eagle, in a past issue of *Baconiana,* says that at the funeral of Sir Thomas Meautys, Bacon's friend, in 1649 at St. Michael's, Bacon's remains were exposed and that a Dr. King of St. Albans had handled the skull, which had become separated. He says the occurrence is well recorded in two books—*The History of King Charles,* by H. L. Esquire (1656) and Fuller's "Worthies" (1662). Apparently Meautys was buried near his beloved master. (Others refute that the body and skull were those of Sir Francis.)

   In another account, Aubrey relates: "This October 1681, it rang over all of St. Albans that Sir Harbottle Grimston, Master of the Rolles, had removed the coffin of this most renowned Lord Chancellor to make room for his owne to lye-in the vault there at St. Michael's Church." Aubrey makes no mention of the coffin's final location after being removed. See "The Tomb of Sir Francis Bacon," at http://www.sirbacon.org/links/tomb.html.

14. Fuller, *Sir Francis Bacon,* p. 345.

15. See Alicia Amy Leith, "Something about Arundel House," in *Baconiana,* vol. XII, no. 46 (April 1914), p. 99.

16. Ibid.

17. Ibid., p. 100; Bowen, *Francis Bacon,* p. 226.

18. See "Highgate," at http://www.sirbacon.org/highgate.htm; Leith, "Something about Arundel House," p. 101.
19. Aubrey, *Brief Lives*, p. 12.
20. Leith, "Something about Arundel House," p. 101.
21. Dodd tells us that Bacon's personal friends report his death as taking place in four different houses. See Dodd, two-volume edition of *Francis Bacon's Personal Life-Story*, p. 542.
22. See Charles Molloy, quoted in Dodd, two-volume edition of *Francis Bacon's Personal Life-Story*, p. 542.
23. See Parker Woodward, "Did Bacon Die in 1626?" in *Baconiana*, vol. XII, no. 46 (April 1914), p. 111.
24. Prescott, *Reminiscences of a Baconian*, pp. 56, 57.
25. Ibid., p. 84.
26. Ibid., pp. 92, 93.
27. Ibid., p. 85. See also Fuller, *Sir Francis Bacon*, p. 345.

ABOUT THOSE CIPHERS

1. *Advancement of Learning*, XVI:6. Project Gutenberg e-text, transcribed from the 1893 Cassell & Company edition.
2. Bacon to James, n.d. [October 22, 1623], quoted in Jardine and Stewart, *Hostage to Fortune*, p. 493.
3. Ibid., pp. 1–3.
4. Gilbert Wats's translation, 1640, of *De Augmentis Scientiarum*, reprinted in Gallup, *Bi-literal Cypher of Sir Francis Bacon*, p. 52. In this and other excerpts from Gallup's work in this chapter, Elizabethan spellings and Gallup's punctuation have been updated to match modern usage. Same-page footnotes are by the editors.
5. Ibid., pp. 118–19.
6. Ibid., p. 120.
7. J. B. Millett, "Dr. Owen's Cipher Method," in *Baconiana*, vol. III, no. 9 (April, 1895), pp. 94–95, 96–97.

ABOUT THE AUTHOR

Virginia Fellows was born in the tiny prairie town of Jordan Valley, Oregon, sixty miles from the closest railroad. Her parents, easterners themselves, had heeded the popular call of their day to "Go west, young man." Later they moved to the more metropolitan area of Boise, Idaho, and there Virginia began her education. She attended Scripps College in Claremont, California, and graduated from the University of Washington at Seattle. Transported to Michigan at the time of her marriage, she continued her education at the University of Michigan while raising four children. She considers several trips to Europe, India, South America and the Pacific islands to have been an important part of that education.

Intrigued from childhood by the mysterious and the unfamiliar, after her family left home, Virginia embarked on the studies of mysticism that led her to spend time at Summit University in Pasadena, California (now located in Montana). It was there that her fascination with the remarkable world of Francis Bacon began. *The Shakespeare Code* explains a few of the amazing facts that she discovered after years of research about this great and only partially understood philosopher. Although she has published numerous articles and pamphlets on the subject, this is her first full-length book.